# Python Microservices
# Development

Build, test, deploy, and scale microservices in Python

**Tarek Ziadé**

BIRMINGHAM - MUMBAI

# Python Microservices Development

First published: July 2017

Production reference: 1210717

Published by Packt Publishing Ltd.
Livery Place
35 Livery Street
Birmingham
B3 2PB, UK.

ISBN 978-1-78588-111-4

www.packtpub.com

# Credits

**Author**
Tarek Ziadé

**Reviewer**
William Kahn-Greene

**Commissioning Editor**
Aaron Lazar

**Acquisition Editor**
Chaitanya Nair

**Content Development Editor**
Rohit Kumar Singh

**Technical Editor**
Pavan Ramchandani

**Copy Editor**
Sonia Mathur

**Project Coordinator**
Vaidehi Sawant

**Proofreader**
Safis Editing

**Indexer**
Mariammal Chettiyar

**Graphics**
Jason Monteiro

**Production Coordinator**
Nilesh Mohite

# About the Author

**Tarek Ziadé** is a Python developer, located in the countryside near Dijon, France. He works at Mozilla in the services team. He founded a French Python user group called Afpy, and he has written several books about Python in French and English. When he is not hacking on his computer or hanging out with his family, he's spending time between his two passions, running and playing the trumpet.

You can visit his personal blog (*Fetchez le Python*) and follow him on Twitter (`@tarek_ziade`). You can also take a look at one of his books on Amazon, *Expert Python Programming*, published by Packt.

*I would like to thank the Packt team for their help, and the following hackers who helped me: Stéfane Fermigier, William Kahn-Greene, Chris Kolosiwsky, Julien Vehent, and Ryan Kelly.*

*I would also like to thank Amina, Milo, Suki, and Freya for their love and patience.*

*I hope you will enjoy this book as much as I've enjoyed writing it!*

# About the Reviewer

**William Kahn-Greene** has been writing Python and building applications on the web since the late 90s. He works in the crash-stats group on the crash ingestion pipeline at Mozilla and also maintains a variety of Python libraries, including *bleach*. When he's waiting for CI to test his code changes, he's building things with wood, tending to his tomato plant, and cooking for four.

# www.PacktPub.com

For support files and downloads related to your book, please visit www.PacktPub.com.

Did you know that Packt offers eBook versions of every book published, with PDF and ePub files available? You can upgrade to the eBook version at www.PacktPub.com and as a print book customer, you are entitled to a discount on the eBook copy. Get in touch with us at service@packtpub.com for more details.

At www.PacktPub.com, you can also read a collection of free technical articles, sign up for a range of free newsletters and receive exclusive discounts and offers on Packt books and eBook.

https://www.packtpub.com/mapt

Get the most in-demand software skills with Mapt. Mapt gives you full access to all Packt books and video courses, as well as industry-leading tools to help you plan your personal development and advance your career.

## Why subscribe?

- Fully searchable across every book published by Packt
- Copy and paste, print, and bookmark content
- On demand and accessible via a web browser

# Customer Feedback

Thanks for purchasing this Packt book. At Packt, quality is at the heart of our editorial process. To help us improve, please leave us an honest review on this book's Amazon page at https://www.amazon.com/dp/1785881116.

If you'd like to join our team of regular reviewers, you can e-mail us at customerreviews@packtpub.com. We award our regular reviewers with free eBooks and videos in exchange for their valuable feedback. Help us be relentless in improving our products!

# Table of Contents

# Preface

If we try to deploy our web applications into the cloud, it requires our code to interact with many third-party services. Using microservice architectures, you can build applications that will allow you to manage these interactions. However, this comes with its own set of challenges, since each set has its own complexity, and getting their interaction right isn't easy. This easy-to-follow guide covers techniques to help you overcome these challenges. You will learn how to best design, write, test, and deploy your microservices. The real-world examples will help Python developers create their own Python microservices using the most efficient methods. By the end of this book, you will have acquired the skills to craft applications that are built as small standard units, using all the proven best practices and avoiding the usual traps. Also, this is a useful guide for the vast community of Python developers who are shifting from monolithic design to the new microservice-based development paradigm.

## What this book covers

Chapter 1, *Understanding Microservices*, defines what microservices are, and their roles in modern web applications. It also introduces Python and explains why it's great for building microservices.

Chapter 2, *Discovering Flask*, introduces Flask and goes through its main features. It showcases the framework with a sample web application that will be the basis for building microservices.

Chapter 3, *Coding, Testing, and Documenting - the Virtuous Cycle*, describes the Test-Driven Development and Continuous Integration approach, and how to use it in practice to build and package Flask applications.

Chapter 4, *Designing Runnerly*, takes you through the app features and user stories, explains how it could be built as a monolithic app, then decomposes it into microservices and explains how they interact with the data. It will also introduce the Open API 2.0 specification (ex-Swagger), which can be used to describe HTTP APIs.

Chapter 5, *Interacting with Other Services*, explains how a service interacts with backend services, how to deal with network splits and other interaction problems, and how to test the service in isolation.

Chapter 6, *Securing Your Services*, explains how to secure your microservices and how to deal with user authentication, service-to-service authentication, as well as user management. It will also introduce the reader to fraud and abuse, and how to mitigate it.

Chapter 7, *Monitoring Your Services*, explains how to add logging and metrics in your code, and how to make sure you have a clear global understanding of what's going on in your application to track down issues and understand your services usage.

Chapter 8, *Bringing It All Together*, describes how to design and build a JavaScript application that leverages and uses the microservices in an end-user interface.

Chapter 9, *Packaging and Running Runnerly*, describes how to package, build, and run the whole Forrest application. As a developer, it's vital to be able to run all the parts that compose your application into a single dev box.

Chapter 10, *Containerized Services*, explains what is virtualization, how to use Docker, and also how to *Dockerize* your services.

Chapter 11, *Deploying on AWS*, introduces you to existing cloud service providers and then to the AWS world, and shows how to instantiate servers and use the major AWS services that are useful to run a microservices-based application. It also introduces CoreOS, a Linux distribution specifically created to deploy Docker containers in the cloud.

Chapter 12, *What Next?*, concludes the book by giving some hints on how your microservices can be built independently from specific cloud providers and virtualization technologies, to avoid the trap of putting all your eggs in the same basket. It emphasizes what you learned in Chapter 9, *Packaging and Running Runnerly*.

# What you need for this book

To execute the commands and applications in this book, you will need Python 3.x, Virtualenv 1.x, and Docker CE installed on your system. Detailed instructions are given in the chapters where needed.

# Who this book is for

If you are a developer who has basic knowledge of Python, the command line, and HTTP-based application principles, and who wants to learn how to build, test, scale, and manage Python 3 microservices, then this book is for you. No prior experience of writing microservices in Python is assumed.

# Conventions

In this book, you will find a number of text styles that distinguish between different kinds of information. Here are some examples of these styles and an explanation of their meaning.

Code words in text, database table names, folder names, filenames, file extensions, pathnames, dummy URLs, user input, and Twitter handles are shown as follows: "The only hint we're using `async` is the `async` keyword, which marks the handle function as being a coroutine."

A block of code is set as follows:

```
import time

def application(environ, start_response):
    headers = [('Content-type', 'application/json')]
    start_response('200 OK', headers)
return bytes(json.dumps({'time': time.time()}), 'utf8')
```

When we wish to draw your attention to a particular part of a code block, the relevant lines or items are set in bold:

```
from greenlet import greenlet
def test1(x, y):
    z = gr2.switch(x+y)
    print(z)
```

Any command-line input or output is written as follows:

```
docker-compose up
```

**New terms** and **important words** are shown in bold.

 Warnings or important notes appear like this.

 Tips and tricks appear like this.

# Reader feedback

Feedback from our readers is always welcome. Let us know what you think about this book-what you liked or disliked. Reader feedback is important for us as it helps us develop titles that you will really get the most out of.

To send us general feedback, simply e-mail `feedback@packtpub.com`, and mention the book's title in the subject of your message.

If there is a topic that you have expertise in and you are interested in either writing or contributing to a book, see our author guide at `www.packtpub.com/authors`.

# Customer support

Now that you are the proud owner of a Packt book, we have a number of things to help you to get the most from your purchase.

# Downloading the example code

You can download the example code files for this book from your account at `http://www.packtpub.com`. If you purchased this book elsewhere, you can visit `http://www.packtpub.com/support` and register to have the files e-mailed directly to you.

You can download the code files by following these steps:

1. Log in or register to our website using your e-mail address and password.
2. Hover the mouse pointer on the **SUPPORT** tab at the top.
3. Click on **Code Downloads & Errata**.
4. Enter the name of the book in the **Search** box.
5. Select the book for which you're looking to download the code files.
6. Choose from the drop-down menu where you purchased this book from.
7. Click on **Code Download**.

Once the file is downloaded, please make sure that you unzip or extract the folder using the latest version of:

- WinRAR / 7-Zip for Windows
- Zipeg / iZip / UnRarX for Mac
- 7-Zip / PeaZip for Linux

The code bundle for the book is also hosted on GitHub at `https://github.com/PacktPubl ishing/Python-Microservices-Development`. We also have other code bundles from our rich catalog of books and videos available at `https://github.com/PacktPublishing/`. Check them out!

# Errata

Although we have taken every care to ensure the accuracy of our content, mistakes do happen. If you find a mistake in one of our books-maybe a mistake in the text or the code-we would be grateful if you could report this to us. By doing so, you can save other readers from frustration and help us improve subsequent versions of this book. If you find any errata, please report them by visiting `http://www.packtpub.com/submit-errata`, selecting your book, clicking on the **Errata Submission Form** link, and entering the details of your errata. Once your errata are verified, your submission will be accepted and the errata will be uploaded to our website or added to any list of existing errata under the Errata section of that title.

To view the previously submitted errata, go to `https://www.packtpub.com/books/conten t/support`and enter the name of the book in the search field. The required information will appear under the **Errata** section.

# Piracy

Piracy of copyrighted material on the Internet is an ongoing problem across all media. At Packt, we take the protection of our copyright and licenses very seriously. If you come across any illegal copies of our works in any form on the Internet, please provide us with the location address or website name immediately so that we can pursue a remedy.

Please contact us at `copyright@packtpub.com` with a link to the suspected pirated material.

We appreciate your help in protecting our authors and our ability to bring you valuable content.

# Questions

If you have a problem with any aspect of this book, you can contact us at
`questions@packtpub.com`, and we will do our best to address the problem.

# Introduction

When I started to work at Mozilla 7 years ago, we began to write web services for some Firefox features. Some of them eventually became microservices. This change did not happen over time, but gradually. The first driver of this shift was the fact that we moved all our services to a cloud provider and started to interact with some of their third-party services. When you host your app in the cloud, a microservice architecture becomes a natural fit. The other driver was the Firefox Account project. We wanted to offer a single identity to our users to interact with our services from Firefox. By doing so, all our services had to interact with the same identity provider, and some server-side pieces started to get redesigned as microservices to be more efficient in that context.

I think a lot of web developers out there have been through a similar experience or are going through it right now. I also believe Python is one of the best languages to write small and efficient microservices; its ecosystem is vibrant and the latest Python 3 features make Python competitive in that field against Node.js, which has had a stellar growth in the last 5 years.

This is what is this book is all about; I wanted to share my experience of writing microservices in Python through a simple use case that I have created for this purpose-- Runnerly, which is available on GitHub for you to study. You can interact with me there, point mistakes if you see any, and we can continue to learn about writing excellent Python apps together.

# 1
# Understanding Microservices

We're always trying to improve how we build software, and since the punched-card era, we have improved a lot, to say the least.

The microservices trend is one improvement that has emerged in the last few years, partially based on companies' willingness to speed up their release cycles. They want to ship new products and new features to their customers as fast as possible. They want to be *agile* by iterating often, and they want to ship, ship, and ship again.

If thousands, or even millions, of customers use your service, pushing in production an experimental feature, and removing it if it does not work, is considered good practice rather than baking it for months before you publish it.

Companies such as Netflix are promoting their continuous delivery techniques where small changes are made very often into production, and tested on a subset of the user base. They've developed tools such as Spinnaker (`http://www.spinnaker.io/`) to automate as many steps as possible to update production, and ship their features in the cloud as independent microservices.

But if you read Hacker News or Reddit, it can be quite hard to detangle what's useful for you and what's just buzzwords-compliant journalistic-style info.

> "Write a paper promising salvation, make it a structured something or a virtual something, or abstract, distributed or higher-order or applicative and you can almost be certain of having started a new cult.
>
> - Edsger W. Dijkstra

This chapter is going to help you understand what are microservices, and will then focus on the various ways in which you can implement them using Python. It's composed of the following few sections:

- A word on Service-Oriented Architecture
- Monolithic approach of building an application
- Microservices approach of building applications
- Benefits of microservices
- Pitfalls in microservices
- Implementing microservices with Python

Hopefully, once you've reached the end of the chapter, you will be able to dive into building microservices with a good understanding of what they are and what they aren't-- and how you can use Python.

# Origins of Service-Oriented Architecture

There are many definitions out there, since there is no official standard for microservices. People often mention **Service-Oriented Architecture** (**SOA**) when they are trying to explain what microservices are.

> *SOA predates microservices, and its core principle is the idea that you organize applications into a discrete unit of functionality that can be accessed remotely and acted upon and updated independently.*

> *- Wikipedia*

Each unit in this preceding definition is a self-contained service, which implements one facet of a business, and provides its feature through some interface.

While SOA clearly states that services should be standalone processes, it does not enforce what protocols should be used for those processes to interact with each other, and stays quite vague about how you deploy and organize your application.

If you read the **SOA Manifesto** (http://www.soa-manifesto.org) that a handful of experts published on the web circa 2009, they don't even mention if the services interact via the network.

SOA services could communicate via **Inter-Process Communication** (**IPC**) using sockets on the same machine, through shared memory, through indirect message queues, or even with **Remote Procedure Calls** (**RPC**). The options are extensive, and at the end of the day, SOA can be everything and anything as long as you are not running all your application code into a single process.

However, it is common to say that microservices are one specialization of SOA, which have started to emerge over the last few years, because they fulfill some of the SOA goals which are to build apps with standalone components that interact with each other.

Now if we want to give a complete definition of what are microservices, the best way to do it is to first look at how most software are architectured.

# The monolithic approach

Let's take a very simple example of a traditional monolithic application: a hotel booking website.

Besides the static HTML content, the website has a booking feature that will let its users book hotels in any city in the world. Users can search for hotels, then book them with their credit cards.

When a user performs a search on the hotel website, the application goes through the following steps:

1. It runs a couple of SQL queries against its hotels' database.
2. An HTTP request to a partner's service is made to add more hotels to the list.
3. An HTML results page is generated using an HTML template engine.

From there, once the user has found the perfect hotel and clicked on it to book it, the application performs these steps:

1. The customer gets created in the database if needed, and has to authenticate.
2. Payment is carried out by interacting with the bank web service.
3. The app saves the payment details in the database for legal reasons.
4. A receipt is generated using a PDF generator.
5. A recap email is sent to the user using the email service.
6. A reservation email is forwarded to the third-party hotel using the email service.
7. A database entry is added to keep track of the reservation.

This process is a simplified model of course, but quite realistic.

The application interacts with a database that contains the hotel's information, the reservation details, the billing, the user information, and so on. It also interacts with external services for sending emails, making payments, and getting more hotels from partners.

In the good old **LAMP** (**Linux-Apache-MySQL-Perl/PHP/Python**) architecture, every incoming request generates a cascade of SQL queries on the database, and a few network calls to external services, and then the server generates the HTML response using a template engine.

The following diagram illustrates this centralized architecture:

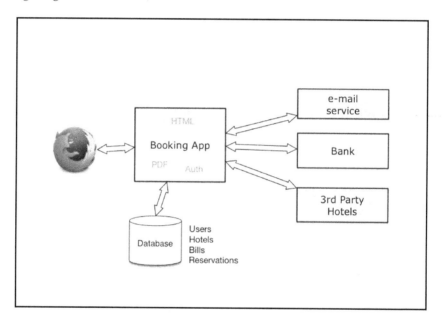

This application is a typical monolith, and it has a lot of obvious benefits.

The biggest one is that the whole application is in a single code base, and when the project coding starts, it makes everything simpler. Building a good test coverage is easy, and you can organize your code in a clean and structured way inside the code base. Storing all the data into a single database also simplifies the development of the application. You can tweak the data model, and how the code will query it.

The deployment is also a no brainer: we can tag the code base, build a package, and run it somewhere. To scale it, we can run several instances of the booking app, and run several databases with some replication mechanism in place.

If your application stays small, this model works well and is easy to maintain for a single team.

But projects are usually growing, and they get bigger than what was first intended. And having the whole application in a single code base brings some nasty issues along the way. For instance, if you need to make a sweeping change that is large in scope such as changing your banking service or your database layer, the whole application gets into a very unstable state. These changes are a big deal in the project's life, and they necessitate a lot of extra testing to deploy a new version. And changes like this *will* happen in a project life.

Small changes can also generate collateral damage because different parts of the system have different uptime and stability requirements. Putting the billing and reservation processes at risk because the function that creates the PDF crashes the server is a bit of a problem.

Uncontrolled growth is another issue. The application is bound to get new features, and with developers leaving and joining the project, the code organization might start to get messy, the tests a bit slower. This growth usually ends up with a spaghetti code base that's hard to maintain, with a hairy database that needs complicated migration plans every time some developer refactors the data model.

Big software projects usually take a couple of years to mature, and then they slowly start to turn into an incomprehensible mess that's hard to maintain. And it does not happen because developers are bad. It happens because as the complexity grows, fewer people fully understand the implications of every small change they make. So they try to work in isolation in one corner of the code base, and when you take the 10,000-foot view of the project, you can see the mess.

We've all been there.

It's not fun, and developers who work on such a project dream of building the application from scratch with the newest framework. And by doing so, they usually fall into the same issues again--the same story is repeated.

The following points summarize the pros and cons of the monolithic approach:

- Starting a project as a monolith is easy, and probably the best approach.
- A centralized database simplifies the design and organization of the data.
- Deploying one application is simple.

- Any change in the code can impact unrelated features. When something breaks, the whole application may break.
- Solutions to scale your application are limited: you can deploy several instances, but if one particular feature inside the app takes all the resources, it impacts everything.
- As the code base grows, it's hard to keep it clean and under control.

There are, of course, some ways to avoid some of the issues described here.

The obvious solution is to split the application into separate pieces, even if the resulting code is still going to run in a single process. Developers do this by building their apps with external libraries and frameworks. Those tools can be in-house or from the **Open Source Software** (**OSS**) community.

Building a web app in Python if you use a framework like **Flask**, lets you focus on the business logic, and makes it very appealing to externalize some of your code into Flask extensions and small Python packages. And splitting your code into small packages is often a good idea to control your application growth.

"*Small is beautiful.*"

*- The UNIX Philosophy*

For instance, the PDF generator described in the hotel booking app could be a separate Python package that uses **Reportlab** and some templates to do the work.

Chances are this package can be reused in some other apps, and maybe, even published to the **Python Package Index** (**PyPI**) for the community.

But you're still building a single application and some problems remain, like the inability to scale parts differently, or any indirect issue introduced by a buggy dependency.

You'll even get new challenges, because you're now using dependencies. One problem you can get is *dependency hell*. If one part of your application uses a library, but the PDF generator can only use a specific version of that library, there are good chances you will eventually have to deal with it with some ugly workaround, or even fork the dependency to have a custom fix there.

Of course, all the problems described in this section do not appear on day 1 when the project starts, but rather pile up over time.

Let's now look at how the same application would look like if we were to use microservices to build it.

# The microservice approach

If we were to build the same application using microservices, we would organize the code into several separate components that run in separate processes. Instead of having a single application in charge of everything, we would split it into many different microservices, as shown in the following diagram:

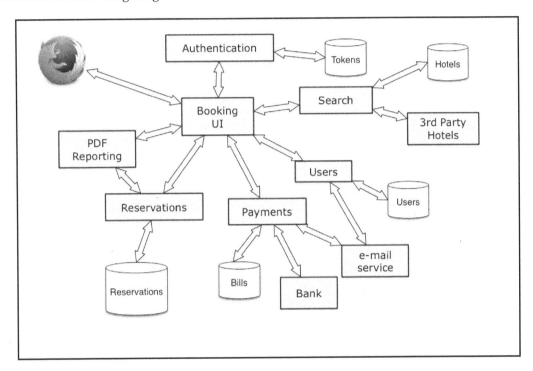

Don't be afraid of the number of components displayed in this diagram. The internal interactions of the monolithic application are just being made visible by separate pieces. We've shifted some of the complexity and ended up with these seven standalone components:

1. **Booking UI**: A frontend service, which generates the web user interface, and interacts with all the other microservices.
2. **PDF reporting service**: A very simple service that would create PDFs for the receipts or any other document given a template and some data.
3. **Search**: A service that can be queried to get a list of hotels given a city name. This service has its own database.

4. **Payments**: A service that interacts with the third-party bank service, and manages a billing database. It also sends e-mails on successful payments.
5. **Reservations:** Stores reservations, and generates PDFs.
6. **Users**: Stores the user information, and interacts with users via emails.
7. **Authentication**: An OAuth 2-based service that returns authentication tokens, which each microservice can use to authenticate when calling others.

Those microservices, along with the few external services like the email service, would provide a feature set similar to the monolithic application. In this design, each component communicates using the HTTP protocol, and features are made available through RESTful web services.

There's no centralized database, as each microservice deals internally with its own data structures, and the data that gets in and out uses a language-agnostic format like JSON. It could use XML or YAML as long as it can be produced and consumed by any language, and travel through HTTP requests and responses.

The Booking UI service is a bit particular in that regard, since it generates the **User Interface (UI)**. Depending on the frontend framework used to build the UI, the Booking UI output could be a mix of HTML and JSON, or even plain JSON if the interface uses a static JavaScript-based client-side tool to generate the interface directly in the browser.

But besides this particular UI case, a web application designed with microservices is a composition of several microservices, which may interact with each other through HTTP to provide the whole system.

In that context, microservices are logical units that focus on a very particular task. Here's a full definition attempt:

> A microservice is a lightweight application, which provides a narrowed list of features with a well-defined contract. It's a *component with a single responsibility*, which can be developed and deployed independently.

This definition does not mention HTTP or JSON, because you could consider a small UDP-based service that exchanges binary data as a microservice for example.

But in our case, and throughout the book, all our microservices are just simple web applications that use the HTTP protocol, and consume and produce JSON when it's not a UI.

# Microservice benefits

While the microservices architecture looks more complicated than its monolithic counterpart, its advantages are multiple. It offers the following:

- Separation of concerns
- Smaller projects to deal with
- More scaling and deployment options

We will discuss them in more detail in the following sections.

# Separation of concerns

First of all, each microservice can be developed independently by a separate team. For instance, building a reservation service can be a full project on its own. The team in charge can make it in whatever programming language and database, as long as it has a well-documented HTTP API.

That also means the evolution of the app is more under control than with monoliths. For example, if the payment system changes its underlying interactions with the bank, the impact is localized inside that service, and the rest of the application stays stable and is probably unaffected.

This loose coupling improves the overall project velocity a lot, as we apply, at the service level, a philosophy similar to the *single responsibility* principle.

The single responsibility principle was defined by Robert Martin to explain that a class should have only one reason to change; in other words, each class should provide a single, well-defined feature. Applied to microservices, it means that we want to make sure that each microservice focuses on a single role.

# Smaller projects

The second benefit is breaking the complexity of the project. When you add a feature to an application such as PDF reporting, even if you do it cleanly, you make the base code bigger, more complicated, and sometimes, slower. Building that feature in a separate application avoids this problem, and makes it easier to write it with whatever tools you want. You can refactor it often, shorten your release cycles, and stay on top of things. The growth of the application remains under your control.

Dealing with a smaller project also reduces risks when improving the application: if a team wants to try out the latest programming language or framework, they can iterate quickly on a prototype that implements the same microservice API, try it out, and decide whether or not to stick with it.

One real-life example in mind is the Firefox Sync storage microservice. There are currently some experiments to switch from the current Python + MySQL implementation to a Go-based one, which stores users' data in standalone SQLite databases. That prototype is highly experimental, but since we have isolated the storage feature in a microservice with a well-defined HTTP API, it's easy enough to give it a try with a small subset of the user base.

# Scaling and deployment

Finally, having your application split into components makes it easier to scale depending on your constraints. Let's say you start getting a lot of customers who book hotels daily, and the PDF generation starts to heat up the CPUs. You can deploy that specific microservice in some servers that have bigger CPUs.

Another typical example are RAM-consuming microservices like the ones that interact with memory databases like **Redis** or **Memcache**. You could tweak your deployments, consequently, by deploying them on servers with less CPU and a lot more RAM.

We can, thus, summarize the benefits of microservices as follows:

- A team can develop each microservice independently, and use whatever technological stack makes sense. They can define a custom release cycle. All they need to define is a language-agnostic HTTP API.
- Developers break the application complexity into logical components. Each microservice focuses on doing one thing well.
- Since microservices are standalone applications, there's a finer control on deployments, which makes scaling easier.

The microservices architecture is good at solving a lot of the problems that may arise once your application starts to grow. However, we need to be aware of some of the new issues they also bring in practice.

# Microservices pitfalls

As said earlier, building an application with microservices has a lot of benefits, but it's not a silver bullet by all means.

You need to be aware of these main problems you might have to deal with when coding microservices:

- Illogical splitting
- More network interactions
- Data storing and sharing
- Compatibility issues
- Testing

These issues will be covered in detail in the following sections.

# Illogical splitting

The first issue of a microservice architecture is how it gets designed. There's no way a team can come up with the perfect microservice architecture in the first shot. Some microservices like the PDF generator are an obvious use case. But as soon as you deal with the business logic, there are good chances that your code will move around before you get a good grasp of how to split things into the right set of microservices.

The design needs to mature with some try-and-fail cycles. And adding and removing microservices can be more painful than refactoring a monolithic application.

You can mitigate this problem by avoiding splitting your app in microservices if the split is not evident.

*Premature splitting is the root of all evil.*

If there's any doubt that the split makes sense, keeping the code in the same app is the safe bet. It's always easier to split apart some of the code into a new microservice later than to merge back to two microservices in the same code base because the decision turned out to be wrong.

For instance, if you always have to deploy two microservices together, or if one change in a microservice impacts the data model of another one, the odds are that you did not split the application correctly, and that those two services should be reunited.

# More network interactions

The second problem is the amount of network interactions added to build the same application. In the monolithic version, even if the code gets messy, everything happens in the same process, and you can send back the result without having to call too many backend services to build the actual response.

That requires extra attention on how each backend service is called, and raises a lot of questions like the following:

- What happens when the Booking UI cannot reach the PDF reporting service because of a network split or a laggy service?
- Does the Booking UI call the other services synchronously or asynchronously?
- How will that impact the response time?

We will need to have a solid strategy to be able to answer all those questions, and we will address those in Chapter 5, *Interacting with Other Services*.

# Data storing and sharing

Another problem is data storing and sharing. An effective microservice needs to be independent of other microservices, and ideally, should not share a database. What does this mean for our hotel booking app?

Again, that raises a lot of questions such as the following:

- Do we use the same users' IDs across all databases, or do we have independent IDs in each service and keep it as a hidden implementation detail?
- Once a user is added to the system, do we replicate some of her information in other services databases via strategies like data pumping, or is that overkill?
- How do we deal with data removal?

These are hard questions to answer, and there are many different ways to solve those problems, as we'll learn throughout the book.

 Avoiding data duplication as much as possible while keeping microservices in isolation is one of the biggest challenges in designing microservices-based applications.

# Compatibility issues

Another problem happens when a feature change impacts several microservices. If a change affects in a backward incompatible way the data that travels between services, you're in for some trouble.

Can you deploy your new service, and will it work with older versions of other services? Or do you need to change and deploy several services at once? Does it mean you've just stumbled on some services that should probably be merged back together?

A good versioning and API design hygiene help to mitigate those issues, as we will discover in the second part of the book when we'll build our application.

# Testing

Last, when you want to do some end-to-end tests and deploy your whole app, you now have to deal with many bricks. You need to have a robust and agile deployment process to be efficient. You need to be able to play with your whole application when you develop it. You can't fully test things out with just one piece of the puzzle.

Hopefully, there are now many tools to facilitate deployments of applications that are built with several components, as we will learn about throughout this book. And all those tools probably helped in the success and adoption of microservices and vice versa.

 Microservices-style architecture boosts deployment tools innovation, and deployment tools lower the bar for the approval of microservices-style architecture.

The pitfalls of using microservices can be summarized as follows:

- Premature splitting of an application into microservices can lead to architectural problems
- Network interactions between microservices add weaknesses spots and additional overhead
- Testing and deploying microservices can be complex
- And the biggest challenge--data sharing between microservices is hard

You should not worry too much about all the pitfalls described in this section for now.

They may seem overwhelming, and the traditional monolithic application may look like a safer bet, but in the long term, splitting your project into microservices will make many of your tasks, as a developer or as an **Operation person** (**Ops**), easier.

# Implementing microservices with Python

Python is an amazingly versatile language.

As you probably already know, it's used to build many different kinds of applications--from simple system scripts that perform tasks on a server to large object-oriented applications that run services for millions of users.

According to a study conducted by Philip Guo in 2014, published on the **Association for Computing Machinery** (**ACM**) website, Python has surpassed Java in top U.S. universities, and is the most popular language to learn computer science.

This trend is also true in the software industry. Python sits now in the top five languages in the TIOBE index (`http://www.tiobe.com/tiobe-index/`), and it's probably even bigger in the web development land, since languages like C are rarely used as main languages to build web applications.

 This book makes the assumption that you are already familiar with the Python programming language. If you are not an experienced Python developer, you can read the book *Expert Python Programming, Second Edition*, where you will learn advanced programming skills in Python.

However, some developers criticize Python for being slow and unfit for building efficient web services. Python is slow, and this is undeniable. But it still is a language of choice for building microservices, and many major companies are happily using it.

This section will give you some background on the different ways you can write microservices using Python, some insights on asynchronous versus synchronous programming, and conclude with some details on Python performances.

This section is composed of five parts:

- The WSGI standard
- Greenlet and Gevent
- Twisted and Tornado
- asyncio
- Language performances

# The WSGI standard

What strikes most web developers who start with Python is how easy it is to get a web application up and running.

The Python web community has created a standard (inspired by the **Common Gateway Interface** or **CGI**) called **Web Server Gateway Interface** (**WSGI**). It simplifies a lot how you can write a Python application in order to serve HTTP requests.

When your code uses that standard, your project can be executed by standard web servers like **Apache** or **nginx**, using WSGI extensions like uwsgi or mod_wsgi.

Your application just has to deal with incoming requests and send back JSON responses, and Python includes all that goodness in its standard library.

You can create a fully functional microservice that returns the server's local time with a vanilla Python module of fewer than 10 lines. It is given as follows:

```
import json
import time

def application(environ, start_response):
    headers = [('Content-type', 'application/json')]
    start_response('200 OK', headers)
    return [bytes(json.dumps({'time': time.time()}), 'utf8')]
```

Since its introduction, the WSGI protocol became an essential standard, and the Python web community widely adopted it. Developers wrote middlewares, which are functions you can hook before or after the WSGI application function itself, to do something within the environment.

Some web frameworks, like **Bottle** (http://bottlepy.org), were created specifically around that standard, and soon enough, every framework out there could be used through WSGI in one way or another.

The biggest problem with WSGI though is its synchronous nature. The application function you saw in the preceding code is called exactly once per incoming request, and when the function returns, it has to send back the response. That means that every time you call the function, it will block until the response is ready.

And writing microservices means your code will have to wait for responses from various network resources all the time. In other words, your application will be idle, and just block the client until everything is ready.

That's an entirely okay behavior for HTTP APIs. We're not talking about building bidirectional applications like web socket-based ones. But what happens when you have several incoming requests that call your application at the same time?

WSGI servers will let you run a pool of threads to serve several requests concurrently. But you can't run thousands of them, and as soon as the pool is exhausted, the next request will block the client's access even if your microservice is doing nothing but idling and waiting for backend services' responses.

That's one of the reasons why non-WSGI frameworks like **Twisted and Tornado,** and in JavaScript land, **Node.js,** became very successful--it's fully async.

When you're coding a Twisted application, you can use callbacks to pause and resume the work done to build a response. That means that you can accept new requests and start to treat them. That model dramatically reduces the idling time in your process. It can serve thousands of concurrent requests. Of course, that does not mean the application will return each single response faster. It just means one process can accept more concurrent requests, and juggle between them as the data is getting ready to be sent back.

There's no simple way with the WSGI standard to introduce something similar, and the community has debated for years to come up with a consensus--and failed. The odds are that the community will eventually drop the WSGI standard for something else.

In the meantime, building microservices with synchronous frameworks is still possible and completely fine if your deployments take into account the *one request == one thread* limitation of the WSGI standard.

There's, however, one trick to boost synchronous web applications--Greenlet, which is explained in the following section.

# Greenlet and Gevent

The general principle of asynchronous programming is that the process deals with several concurrent execution contexts to simulate parallelism.

Asynchronous applications use an event loop that pauses and resumes execution contexts when an event is triggered--only one context is active, and they take turns. Explicit instruction in the code will tell the event loop that this is where it can pause the execution.

When that occurs, the process will look for some other pending work to resume. Eventually, the process will come back to your function and continue it where it stopped. Moving from an execution context to another is called **switching**.

The **Greenlet** project (https://github.com/python-greenlet/greenlet) is a package based on the **Stackless** project, a particular CPython implementation, and provides *greenlets*.

Greenlets are *pseudo-threads* that are very cheap to instantiate, unlike real threads, and that can be used to call Python functions. Within those functions, you can *switch*, and give back the control to another function. The switching is done with an event loop, and allows you to write an asynchronous application using a thread-like interface paradigm.

Here's an example from the Greenlet documentation:

```python
from greenlet import greenlet
def test1(x, y):
    z = gr2.switch(x+y)
    print(z)

def test2(u):
    print (u)
    gr1.switch(42)

gr1 = greenlet(test1)
gr2 = greenlet(test2)
gr1.switch("hello", " world")
```

The two greenlets in the preceding example explicitly switch from one to the other.

For building microservices based on the WSGI standard, if the underlying code uses greenlets, we could accept several concurrent requests, and just switch from one to another when we know a call is going to block the request--like I/O requests.

However, switching from one greenlet to another has to be done explicitly, and the resulting code can quickly become messy and hard to understand. That's where Gevent can become very useful.

The **Gevent** project (http://www.gevent.org/) is built on top of Greenlet, and offers an implicit and automatic way of switching between greenlets, among many other things.

It provides a cooperative version of the *socket* module, which uses greenlets to automatically pause and resume the execution when some data is made available in the socket. There's even a *monkey patch* feature, which automatically replaces the standard library socket with Gevent's version. That makes your standard synchronous code magically asynchronous every time it uses sockets--with just one extra line:

```
from gevent import monkey; monkey.patch_all()

def application(environ, start_response):
    headers = [('Content-type', 'application/json')]
    start_response('200 OK', headers)
    # ...do something with sockets here...
    return result
```

This implicit magic comes at a price though. For Gevent to work well, all the underlying code needs to be compatible with the patching that Gevent does. Some packages from the community will continue to block or even have unexpected results because of this--in particular, if they use C extensions, and bypass some of the features of the standard library Gevent patched.

But it works well for most cases. Projects that play well with Gevent are dubbed *green*, and when a library is not functioning well, and the community asks its authors to *make it green*, it usually happens.

That's what was used to scale the Firefox Sync service at Mozilla, for instance.

# Twisted and Tornado

If you are building microservices where increasing the number of concurrent requests you can hold is important, it's tempting to drop the WSGI standard, and just use an asynchronous framework like **Tornado** (http://www.tornadoweb.org/) or **Twisted** (https://twistedmatrix.com/trac/).

Twisted has been around for ages. To implement the same microservices, you need to write a slightly more verbose code like this:

```
import time
import json
from twisted.web import server, resource
from twisted.internet import reactor, endpoints

class Simple(resource.Resource):
    isLeaf = True
    def render_GET(self, request):
```

```
request.responseHeaders.addRawHeader(b"content-type",
                                    b"application/json")
    return bytes(json.dumps({'time': time.time()}), 'utf8')

site = server.Site(Simple())
endpoint = endpoints.TCP4ServerEndpoint(reactor, 8080)
endpoint.listen(site)
reactor.run()
```

While Twisted is an extremely robust and efficient framework, it suffers from a few problems when building HTTP microservices, which are as follows:

- You need to implement each endpoint in your microservice with a class derived from a `Resource` class, and that implements each supported method. For a few simple APIs, it adds a lot of boilerplate code.
- Twisted code can be hard to understand and debug due to its asynchronous nature.
- It's easy to fall into **callback hell** when you chain too many functions that get triggered successively one after the other--and the code can get messy.
- Properly testing your Twisted application is hard, and you have to use a Twisted-specific unit testing model.

Tornado is based on a similar model, but does a better job in some areas. It has a lighter routing system, and does everything possible to make the code closer to plain Python. Tornado also uses a callback model, so debugging can be hard.

But both frameworks are working hard at bridging the gap to rely on the new async features introduced in Python 3.

# asyncio

When Guido van Rossum started to work on adding async features in Python 3, part of the community pushed for a Gevent-like solution, because it made a lot of sense to write applications in a synchronous, sequential fashion rather than having to add explicit callbacks like in Tornado or Twisted.

But Guido picked the explicit technique, and experimented in a project called **Tulip** inspired by Twisted. Eventually, the **asyncio** module was born out of that side project and added into Python.

In hindsight, implementing an explicit event loop mechanism in Python instead of going the Gevent way makes a lot of sense. The way the Python core developers coded asyncio, and how they elegantly extended the language with the `async` and `await` keywords to implement coroutines, made asynchronous applications built with vanilla Python 3.5+ code look very elegant and close to synchronous programming.

 Coroutines are functions that can suspend and resume their execution. `Chapter 12`, *What Next?*, explains in detail how they are implemented in Python and how to use them.

By doing this, Python did a great job at avoiding the callback syntax mess we sometimes see in Node.js or Twisted (Python 2) applications.

And beyond coroutines, Python 3 has introduced a full set of features and helpers in the asyncio package to build asynchronous applications, refer to `https://docs.python.org/3/library/asyncio.html`.

Python is now as expressive as languages like **Lua** to create coroutine-based applications, and there are now a few emerging frameworks that have embraced those features, and will only work with Python 3.5+ to benefit from this.

KeepSafe's **aiohttp** (`http://aiohttp.readthedocs.io`) is one of them, and building the same microservice, fully asynchronous, with it would simply need these few elegant lines:

```python
from aiohttp import web
import time

async def handle(request):
    return web.json_response({'time': time.time()})

if __name__ == '__main__':
    app = web.Application()
    app.router.add_get('/', handle)
    web.run_app(app)
```

In this small example, we're very close to how we would implement a synchronous app. The only hint we're using async is the `async` keyword, which marks the handle function as being a coroutine.

And that's what's going to be used at every level of an async Python app going forward. Here's another example using `aiopg`, a PostgreSQL library for asyncio from the project documentation:

```
import asyncio
import aiopg

dsn = 'dbname=aiopg user=aiopg password=passwd host=127.0.0.1'

async def go():
    pool = await aiopg.create_pool(dsn)
    async with pool.acquire() as conn:
        async with conn.cursor() as cur:
            await cur.execute("SELECT 1")
            ret = []
            async for row in cur:
                ret.append(row)
            assert ret == [(1,)]

loop = asyncio.get_event_loop()
loop.run_until_complete(go())
```

With a few `async` and `await` prefixes, the function that performs an SQL query and sends back the result looks a lot like a synchronous function.

But asynchronous frameworks and libraries based on Python 3 are still emerging, and if you are using asyncio or a framework like aiohttp, you will need to stick with particular asynchronous implementations for each feature you need.

If you need to use a library that is not asynchronous in your code, to use it from your asynchronous code means that you will need to go through some extra and challenging work if you want to prevent blocking the event loop.

If your microservices deal with a limited number of resources, it could be manageable. But it's probably a safer bet at the time of this writing to stick with a synchronous framework that's been around for a while rather than an asynchronous one. Let's enjoy the existing ecosystem of mature packages, and wait until the asyncio ecosystem gets more sophisticated.

And there are many great synchronous frameworks to build microservices with Python, like **Bottle**, **Pyramid** with **Cornice**, or **Flask**.

There are good chances that the second edition of this book will use an asynchronous framework. But for this edition, we'll use the Flask framework throughout the book. It's been around for some time, and is very robust and mature. However, keep in mind that whatever Python web framework you use, you should be able to transpose all the examples in this book. This is because most of the coding involved when building microservices is very close to plain Python, and the framework is mostly to route the requests and offer a few helpers.

# Language performances

In the previous sections, we've been through the two different ways to write microservices: asynchronous versus synchronous, and whatever technique you use, the speed of Python directly impacts the performance of your microservice.

Of course, everyone knows Python is slower than Java or Go, but execution speed is not always the top priority. A microservice is often a thin layer of code that sits most of its life waiting for some network responses from other services. Its core speed is usually less important than how fast your SQL queries will take to return from your Postgres server, because the latter will represent most of the time spent to build the response.

But wanting an application that's as fast as possible is legitimate.

One controversial topic in the Python community around speeding up the language is how the **Global Interpreter Lock** (**GIL**) mutex can ruin performances, because multi-threaded applications cannot use several processes.

The GIL has good reasons to exist. It protects non-thread-safe parts of the CPython interpreter, and exists in other languages like Ruby. And all attempts to remove it so far have failed to produce a faster CPython implementation.

Larry Hasting is working on a GIL-free CPython project called **Gilectomy** (`https://github.com/larryhastings/gilectomy`). Its minimal goal is to come up with a GIL-free implementation, which can run a single-threaded application as fast as CPython. As of the time of this writing, this implementation is still slower that CPython. But it's interesting to follow this work, and see if it reaches speed parity one day. That would make a GIL-free CPython very appealing.

For microservices, besides preventing the usage of multiple cores in the same process, the GIL will slightly degrade performances on high load because of the system calls overhead introduced by the mutex.

However, all the scrutiny around the GIL has been beneficial: work has been done in the past years to reduce GIL contention in the interpreter, and in some areas, Python's performance has improved a lot.

Bear in mind that even if the core team removes the GIL, Python is an interpreted and garbage collected language and suffers performance penalties for those properties.

Python provides the `dis` module if you are interested to see how the interpreter decomposes a function. In the following example, the interpreter will decompose a simple function that yields incremented values from a sequence in no less than 29 steps:

```
>>> def myfunc(data):
...     for value in data:
...         yield value + 1
...
>>> import dis
>>> dis.dis(myfunc)
  2           0 SETUP_LOOP              23 (to 26)
              3 LOAD_FAST                0 (data)
              6 GET_ITER
        >>    7 FOR_ITER                15 (to 25)
             10 STORE_FAST               1 (value)

  3          13 LOAD_FAST                1 (value)
             16 LOAD_CONST               1 (1)
             19 BINARY_ADD
             20 YIELD_VALUE
             21 POP_TOP
             22 JUMP_ABSOLUTE            7
        >>   25 POP_BLOCK
        >>   26 LOAD_CONST               0 (None)
             29 RETURN_VALUE
```

A similar function written in a statically compiled language will dramatically reduce the number of operations required to produce the same result. There are ways to speed up Python execution, though.

One is to write a part of your code into compiled code by building C extensions, or using a static extension of the language like Cython (http://cython.org/), but that makes your code more complicated.

Another solution, which is the most promising one, is by simply running your application using the **PyPy** interpreter (http://pypy.org/).

PyPy implements a **Just-In-Time** (**JIT**) compiler. This compiler directly replaces, at runtime, pieces of Python with machine code that can be directly used by the CPU. The whole trick for the JIT is to detect in real time, ahead of the execution, when and how to do it.

Even if PyPy is always a few Python versions behind CPython, it has reached a point where you can use it in production, and its performances can be quite amazing. In one of our projects at Mozilla that needs fast execution, the PyPy version was almost as fast as the Go version, and we've decided to use Python there instead.

 The Pypy Speed Center website is a great place to look at how PyPy compares to CPython ( http://speed.pypy.org/).

However, if your program uses C extensions, you will need to recompile them for PyPy, and that can be a problem. In particular, if other developers maintain some of the extensions you are using.

But if you build your microservice with a standard set of libraries, chances are that it will work out of the box with the PyPy interpreter, so that's worth a try.

In any case, for most projects, the benefits of Python and its ecosystem largely surpass the performance issues described in this section, because the overhead in a microservice is rarely a problem. And if performance is a problem, the microservice approach allows you to rewrite performance-critical components without affecting the rest of the system.

# Summary

In this chapter, we've compared the monolithic versus microservice approach to building web applications, and it became apparent that it's not a binary world where you have to pick one model on day one and stick with it.

You should see microservices as an improvement of an application that started its life as a monolith. As the project matures, parts of the service logic should migrate into microservices. It is a useful approach as we've learned in this chapter, but it should be done carefully to avoid falling into some common traps.

Another important lesson is that Python is considered to be one of the best languages to write web applications, and therefore, microservices--for the same reasons, it's a language of choice in other areas, and also because it provides tons of mature frameworks and packages to do the work.

We've rapidly looked through the chapter at several frameworks, both synchronous and asynchronous, and for the rest of the book, we'll be using Flask.

The next chapter will introduce this fantastic framework, and if you are not familiar with it, you will probably love it.

Lastly, Python is a slow language, and that can be a problem in very specific cases. But knowing what makes it slow, and the different solutions to avoid this issue will usually be enough to make that problem not relevant.

# 2
# Discovering Flask

**Flask** was started around 2010, leveraging the **Werkzeug** WSGI toolkit (http://werkzeug.pocoo.org/), which provides the foundations for interacting with HTTP requests via the WSGI protocol, and various tools such as a routing system.

Werkzeug is equivalent to **Paste**, which provided similar features. The **Pylons** project (http://pylonsproject.org), which is the umbrella organization for projects like Pyramid -- another web framework-- integrated Paste and its various components at some point.

Together with **Bottle** (http://bottlepy.org/) and a handful of other projects, they composed the *Python microframeworks ecosystem*.

All those projects have a similar goal--they want to offer to the Python community simple tools to build web applications faster.

However, the term *microframework* can be a bit misleading. It does not mean you can only create micro applications. Using those tools, you can build any application--even a large one. The prefix *micro* here means that the framework tries to take as few decisions as possible. It lets you freely organize your application code as you want, and use whatever libraries you want.

A microframework acts as the glue code that delivers requests to your system, and sends back responses. It does not enforce any particular paradigm on your project.

A typical example of this philosophy is when you need to interact with an SQL database. A framework like Django is *batteries-included*, and provides everything you need to build your web app including an **Object-Relational Mapper** (**ORM**) to bind objects with database query results. The rest of the framework tightly integrates with the ORM.

If you want to use an alternative ORM like **SQLAlchemy (SA)** in Django to benefit from some of its great features, you'd not be taking the easiest path, because the whole idea of Django is to provide an entire working system, and let the developer focus on building original features.

Flask, on the other hand, does not care what library you use to interact with your data. The framework will only try to make sure it has enough hooks to be extended by external libraries to provide all kinds of features. In other words, using SQLAlchemy in Flask, and making sure you're doing the right thing with SQL sessions and transactions, will mostly consist of adding a package like **Flask-SQLAlchemy** in your project. And if you don't like how that particular library integrates SLQAlchemy, you're free to use another one, or to build your integration.

Of course, that's not a silver bullet. Being completely free in your choices also means it's easier to make poor decisions, and build an application that relies on defective libraries or one that's not well designed.

But fear not! This chapter will make sure you know what Flask has to offer, and how to organize your code for building microservices.

This chapter covers the following topics:

- Which Python?
- How Flask handles requests
- Flask built-in features
- A microservice skeleton

The goal of this chapter is to give you all the information needed to build microservices with Flask. By doing so, it inevitably duplicates some of the information you can find in Flask's official documentation--but focuses on providing interesting details and anything relevant when building microservices. Flask has a good online documentation. Make sure you take a look at its user guide at `http://flask.pocoo.org/docs`, which should be a great complement to this chapter. The code base in GitHub, located at `https://github.com/pallets/flask`, is very well documented as well-- and the source code is always the ultimate source of truth when you need to understand how something works.

# Which Python?

Before we start digging into Flask, there's one question we should answer. What Python version should be used at this point with Flask, since it supports both?

We're now in 2017, and as we've seen in the previous chapter, Python 3 has made some incredible progress. Packages that don't support Python 3 are now less common. Unless you're building something very specific, you should not have any problem with Python 3.

And building microservices means each app will run in isolation, so it would be entirely imaginable to run some in Python 2 and some in Python 3 depending on your constraints. You can even using PyPy.

Despite the initial pushbacks the Flask creator had on some of the Python 3 language decisions, the documentation explicitly says at this point that new projects should start using Python 3; refer to `http://flask.pocoo.org/docs/latest/python3/#python3-suppo rt`.

Since Flask is not using any new bleeding-edge Python 3 language features, your code will probably be able to run in Python 2 and 3 anyway. In the worst case, you can use a tool like **Six** (`http://pythonhosted.org/six/`) to make your code compatible with both versions if you need to.

The general advice is to use Python 3 unless you have some constraints that require Python 2. Python 2 will not be supported anymore after 2020; see `https://pythonclock.org/`.

> This book uses the latest Python 3.5 stable release for all its code examples, but they are likely to work on the last Python 3.x versions.
> At this point, you should make sure you have a working Python 3 environment with **Virtualenv** (`https://virtualenv.pypa.io`) installed. Every code example in the book runs in a terminal.

# How Flask handles requests

The framework entry point is the `Flask` class in the `flask.app` module. Running a Flask application means running one single instance of this class, which will take care of handling incoming **Web Server Gateway Interface** (**WSGI**) requests, dispatch them to the right code, and then return a response.

WSGI is a specification that defines the interface between web servers and Python applications. The incoming request is described in a single mapping, and frameworks such as Flask take care of routing the call to the right callable.

The class offers a *route* method, which can decorate your functions. When you decorate a function with it, it becomes a *view*, and it's registered into Werkzeug's routing system. That system uses a small rule engine to match views with incoming requests, and will be described later in this chapter.

Here's a very basic example of a fully functional Flask application:

```python
from flask import Flask, jsonify

app = Flask(__name__)

@app.route('/api')
def my_microservice():
    return jsonify({'Hello': 'World!'})

if __name__ == '__main__':
    app.run()
```

That app returns a JSON mapping when called on /api. Every other endpoint would return a 404 Error.

The __name__ variable, whose value will be __main__ when you run that single Python module, is the name of the application package. It's used by Flask to instantiate a new logger with that name, and to find where the file is located on the disk. Flask will use the directory as the root for helpers like the config that's associated with your app, and to determine default locations for the static and templates directories.

If you run that module in a shell, the Flask app will run its web server, and start listen to incoming connections on the 5000 port:

```
$ python flask_basic.py
* Running on http://127.0.0.1:5000/ (Press CTRL+C to quit)
```

Calling /api with the curl command will return a valid JSON response with the right headers, thanks to the jsonify() function, which takes care of converting the Python dict into a valid JSON response with the proper Content-Type header.

The `curl` command is going to be used a lot in this book. If you are under Linux or macOS, it should be pre-installed; refer to `https://curl.haxx.s e/`.

```
$ curl -v http://127.0.0.1:5000/api
*    Trying 127.0.0.1...
...
< HTTP/1.0 200 OK
< Content-Type: application/json
< Content-Length: 24
< Server: Werkzeug/0.11.11 Python/3.5.2
< Date: Thu, 22 Dec 2016 13:54:41 GMT
<
{
   "Hello": "World!"
}
```

The `jsonify()` function creates a `Response` object, and dumps the mapping in its body.

While many web frameworks explicitly pass a `request` object to your code, Flask provides an implicit global `request` variable, which points to the current `Request` object it built with the incoming call by parsing the HTTP call into a WSGI environment dictionary.

This design decision makes the simpler views code very concise: like in our example, if you don't have to look at the request content to reply, there's no need to have it around. As long as your view returns what the client should get and Flask can serialize it, everything is pretty much transparent.

For other views, they can just import that variable and use it.

The `request` variable is global, but unique, to each incoming request and is thread safe. Flask uses a mechanism called context locals, which we will explain later.

Let's add some `print` method calls here and there so that we can see what's happening under the hood:

```
from flask import Flask, jsonify, request

app = Flask(__name__)

@app.route('/api')
def my_microservice():
```

```
print(request)
print(request.environ)
response = jsonify({'Hello': 'World!'})
print(response)
print(response.data)
return response

if __name__ == '__main__':
    print(app.url_map)
    app.run()
```

Running that new version and hitting it with the `curl` command in another shell, you get a lot of details, like the following:

```
$ python flask_details.py
Map([<Rule '/api' (GET, OPTIONS, HEAD) -> my_microservice>,
    <Rule '/static/<filename>' (GET, OPTIONS, HEAD) -> static>])
* Running on http://127.0.0.1:5000/ (Press CTRL+C to quit)

<Request 'http://127.0.0.1:5000/api' [GET]>

{'wsgi.url_scheme': 'http', 'HTTP_ACCEPT': '*/*',
 'wsgi.run_once': False, 'PATH_INFO': '/api', 'SCRIPT_NAME': '',
 'wsgi.version': (1, 0), 'SERVER_SOFTWARE': 'Werkzeug/0.11.11',
 'REMOTE_ADDR': '127.0.0.1',
 'wsgi.input': <_io.BufferedReader name=5>,
 'SERVER_NAME': '127.0.0.1', 'CONTENT_LENGTH': '',
 'werkzeug.request': <Request 'http://127.0.0.1:5000/api' [GET]>,
 'SERVER_PORT': '5000', 'HTTP_USER_AGENT': 'curl/7.51.0',
 'wsgi.multiprocess': False, 'REQUEST_METHOD': 'GET',
 'SERVER_PROTOCOL': 'HTTP/1.1', 'REMOTE_PORT': 22135,
 'wsgi.multithread': False, 'werkzeug.server.shutdown': <function
    WSGIRequestHandler.make_environ.<locals>.shutdown_server at
    0x1034e12f0>,
 'HTTP_HOST': '127.0.0.1:5000', 'QUERY_STRING': '',
 'wsgi.errors': <_io.TextIOWrapper name='<stderr>' mode='w'
    encoding='UTF-8'>, 'CONTENT_TYPE': ''}

<Response 24 bytes [200 OK]>
b'{n  "Hello": "World!"n}n'
127.0.0.1 - - [22/Dec/2016 15:07:01] "GET /api HTTP/1.1" 200
```

Let's explore what's happening here on the call:

- Routing: Flask creates the Map class
- Request: Flask passes a Request object to the view
- Response: A Response object is sent back with the response content

# Routing

The routing happens in app.url_map, which is an instance of Werkzeug's Map class. That class uses regular expressions to determine if a function decorated by @app.route matches the incoming request. The routing only looks at the path you provided in the route call to see if it matches the client's request.

By default, the mapper will only accept GET, OPTIONS, and HEAD calls on a declared route. Calling a valid endpoint with an unsupported method will return a 405 Method Not Allowed response together with the list of supported methods in the Allow header:

```
$ curl -v -XDELETE localhost:5000/api
* Connected to localhost (127.0.0.1) port 5000 (#0)
> DELETE /api/person/1 HTTP/1.1
> Host: localhost:5000
> User-Agent: curl/7.51.0
> Accept: */*
>
* HTTP 1.0, assume close after body
< HTTP/1.0 405 METHOD NOT ALLOWED
< Content-Type: text/html
< Allow: GET, OPTIONS, HEAD
< Content-Length: 178
< Server: Werkzeug/0.11.11 Python/3.5.2
< Date: Thu, 22 Dec 2016 21:35:01 GMT
<
<!DOCTYPE HTML PUBLIC "-//W3C//DTD HTML 3.2 Final//EN">
<title>405 Method Not Allowed</title>
<h1>Method Not Allowed</h1>
<p>The method is not allowed for the requested URL.</p> *
   Curl_http_done: called premature == 0
   Closing connection 0
```

If you want to support specific methods, you can pass them to the route decorator with the methods argument as follows:

```
@app.route('/api', methods=['POST', 'DELETE', 'GET'])
def my_microservice():
    return jsonify({'Hello': 'World!'})
```

Note that the OPTIONS and HEADS methods are implicitly added in all rules, since it is automatically managed by the request handler. You can deactivate this behavior by setting a provide_automatic_options attribute to False to the function. This can be useful when you want to add custom headers in the response when OPTIONS is called, like when dealing with CORS where you need to add several Access-Control-Allow-* headers.

## Variables and converters

Another feature provided by the routing system is variables.

You can use variables using the <VARIABLE_NAME> syntax. This notation is pretty standard (Bottle uses the same), and allows you to describe endpoints with dynamic values.

For example, if you want to create a function that handles all requests to /person/N, with N being the unique ID of a person, you could use /person/<person_id>.

When Flask calls your function, it converts the value it finds in the URL section as the person_id argument:

```
@app.route('/api/person/<person_id>')
def person(person_id):
    response = jsonify({'Hello': person_id})
    return response

$ curl localhost:5000/api/person/3
{
  "Hello": "3"
}
```

If you have several routes that match the same URL, the mapper uses a particular set of rules to determine which one it calls. This is the implementation description taken from Werkzeug's routing module:

1. Rules without any arguments come first for performance. This is because we expect them to match faster and some common rules usually don't have any arguments (index pages, and so on).
2. The more complex rules come first, so the second argument is the negative length of the number of weights.
3. Lastly, we order by the actual weights.

Werzeug's Rules have, therefore, weights that are used to sort them, and this is not used or surfaced in Flask. So, it boils down to picking views with more variables first, then the others --in order of appearance--when Python imports the different modules. The rule of thumb is to make sure that every declared route in your app is unique, otherwise, tracking which one gets picked will give you headaches.

There's also a basic converter that will convert the variable to a particular type. For instance, if you want an integer, you would use `<int:VARIABLE_NAME>`. In the person example, that translates to `/person/<int:person_id>`.

If a request matches a route, but a converter fails to change a value, Flask will return a `404 Error` unless another route matches the same path.

Built-in converters are `string` (the default, a Unicode string), `int`, `float`, `path`, `any`, and `uuid`.

The `path` converter is like the default converter, but includes slashes. It's similar to the `[^/].*?` regular expression.

The `any` converter allows you to combine several values. It's a bit too smart, and rarely used. The `uuid` converter matches the UUIDs strings.

It's quite easy to create your custom converter. For example, if you want to match users' IDs with usernames, you could create a converter that looks up a database, and converts the integer into a username.

To do this, you need to create a class derived from the `BaseConverter` class, which implements two methods: the `to_python()` method to convert the value to a Python object for the view, and the `to_url()` method to go the other way (used by `url_for()` described in the next section uses `to_url()`):

```python
from flask import Flask, jsonify, request
from werkzeug.routing import BaseConverter, ValidationError

_USERS = {'1': 'Tarek', '2': 'Freya'}
_IDS = {val: id for id, val in _USERS.items()}

class RegisteredUser(BaseConverter):
    def to_python(self, value):
        if value in _USERS:
            return _USERS[value]
        raise ValidationError()

    def to_url(self, value):
        return _IDS[value]

app = Flask(__name__)
app.url_map.converters['registered'] = RegisteredUser

@app.route('/api/person/<registered:name>')
def person(name):
    response = jsonify({'Hello hey': name})
    return response

if __name__ == '__main__':
    app.run()
```

The `ValidationError` method is raised in case the conversion fails, and the mapper will consider that the route simply does not match that request.

Let's try a few calls to see how that works in practice:

```
$ curl localhost:5000/api/person/1
{
  "Hello hey": "Tarek"
}

$ curl localhost:5000/api/person/2
{
  "Hello hey": "Freya"
}

$ curl localhost:5000/api/person/3
```

```
<!DOCTYPE HTML PUBLIC "-//W3C//DTD HTML 3.2 Final//EN">
<title>404 Not Found</title>
<h1>Not Found</h1>
<p> The requested URL was not found on the server.  If you entered
    the URL manually please check your spelling and try again.</p>
```

But beware that this was just an example to demonstrate the power of converters. In real applications, we would need to be careful not to rely on too many converters, because it would be painful to change all the routes when the code evolves.

> The best practice for routing is to keep it as static and straightforward as possible, and see it as mere labels you put on your functions.

# The url_for function

The last interesting feature of Flask's routing system is the `url_for()` function. Given any view, it will return its actual URL.

Here's an example with the previous app:

```
>>> from flask_converter import app
>>> from flask import url_for
>>> with app.test_request_context():
...     print(url_for('person', name='Tarek'))
...
/api/person/1
```

> The previous example uses the **Read-Eval-Print Loop** (**REPL**), which you can get by running the Python executable directly.

This feature is quite useful in templates when you want to display the URLs of some views depending on the execution context. Instead of hardcoding some links, you can just point the function name to `url_for` to get it.

# Request

When a request comes in, Flask calls the view inside a thread-safe block, and uses Werzeug's **local** helper (http://werkzeug.pocoo.org/docs/latest/local/). This helper does a job similar to Python's **threading.local** (https://docs.python.org/3/library/threading.html#thread-local-data), and makes sure that each thread has an isolated environment, specific to that request.

In other words, when you access the global request object in your view, you are guaranteed that it's unique to your thread, and will not leak data to another thread in a multi-threaded environment.

As we've seen earlier, Flask uses the incoming WSGI environment data to create the request object. That object is a `Request` class instance, which merges several `mixin` classes in charge of parsing specific headers from the incoming environment.

> Check out the WSGI **PEP** (**Python Environment Proposal**) to get more details on what's in a WSGI environment at https://www.python.org/de v/peps/pep-0333/#environ-variables.

The bottom line is that a view can introspect the incoming request through the request object attributes without having to deal with some parsing. The work done by Flask is quite high level. For instance, the `Authorization` header is looked at and decomposed automatically when possible.

In the following example, an `HTTP Basic Auth` that is sent by the client is always converted to a base64 form when sent to the server. Flask will detect the `Basic` prefix, and will parse it into `username` and `password` fields in the `request.authorization` attribute:

```
from flask import Flask, request

app = Flask(__name__)

@app.route("/")
def auth():
    print("The raw Authorization header")
    print(request.environ["HTTP_AUTHORIZATION"])
    print("Flask's Authorization header")
    print(request.authorization)
    return ""

if __name__ == "__main__":
    app.run()
```

```
$ curl http://localhost:5000/ -u tarek:password

$ bin/python flask_auth.py
* Running on http://127.0.0.1:5000/ (Press CTRL+C to quit)
The raw Authorization header
Basic dGFyZWs6cGFzc3dvcmQ=
Flask's Authorization header
{'username': 'tarek', 'password': 'password'}
127.0.0.1 - - [26/Dec/2016 11:33:04] "GET / HTTP/1.1" 200 -
```

This behavior makes it easy to implement a pluggable authentication system on top of the request object.

Other common request elements like cookies, files, and so on are all accessible via other attributes, as we will discover throughout the book.

# Response

In the previous examples, we've used the jsonify() function, which creates a Response object from the mapping returned by the view.

The Response object is, technically, a standard WSGI application you could use directly. It's wrapped by Flask, and called with the WSGI's environ, and the start_response function is received from the web server.

When Flask picks a view via its URL mapper, it expects it to return a callable object that can receive the environ and start_response arguments.

> This design may seem a little awkward since the WSGI environ is already parsed into a Request object by the time the Response object is called with the WSGI environ again. But, in practice, this is just an implementation detail. When your code needs to interact with the request, it can use the global Request object, and ignore what's happening inside the Response class.

In case the returned value is not a callable, Flask will try to convert it into a `Response` object if it's one of the following cases:

- **str**: The data gets encoded as UTF-8 and used as the HTTP response body.
- **bytes/bytesarray**: Used as the body.
- **A (response, status, headers) tuple**: Where *response* can be a `Response` object or one of the previous types. *status* is an integer value that overwrites the *response* status, and *headers* is a mapping that extends the *response* headers.
- **A (response, status) tuple**: Like the previous one, but without specific headers
- **A (response, headers) tuple**: Like the preceding one, but with just extra headers.

Any other case will lead to an exception.

In most cases, when building microservices, we'll use the built-in `jsonify()` function, but in case you need your endpoints to produce another content type, creating a function that will convert the generated data into a `Response` class is easy enough.

Here's an example with YAML: the `yamlify()` function will return a (response, status, headers) tuple, which will be converted by Flask into a proper `Response` object.

```python
from flask import Flask
import yaml      # requires PyYAML

app = Flask(__name__)

def yamlify(data, status=200, headers=None):
    _headers = {'Content-Type': 'application/x-yaml'}
    if headers is not None:
        _headers.update(headers)
    return yaml.safe_dump(data), status, _headers

@app.route('/api')
def my_microservice():
    return yamlify(['Hello', 'YAML', 'World!'])
if __name__ == '__main__':
    app.run()
```

The way Flask handles requests can be summarized as follows:

1. When the application starts, any function decorated with `@app.route()` is registered as a view, and stored into the `app.url_map`.
2. A call is dispatched to the right view depending on its endpoint and method.

3. A `Request` object is created in a thread-safe thread-local execution context.

4. A `Response` object wraps the content to send back.

These four steps are roughly all you need to know to start building apps using Flask. The next section will summarize the most important built-in features that Flask offers alongside this request-response mechanism.

# Flask built-in features

The previous section gave us a good understanding of how Flask processes a request, and that's good enough to get you started.

But Flask comes with more helpers, which are quite useful. We'll discover the following main ones in this section:

- **The session object**: Cookie-based data
- **Globals**: Storing data in the request context
- **Signals**: Sending and intercepting events
- **Extensions and middlewares**: Adding features
- **Templates**: Building text-based content
- **Configuring**: Grouping your running options in a config file
- **Blueprints**: Organizing your code in namespaces
- **Error handling and debugging**: Dealing with errors in your app

# The session object

Like the `request` object, Flask creates a `session` object, which is unique to the request context.

It's a dict-like object, which Flask serializes into a *cookie* on the user side. The data contained into the session mapping is dumped into a JSON mapping, then compressed using **zlib** when that makes it smaller, and finally encoded in base64.

When the session gets serialized, the **itsdangerous** (`https://pythonhosted.org/itsdange rous/`) library signs the content using the `secret_key` value defined at the application level. The signing uses **HMAC** (`https://en.wikipedia.org/wiki/Hash-based_message_a uthentication_code`) and **SHA1**.

This signature, which is added as a suffix in the data, ensures that the client cannot tamper with the data that is stored in a cookie unless they know the secret key to sign the data. Note that the data itself is not encrypted.

Flask will let you customize the signing algorithm to use, but *HMAC + SHA1* is good enough when you need to store data in cookies.

However, when you're building microservices that are not producing HTML, you rarely rely on cookies since they are specific to web browsers. But the idea of keeping a volatile key-value storage per user can be extremely useful to speed up some of the server-side work. For instance, if you need to perform some database look-ups to get some information about a user every time they connect, caching this information in a session-like object on the server side makes a lot of sense.

# Globals

As discussed earlier in this chapter, Flask provides a mechanism to store global variables that are unique to a particular thread and request context. That's used for request and session, but is also available to store any custom object.

The flask.g variable contains all globals, and you can set whatever attributes you want on it.

In Flask, the @app.before_request decorator can be used to point a function that the app will call every time a request is made just before it dispatches the request to a view.

It's a typical pattern in Flask to use before_request to set values in the globals. That way, all the functions that are called within the request context can interact with g and get the data.

In the following example, we copy the username provided when the client performs an HTTP basic authentication in the user attribute:

```
from flask import Flask, jsonify, g, request

app = Flask(__name__)

@app.before_request
def authenticate():
    if request.authorization:
        g.user = request.authorization['username']
    else:
        g.user = 'Anonymous'
```

```
@app.route('/api')
def my_microservice():
    return jsonify({'Hello': g.user})

if __name__ == '__main__':
    app.run()
```

When a client requests the /api view, the authenticate function will set g.user depending on the provided headers:

```
$ curl http://127.0.0.1:5000/api
{
  "Hello": "Anonymous"
}
$ curl http://127.0.0.1:5000/api --user tarek:pass
{
  "Hello": "tarek"
}
```

Any data you may think of that's specific to a request context, and could be shared throughout your code, can be shared via flask.g.

# Signals

Flask integrates with **Blinker** (https://pythonhosted.org/blinker/), which is a signal library that lets you subscribe a function to an event.

Events are instances of the blinker.signal class created with a unique label, and Flask instantiates ten of them in 0.12. Flask triggers signals at critical moments during the processing of a request. Refer to http://flask.pocoo.org/docs/latest/api/#core-signals-list for the full list.

Registering to a particular event is done by calling the signal's connect method. Signals are triggered when some code calls the signal's send method. The send method accepts extra arguments to pass data to all the registered functions.

In the following example, we register the finished function to the request_finished signal. That function will receive the response object:

```
from flask import Flask, jsonify, g, request_finished
from flask.signals import signals_available

if not signals_available:
    raise RuntimeError("pip install blinker")
```

```
app = Flask(__name__)
```

*→ variable args in a dict*

```
def finished(sender, response, **extra):
    print('About to send a Response')
    print(response)

request_finished.connect(finished)

@app.route('/api')
def my_microservice():
    return jsonify({'Hello': 'World'})

if __name__ == '__main__':
    app.run()
```

Notice that the signal feature will only work if you install Blinker, which is not installed by default as a dependency when you install Flask.

Some signals implemented in Flask are not useful in microservices, such as the ones occurring when the framework renders a template. But there are some interesting signals that Flask triggers throughout the request life, which can be used to log what's going on

For instance, the `got_request_exception` signal is triggered when an exception occurs before the framework does something with it. That's how Sentry's (`https://sentry.io`) Python client (**Raven**) hooks itself onto Flask to log exceptions.

It can also be interesting to implement custom signals in your apps when you want to trigger some of your features with events and decouple the code.

For example, if your microservice produces PDF reports, and you want to have the reports cryptographically signed, you could trigger a `report_ready` signal, and have a signer register to that event.

One important aspect of the Blinker implementation is that all registered functions are called in no particular order and *synchronously* on the `signal.send` calls. So, if your application starts to use a lot of signals, all the triggering could become an important part of the time spent processing a request, and create bottlenecks.

If you need to do work that doesn't impact the response, consider using a queue like **RabbitMQ** (`https://www.rabbitmq.com/`) to queue up the task and have a separate service do that work.

# Extensions and middlewares

Flask extensions are simply Python projects that, once installed, provide a package or a module named `flask_something`. In previous versions, it was `flask.ext.something`.

The project has to follow a few guidelines, as described at `http://flask.pocoo.org/docs/latest/extensiondev`. These guidelines are more or less good practices that could apply to any Python project. Flask has a curated list of extensions maintained at `http://flask.pocoo.org/extensions/`, which is a good first stop when you are looking for extra features. What's provided by the extension is up to the developers, and not much is enforced besides the guidelines described in Flask documentation.

The other mechanism to extend Flask is to use WSGI middlewares. A WSGI middleware is a pattern to extend WSGI apps by wrapping the calls made to the WSGI endpoint.

In the example that follows, the middleware fakes a `X-Forwarded-For` header, so the Flask application thinks it's behind a proxy like nginx. This is a useful middleware in a testing environment when you want to make sure your application behaves properly when it tries to get the remote IP address, since the `remote_addr` attribute will get the IP of the proxy, not the real client:

```python
from flask import Flask, jsonify, request
import json

class XFFMiddleware(object):
    def __init__(self, app, real_ip='10.1.1.1'):
        self.app = app
        self.real_ip = real_ip

    def __call__(self, environ, start_response):
        if 'HTTP_X_FORWARDED_FOR' not in environ:
            values = '%s, 10.3.4.5, 127.0.0.1' % self.real_ip
            environ['HTTP_X_FORWARDED_FOR'] = values
        return self.app(environ, start_response)

app = Flask(__name__)
app.wsgi_app = XFFMiddleware(app.wsgi_app)

@app.route('/api')
def my_microservice():
    if "X-Forwarded-For" in request.headers:
        ips = [ip.strip() for ip in
                request.headers['X-Forwarded-For'].split(',')]
        ip = ips[0]
    else:
        ip = request.remote_addr
```

```
        return jsonify({'Hello': ip})

if __name__ == '__main__':
    app.run()
```

 Notice that we use `app.wsgi_app` here to wrap the WSGI app. In Flask, the app object is not the WSGI application itself as we've seen earlier.

Tampering with the WSGI `environ` before your application gets it is fine, but if you want to implement anything that will impact the response, doing it inside a WSGI middleware is going to make your work very painful.

The WSGI protocol requires that the `start_response` function gets called with the response status code, and headers before the app sends back the actual body content. Unfortunately, a single function call on your application triggers this two-step mechanism. So, changing the results on the fly from outside the app requires some callback magic to work.

A good example is when you want to modify the response body. That impacts the `Content-Length` header, so your middleware will need to intercept the headers sent by the app, and rewrite them *after* the body has been modified.

And this is just one problem of the WSGI protocol design; there are many other issues around it.

Unless you want your functionality to work for other WSGI frameworks, there are no good reasons to extend your apps with WSGI middlewares. It's much better to write a Flask extension that will interact from within the Flask application.

# Templates

Sending back JSON or YAML documents is easy enough, since we're just serializing data. And most microservices produce machine-parseable data. But in some cases, we might need to create documents with some layout--whether it's an HTML page, or a PDF report, or an email.

For anything that's text-based, Flask integrates a template engine called **Jinja** (`http://jinja.pocoo.org`). The main reason Flask incorporates Jinja is to produce HTML documents, so you will find helpers like `render_template`, which generate responses by picking a Jinja template, and provide the output given some data.

But Jinja is not unique to HTML or other tag-based documents. It can create any document as long as it's text-based.

For example, if your microservice sends emails, instead of relying on the standard library's `email` package to produce the email content, which can be cumbersome, you could use Jinja.

The following is an example of an email template:

```
Date: {{date}}
From: {{from}}
Subject: {{subject}}
To: {{to}}
Content-Type: text/plain


Hello {{name}},

We have received your payment!

Below is the list of items we will deliver for lunch:

{% for item in items %}- {{item['name']}} ({{item['price']}} Euros)
{% endfor %}

Thank you for your business!

--
Tarek's Burger
```

Jinja uses double brackets for marking variables that will be replaced by a value. Variables can be anything that's passed to Jinja at execution time.

You can also use Python's `if` and `for` blocks directly in your templates with the `{% for x in y % }... {% endfor %}` and `{% if x %}...{% endif %}` notations.

The following is a Python script that uses the email template to produce an entirely valid RFC 822 message, which you can send via SMTP:

```
from datetime import datetime
from jinja2 import Template
from email.utils import format_datetime

def render_email(**data):
    with open('email_template.eml') as f:
        template = Template(f.read())
    return template.render(**data)
```

```
data = {'date': format_datetime(datetime.now()),
        'to': 'bob@example.com',
        'from': 'tarek@ziade.org',
        'subject': "Your Tarek's Burger order",
        'name': 'Bob',
        'items': [{'name': 'Cheeseburger', 'price': 4.5},
                  {'name': 'Fries', 'price': 2.},
                  {'name': 'Root Beer', 'price': 3.}]}

print(render_email(**data))
```

The `render_email` function uses the `Template` class to generate the email using the provided data.

 Jinja is quite powerful, and comes with many features we won't describe here, since it's out of the chapter's scope. But if you need to do some templating work in your microservices, it's a good choice, and it's present in Flask. Check out `http://jinja.pocoo.org/docs` for a full documentation on Jinja features.

# Configuration

When building applications, you will need to expose options to run them, like the information to connect to a database or any other variable that is specific to a deployment.

Flask uses a mechanism similar to Django in its configuration approach. The `Flask` object comes with an object called `config`, which contains some built-in variables, and which can be updated when you start your Flask app via your configuration objects.

For example, you can define a `Config` class in a `prod_settings.py` file as follows:

```
class Config:
    DEBUG = False
    SQLURI = 'postgres://tarek:xxx@localhost/db'
```

And then, load it from your app object using `app.config.from_object`:

```
>>> from flask import Flask
>>> app = Flask(__name__)
>>> app.config.from_object('prod_settings.Config')
>>> print(app.config)
<Config {'SESSION_COOKIE_HTTPONLY': True, 'LOGGER_NAME': '__main__',
         'APPLICATION_ROOT': None, 'MAX_CONTENT_LENGTH': None,
         'PRESERVE_CONTEXT_ON_EXCEPTION': None,
         'LOGGER_HANDLER_POLICY': 'always',
```

```
'SESSION_COOKIE_DOMAIN': None, 'SECRET_KEY': None,
'EXPLAIN_TEMPLATE_LOADING': False,
'TRAP_BAD_REQUEST_ERRORS': False,
'SESSION_REFRESH_EACH_REQUEST': True,
'TEMPLATES_AUTO_RELOAD': None,
'JSONIFY_PRETTYPRINT_REGULAR': True,
'SESSION_COOKIE_PATH': None,
'SQLURI': 'postgres://tarek:xxx@localhost/db',
'JSON_SORT_KEYS': True, 'PROPAGATE_EXCEPTIONS': None,
'JSON_AS_ASCII': True, 'PREFERRED_URL_SCHEME': 'http',
'TESTING': False, 'TRAP_HTTP_EXCEPTIONS': False,
'SERVER_NAME': None, 'USE_X_SENDFILE': False,
'SESSION_COOKIE_NAME': 'session', 'DEBUG': False,
'JSONIFY_MIMETYPE': 'application/json',
'PERMANENT_SESSION_LIFETIME': datetime.timedelta(31),
'SESSION_COOKIE_SECURE': False,
'SEND_FILE_MAX_AGE_DEFAULT': datetime.timedelta(0, 43200)}>
```

However, there are two significant drawbacks when using Python modules as configuration files.

First, it can be tempting to add into those configuration modules some code that's more complex than simple flat classes; and by doing so, it means you will have to treat those modules like the rest of the application code. That's usually not what happens when applications are deployed: the configuration files are managed separately from the code.

Secondly, if another team is in charge of managing the configuration file of your application, they will need to edit the Python code to do so. While this is usually fine, it makes it easier to introduce some problems. For instance, it's harder to make Puppet templates out of Python modules rather than flat, static configuration files.

Since Flask exposes its configuration via `app.config`, it's pretty simple to load additional options from a YAML file, or any other text-based file.

The INI format is the most-used format in the Python community, because there's an INI parser included in the standard library, and because it's pretty universal.

Many Flask extensions exist to load the configuration from an INI file, but using the standard library `ConfigParser` is trivial. Although, there's one major caveat from using INI files: variables values are all strings, and your application needs to take care of converting them to the right type.

The **Konfig** project (`https://github.com/mozilla-services/konfig`) is a small layer on top of `ConfigParser`, which automates the conversion of simple types like integers and Booleans.

Using it with Flask is straightforward:

```
$ more settings.ini
[flask]
DEBUG = 0
SQLURI = postgres://tarek:xxx@localhost/db

$ python
>>> from konfig import Config
>>> from flask import Flask
>>> c = Config('settings.ini')
>>> app = Flask(__name__)
>>> app.config.update(c.get_map('flask'))
>>> app.config['SQLURI']
'postgres://tarek:xxx@localhost/db
```

# Blueprints

When you write microservices that have more than a single endpoint, you will end up with a handful of decorated functions--maybe, a few per endpoint. The first logical step to organize your code is to have one module per endpoint, and when you create your app instance, to make sure they get imported so that Flask registers the views.

For example, if your microservice manages a company employees database, you could have one endpoint to interact with all employees, and one with teams. You could organize your application in these three modules:

- `app.py`: To contain the Flask `app` object, and to run the app
- `employees.py`: To provide all the views related to employees
- `teams.py`: To provide all the views related to teams

From there, `employee` and `teams` can be seen as a subset of the app, and might have a few specific utilities and configuration.

Blueprints take that logic a step further by providing a way to group your views into namespaces. You can create a `Blueprint` object which looks like a Flask app object, and then use it to arrange some views. The initialization process can then register blueprints with `app.register_blueprint`. That call will make sure that all the views defined in the blueprint are part of the app.

A possible implementation of the employee's blueprint could be as follows:

```
from flask import Blueprint, jsonify

teams = Blueprint('teams', __name__)

_DEVS = ['Tarek', 'Bob']
_OPS = ['Bill']
_TEAMS = {1: _DEVS, 2: _OPS}

@teams.route('/teams')
def get_all():
    return jsonify(_TEAMS)

@teams.route('/teams/<int:team_id>')
def get_team(team_id):
    return jsonify(_TEAMS[team_id])
```

The main module (`app.py`) can then import this file, and register its blueprint with `app.register_blueprint(teams)`.

This mechanism is also interesting when you want to reuse a generic set of views in another application, or several times in the same application.

The Flask-Restless (`https://flask-restless.readthedocs.io`) extension, for instance, which is a **Create, Read, Update, and Delete (CRUD)** tool that automatically exposes a database through a REST API by introspecting SQLAlchemy models, generates one blueprint per SQLAlchemy model.

The following is from the Flask-Restless documentation (`Person` is SQLAlchemy model):

```
blueprint = manager.create_api_blueprint(Person, methods=['GET',
'POST'])
app.register_blueprint(blueprint)
```

# Error handling and debugging

When something goes wrong in your application, it's important to be able to control what responses will the clients will receive. In HTML web apps, you usually get specific HTML pages when you encounter a 404 or a 50x error, and that's how Flask works out of the box. But when building microservices, you need to have more control on what should be sent back to the client--that's where *custom error handlers* come in handy.

The other important feature is the ability to debug what's wrong with your code when an unexpected error occurs. And Flask comes with a built-in debugger we'll discover in this section, which can be activated when your app runs in the *debug mode*.

# Custom error handler

When your code does not handle an exception, Flask returns an HTTP 500 response without providing any specific information, like the traceback. Producing a generic error is a safe default behavior to avoid leaking any private information to the users in the error body.

The default 500 response is a simple HTML page along with the right status code:

```
$ curl http://localhost:5000/api
<!DOCTYPE HTML PUBLIC "-//W3C//DTD HTML 3.2 Final//EN">
<title>500 Internal Server Error</title>
<h1>Internal Server Error</h1>
<p>The server encountered an internal error and was unable to complete your
request.  Either the server is overloaded or there is an error in the
application.</p>
```

When implementing microservices using JSON, it's a good practice to make sure that every response sent to the clients, including any exception, is JSON formatted. Consumers of your microservice will expect every response to be machine-parseable.

Flask lets you customize the app error handling via a couple of functions. The first one is the `@app.errorhandler` decorator, which works like `@app.route`. But instead of providing an endpoint, the decorator links a function to a specific error code.

In the following example, we use it to connect a function that will return a JSON-formatted error when Flask returns a 500 server response (any code exception):

```
from flask import Flask, jsonify

app = Flask(__name__)

@app.errorhandler(500)
def error_handling(error):
    return jsonify({'Error': str(error)}, 500)

@app.route('/api')
def my_microservice():
    raise TypeError("Some Exception")

if __name__ == '__main__':
    app.run()
```

Flask will call this error view no matter what exception the code raises.

However, in case your application issues an HTTP 404 or any other 4xx or 5xx response, you will be back to the default HTML responses that Flask sends.

To make sure your app sends JSON for every 4xx and 50x, we need to register that function to each error code.

One place where you can find the list of errors is in the `abort.mapping` dict. In the following code snippet, we register the `error_handling` function to every error using `app.register_error_handler`, which is similar to the `@app.errorhandler` decorator:

```python
from flask import Flask, jsonify, abort
from werkzeug.exceptions import HTTPException, default_exceptions

def JsonApp(app):
    def error_handling(error):
        if isinstance(error, HTTPException):
            result = {'code': error.code, 'description':
                        error.description, 'message': str(error)}
        else:
            description = abort.mapping[500].description
            result = {'code': 500, 'description': description,
                        'message': str(error)}

        resp = jsonify(result)
        resp.status_code = result['code']
        return resp

    for code in default_exceptions.keys():
        app.register_error_handler(code, error_handling)

    return app

app = JsonApp(Flask(__name__))

@app.route('/api')
def my_microservice():
    raise TypeError("Some Exception")

if __name__ == '__main__':
    app.run()
```

The `JsonApp` function wraps a Flask app instance, and sets up the custom JSON error handler for every 4xx and 50x error that might occur.

# The debug mode

The Flask application `run` method has a `debug` option, which, when used, runs it in the debug mode:

```
app.run(debug=True)
```

The debug mode is a special mode, where the built-in debugger takes precedence on any error, and allows you to interact with the app from a browser:

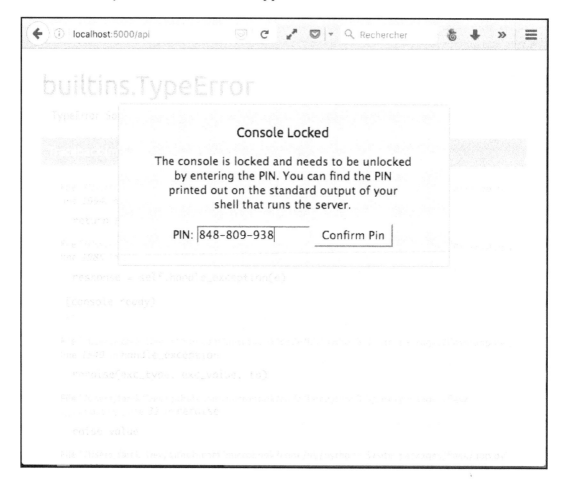

The console in the web-debugger will let you interact with the current app, and inspect variables or execute any Python code that is in the current execution frame.

Flask will even let you configure a third-party debugger. JetBrains's **PyCharm** (`https://ww w.jetbrains.com/pycharm`), for example, is a commercial IDE for Python, which offers a powerful visual debugger that can be set up to run with Flask.

 Since the debug mode allows remote code execution, it's a security hazard even though you need to provide a PIN to access the console. In 2015, the Patreon online service got hacked via the Flask debugger. You need to be extremely cautious not to run the debug mode in production. The **Bandit** security linter (`https://wiki.openstack.org/wiki/Security/Projects /Bandit`) tracks Flask applications that are executed with a plain debug flag, and can be used to prevent deploying an application with that flag.

The plain old `pdb` module is also a good option when you are tracking down a problem by inserting a `pdb.set_trace()` call in your code.

# A microservice skeleton

So far in this chapter, we've looked at how Flask works, and at most of the built-in features it provides--and we will be using them throughout this book.

One topic we have not covered yet is how to organize the code in your projects, and how to instantiate your Flask app. Every example so far used a single Python module and the `app.run()` call to run the service.

Having everything in a module is, of course, a terrible idea unless your code is just a few lines. And since we will want to release and deploy the code, it's better to have it inside a Python package so that we can use standard packaging tools like **Pip** and **Setuptools**.

It's also a good idea to organize views into blueprints, and have one module per blueprint.

Lastly, the `run()` call can be removed from the code, since Flask provides a generic runner that looks for an app variable given a module pointed by the `FLASK_APP` environment variable. Using that runner offers extra options like the ability to configure the host and port that will be used to run the app.

The microservice project on GitHub (`https://github.com/Runnerly/microservice`) was created for this book, and is a generic Flask project that you can use to start a microservice. It implements a simple layout, which works well for building microservices.

You can install it and run it, then modify it.

 This project uses **Flakon** (`https://github.com/Runnerly/flakon`), which is a minimalistic helper that takes care of configuring and instantiating a Flask application with an INI file and a default JSON behavior. Flakon was also created for this book to let you focus on building microservices with the minimal amount of boilerplate code. Flakon is opinionated, so if its decisions do not suit you, you can just remove it from your project, and build your function that creates an app; or use one of the existing open source projects that provide this kind of feature.

The `microservice` project skeleton contains the following structure:

- `setup.py`: Distutils' setup file, which is used to install and release the project
- `Makefile`: A Makefile that contains a few useful targets to make, build, and run the project
- `settings.ini`: The application default settings in the INI file
- `requirements.txt`: The project dependencies following the pip format
- `myservices/`: The actual package
    - `__init__.py`
    - `app.py`: The app module, which contains the app itself
    - `views/`: A directory containing the views organized in blueprints
        - `__init__.py`
        - `home.py`: The home blueprint, which serves the root endpoint
    - `tests`: The directory containing all the tests
        - `__init__.py`
        - `test_home.py`: Tests for the home blueprint views

In the following code, the `app.py` file instantiates a Flask app using Flakon's `create_app` helper; that takes a few options like a list of blueprints, which get registered:

```
import os
from flakon import create_app
from myservice.views import blueprints

_HERE = os.path.dirname(__file__)
_SETTINGS = os.path.join(_HERE, '..', 'settings.ini')

app = create_app(blueprints=blueprints, settings=_SETTINGS)
```

The `home.py` view uses Flakon's `JsonBlueprint` class, which implements the error handling we've seen in the previous section. It also automatically calls `jsonify()` on the object returned by the view if its a dictionary, like how the Bottle framework does:

```
from flakon import JsonBlueprint

home = JsonBlueprint('home', __name__)

@home.route('/')
def index():
    """Home view.

    This view will return an empty JSON mapping.
    """
    return {}
```

This example application can run via Flask's built-in command line, using the package name:

```
$ FLASK_APP=myservice flask run
 * Serving Flask app "myservice"
 * Running on http://127.0.0.1:5000/ (Press CTRL+C to quit)
```

From there, building JSON views for your microservice consists of adding modules in `microservice/views`, and their corresponding tests.

# Summary

This chapter gave us a pretty detailed overview of the Flask framework, and how it can be used to build microservices.

The main takeaways are as follows:

- Flask wraps a simple request-response mechanism around the WSGI protocol, which lets you write your applications in almost vanilla Python.

- Flask is easy to extend, and it works with Python 3.

- Flask comes with nice built-in features: blueprints, globals, signals, a template engine, error handlers, and a debugger.

- The microservice project is a Flask skeleton, which will be used to write microservices throughout this book. It's a simple app that uses an INI file for its configuration, and makes sure everything produced by the app is JSON.

The next chapter will focus on development methodology: how to continuously code, test, and, document your microservices.

# 3
# Coding, Testing, and Documenting - the Virtuous Cycle

Every software project that's deployed suffers from bugs that are inevitable--and bugs are time and money consuming.

Using a **Test-Driven Development** (**TDD**) approach, where you write tests alongside the code you are creating, will not always improve the quality of your project, but it will make your team more agile. This means that the developers who need to fix a bug, or refactor a part of an application, will be able to do a faster and better job when relying on a battery of tests. If they break a feature, the tests should warn them about it.

Writing tests is time-consuming at first, but in the long run, it's often the best approach to make a project grow. Of course, it's always possible to write bad tests and end up with poor results, or create a test suite that's horrible to maintain and takes too long to run. The best tools and processes in the world won't prevent a sloppy developer from producing bad software:

The software industry has long debated on the virtues of TDD. But in the last decade, most of the research papers that tried to measure the benefits of TDD concluded that software built with it costs less money in the long term, and is as good, or better, in terms of quality. This page links to a few research papers on this topic at http://biblio.gdinwiddie.com/biblio/StudiesOfTestDrivenDevelopment.

Writing tests is also a good way to get some perspective on your code. Does the API you've designed make sense? Do things fit well together? And when the team grows or changes, tests are the best source of information. Unlike documentation, they should reflect what the current version of the code does.

But documentation is still an important part of a project even though it's hard and time-consuming to maintain. It's the first stop for anyone using your software or joining the team to work on it. How is the application installed and configured? How to run tests or add features? How is it designed the way it is, and why?

After a while, it's pretty rare to see a project's documentation fully up-to-date with what the code has become unless some dedicated people work on it. And it can be an immense frustration for developers to find out that the code examples in the documentation are broken after some refactoring. But there are ways to mitigate these issues; for instance, code extracts in the documentation could be part of the test suite to make sure they work.

In any case, no matter how much energy you spend on tests and documentation, there's one golden rule: *testing, documenting, and coding your projects should be done continuously*. In other words, changes in the code should ideally be reflected in the tests and documentation as they happen.

After providing a few general tips on how to test in Python, this chapter focuses on what testing and documentation tools can be used in the context of building microservices with Flask, and how to set up continuous integration with some popular online services.

It's organized into five parts:

- The different kind of tests
- Using WebTest against your microservice
- Using pytest and Tox
- Developer documentation
- Continuous integration

# Different kinds of tests

There are many different kinds of tests, and it can be confusing sometimes to know what we're talking about. For instance, when people refer to *functional tests*, they may refer to different kinds of tests depending on the project's nature.

In the microservice land, we can classify tests into these five distinct goals:

- **Unit tests**: Make sure a class or a function works as expected in isolation
- **Functional tests**: Verify that the microservice does what it says from the consumer's point of view, and behaves correctly even on bad requests
- **Integration tests**: Verify how a microservice integrates with all its network dependencies
- **Load tests**: Measure the microservice performances
- **End-to-end tests**: Verify that the whole system works with an end-to-end test

We will see these in detail in the following sections.

# Unit tests

Unit tests are the simplest tests to add to a project, and the standard library comes with everything needed to write some. In a project based on Flask, there usually are, alongside the views, some functions and classes, which can be unit-tested in isolation.

However, the concept of *separation* is quite vague for a Python project, because we don't use contracts or interfaces like in other languages, where the implementation of the class is separated from its definition.

Testing in isolation in Python usually means that you instantiate a class or call a function with specific arguments, and verify that you get the expected result. When the class or function calls another piece of code that's not built in Python or its standard library, it's not in isolation anymore.

In some cases, it will be useful to *mock* those calls to achieve isolation. **Mocking** means replacing a piece of code with a mock version, which takes specified input, yields specified outputs, and fakes the behavior in between. But mocking is often a dangerous exercise, because it's easy to implement a different behavior in your mocks and end up with some code that works with your mocks but not the real thing. That problem often occurs when you update your project's dependencies, and your mocks are not updated to reflect the new behaviors, which might have been introduced in some library.

So, limiting the usage of mocks to the three following use cases is good practice:

- **I/O operations**: When the code performs calls to third-party services or a resource (socket, files, and so on), and you can't run them from within your tests
- **CPU intensive operations**: When the call computes something that would make the test suite too slow
- **Specific behaviors to reproduce**: When you want to write a test to try out your code under specific behaviors (for example, a network error or changing the date or time by mocking the date time and time modules)

Consider the following class, which can be used to query a bug list via the Bugzilla REST API, using the `requests` (`http://docs.python-requests.org`) library:

```python
import requests

class MyBugzilla:
    def __init__(self, account, server =
                    'https://bugzilla.mozilla.org'):
        self.account = account
        self.server = server
        self.session = requests.Session()
```

```
def bug_link(self, bug_id):
    return '%s/show_bug.cgi?id=%s' % (self.server, bug_id)

def get_new_bugs(self):
    call = self.server + '/rest/bug'
    params = {'assigned_to': self.account,
              'status': 'NEW',
              'limit': 10}
    try:
        res = self.session.get(call, params=params).json()
    except requests.exceptions.ConnectionError:
        # oh well
        res = {'bugs': []}

    def _add_link(bug):
        bug['link'] = self.bug_link(bug)
        return bug

    for bug in res['bugs']:
        yield _add_link(bug)
```

This class has a bug_link() method, which we can test in isolation, and one
get_new_bugs() method, which performs calls to the Bugzilla server. It would be too
complicated to run our Bugzilla server when the test is executed, so we can mock the calls
and provide our JSON values for the class to work in isolation.

This technique is used in the following example with request_mock (http://requests-mo
ck.readthedocs.io), which is a handy library to mock request network calls:

```
import unittest
from unittest import mock
import requests
from requests.exceptions import ConnectionError
import requests_mock
from bugzilla import MyBugzilla


class TestBugzilla(unittest.TestCase):
    def test_bug_id(self):
        zilla = MyBugzilla('tarek@mozilla.com', server =
                            ='http://example.com')
        link = zilla.bug_link(23)
        self.assertEqual(link, 'http://example.com/show_bug.cgi?id=23')

    @requests_mock.mock()
    def test_get_new_bugs(self, mocker):
        # mocking the requests call and send back two bugs
```

```
        bugs = [{'id': 1184528}, {'id': 1184524}]
        mocker.get(requests_mock.ANY, json={'bugs': bugs})

        zilla = MyBugzilla('tarek@mozilla.com',
                            server ='http://example.com')
        bugs = list(zilla.get_new_bugs())
        self.assertEqual(bugs[0]['link'],
                        'http://example.com/show_bug.cgi?id=1184528')

    @mock.patch.object(requests.Session, 'get',
                    side_effect=ConnectionError('No network'))
    def test_network_error(self, mocked):
        # faking a connection error in request if the web is down
        zilla = MyBugzilla('tarek@mozilla.com',
                           server='http://example.com')

        bugs = list(zilla.get_new_bugs())
        self.assertEqual(len(bugs), 0)

if __name__ == '__main__':
    unittest.main()
```

 You should keep an eye on all your mocks as the project grows, and make sure they are not the only kind of tests that cover a particular feature. For instance, if the Bugzilla project comes up with a new structure for its REST API, and the server your project uses is updated, your tests will happily pass with your broken code until the mocks reflect the new behavior.

The test_network_error() method is a second test which fakes a network error by triggering requests' connection error, using Python's mock patch decorator. This test ensures the class behaves as expected when there's no network.

This kind of unit test is usually enough to cover most of your classes' and functions' behaviors.

This test class will probably cover more cases as the project grows and new situations occur. For instance, what happens if the server sends back a malformed JSON body?

But there's no need to have tests for all the failures you can come up with on day one. In a microservice project, unit tests are not a priority, and aiming at 100% test coverage (where every line of your code is called somewhere in your tests) in your unit tests will add a lot of maintenance work for little benefits.

It's better to focus on building a robust set of functional tests.

# Functional tests

Functional tests for a microservice project are all the tests that interact with the published API by sending HTTP requests and asserting the HTTP responses.

This definition is broad enough to include any test that can call the app, from *fuzzing tests* (you send gibberish to your app and see what happens) to *penetration tests* (you try to break the app security), and so on.

As developers, the two most important kinds of functional tests we should focus on are these:

- Tests that verify that the application does what it was built for
- Tests that ensure an abnormal behavior that was fixed is not happening anymore

The way those scenarios are organized in the tests class is up to the developers, but the general pattern is to create an instance of the application in the test class and then interact with it.

In that context, the network layer is not used, and the application is called directly by the tests, but the same request-response cycle happens, so it's realistic enough. However, we would still mock out any network calls happening within the application.

Flask includes a `FlaskClient` class to build requests, which can be instantiated directly from the `app` object via its `test_client()` method.

The following is an example of a test against the first app we showed in this chapter, which sends back a JSON body on `/api/`:

```
import unittest
import json
from flask_basic import app as tested_app

class TestApp(unittest.TestCase):
    def test_help(self):
        # creating a FlaskClient instance to interact with the app
```

```
        app = tested_app.test_client()

        # calling /api/ endpoint
        hello = app.get('/api')

        # asserting the body
        body = json.loads(str(hello.data, 'utf8'))
        self.assertEqual(body['Hello'], 'World!')

if __name__ == '__main__':
    unittest.main()
```

The `FlaskClient` class has one method per HTTP verb, and sends back `Response` objects that can be used to assert the results. In the preceding example, we used `.get()`.

There's a `testing` flag in the `Flask` class, which you can use to propagate exceptions to the test, but some prefer not to use it by default to get back from the app what a real client would get--for instance, to make sure the body of 5xx or 4xx errors are converted to JSON for API consistency.

In the following example, the `/api/` call produces an exception, and we're making sure the client gets a proper 500 with a structured JSON body in `test_raise()`.

The `test_proper_404()` test method does the same tests on a non-existent path:

```
import unittest
import json
from flask_error import app as tested_app

_404 = ('The requested URL was not found on the server.  '
        'If you entered the URL manually please check your '
        'spelling and try again.')

class TestApp(unittest.TestCase):
    def setUp(self):
        # creating a client to interact with the app
        self.app = tested_app.test_client()

    def test_raise(self):
        # this won't raise a Python exception but return a 500
        hello = self.app.get('/api')
        body = json.loads(str(hello.data, 'utf8'))
        self.assertEqual(body['code'], 500)

    def test_proper_404(self):
        # calling a non existing endpoint
        hello = self.app.get('/dwdwqqwdwqd')
```

```
    # yeah it's not there
    self.assertEqual(hello.status_code, 404)

    # but we still get a nice JSON body
    body = json.loads(str(hello.data, 'utf8'))
    self.assertEqual(body['code'], 404)
    self.assertEqual(body['message'], '404: Not Found')
    self.assertEqual(body['description'], _404)

if __name__ == '__main__':
    unittest.main()
```

An alternative to the `FlaskClient` method is **WebTest** (`http://webtest.pythonpaste.org`), which offers a few more features out of the box. It's covered later in this chapter.

# Integration tests

Unit tests and functional tests focus on testing your service code without calling other network resources, whether they are other microservices from your application or third-party services like databases, queues, and so on. For the sake of speed, isolation, and simplicity, network calls are mocked.

Integration tests are functional tests without any mocking, and should be able to run on a real deployment of your application. For example, if your service interacts with Redis and RabbitMQ, they will be called by your service as normal when the integration tests are run.

The benefit is to avoid falling into the problems that were described earlier when mocking network interactions. You will be sure that your application works in a production execution context only if you try it for real.

The caveat is that running tests against an actual deployment makes it harder to set up tests data, or to clean up whatever data was produced from within the service during the test. Patching the application behavior to reproduce a problem is also a difficult task.

But along with unit and functional tests, integration tests are an excellent complement to verify your application behavior.

Typically, integration tests are executed on a development or staging deployment of your service, but if it's easy to do, you can also have a dedicated testing deployment, which will be used for that sole purpose.

You can use whatever tool you want to write your integration test. A curl script, for instance, might sometimes be enough on some microservices.

But it's nicer if integration tests can be written in Python, and can be part of your project's tests collection. To do this, a Python script that uses requests to call your microservice can do the trick. Or better, in case you provide a client library for your microservice, it's a good way to test it.

 What differentiates integration tests from functional tests is mostly the fact that it's a real server that gets called. What if we could write functional tests that can either be run on a local Flask application or against an actual deployment? This is possible with WebTest, as we will find out later in this chapter.

# Load tests

The goal of a load test is to understand your service's bottlenecks under stress and to plan for the future, not to do premature optimizations.

Maybe the first version of your service will be fast enough for what it will be used for, but understanding its limits will help you determining how you want to deploy it and if its design is future-proof in case the load increases.

It's a common mistake to spend a lot of time on making each microservice as fast as possible, and end up with an application that relies on a single point of failure because your design makes it hard to deploy several instances of one particular microservice.

Writing load tests can help you answer the following questions:

- How many users can one instance of my service serve when I deploy it on this machine?
- What's the average response time when there are 10, 100 or 1,000 concurrent requests? Can I handle that much concurrency?
- When my service is under stress, is it running out of RAM or is it mainly CPU-bound?
- Can I add other instances of the same service and scale horizontally?
- If my microservice calls other services, can I use pools of connectors, or do I have to serialize all the interactions through a single connection?
- Can my service run for multiple days at a time without degradation?
- Is my service working properly after a usage peak?

Depending on the kind of load you want to achieve, there are many tools available, from simple command-line tools to heavier distributed load systems.

For performing a simple load test that does not require any particular scenario, **Boom** (http s://github.com/tarekziade/boom) is an **Apache Bench** (**AB**) equivalent written in Python, which can be used to hit your endpoints.

In the following example, Boom performs a 10-second load test against a Flask web server on the /api/ endpoint, using 100 concurrent users--and ends up with 286 **requests per second** (**RPS**):

```
$ boom http://127.0.0.1:5000/api -c 100 -d 10 -q

-------- Results --------
Successful calls          2866
Total time                10.0177 s
Average                   0.3327 s
Fastest                   0.2038 s
Slowest                   0.4782 s
Amplitude                 0.2744 s
Standard deviation        0.035476
RPS                       286
BSI                       Pretty good

-------- Status codes --------
Code 200                  2866 times.

-------- Legend --------
RPS: Request Per Second
BSI: Boom Speed Index
```

These numbers don't mean much, as they will vary a lot depending on the deployment, and from where you run them. For instance, if your Flask application is served behind nginx with several workers, it will handle better the stream of incoming connections.

But this small test alone can often catch problems early on, in particular when your code is opening socket connections itself. If something's wrong in the microservice design, it's quite easy to detect it with a tool like Boom.

If you need to write interactive scenarios, another small command-line tool is **Molotov** (htt ps://github.com/tarekziade/molotov), which gives you the ability to write Python functions where you can query a microservice and check the responses.

In the following example, each function is a possible scenario that gets picked by Molotov to run against the server:

```
import json
from molotov import scenario

@scenario(5)
async def scenario_one(session):
    res = await session.get('http://localhost:5000/api').json()
    assert res['Hello'] == 'World!'
@scenario(30)
async def scenario_two(session):
    somedata = json.dumps({'OK': 1})
    res = await session.post('http://localhost:5000/api',
                            data=somedata)
    assert res.status_code == 200
```

Both tools will give you some metrics, but they are not very accurate because of the network and client CPU variance on the box they are launched from. For instance, the test itself will stress the machine resources, and that will impact the metrics.

When performing a load test, it's better to add some metrics on the server side. At the Flask level, you can use a small tool like **flask-profiler** (https://github.com/muatik/flask-pro filer), which collects how long each request takes, and offers a dashboard that will let you browse the collected times--its overhead is minimal.

 You can also send detail metrics via **StatsD** (https://github.com/etsy/s tatsd), and use a dedicated dashboard application like **Graphite** (http ://graphite.readthedocs.io). Metrics are covered in Chapter 6, *Monitoring Your Services*.

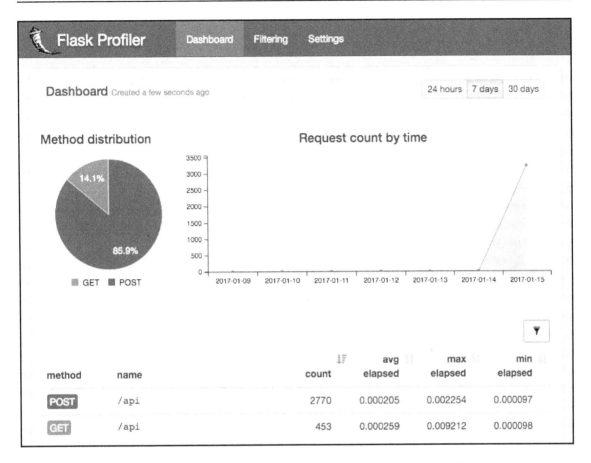

If you need to do a heavier load test, you will need to use a load testing framework, which can distribute the tests across several agents. One of the possible tools is **locust.io** (`http://docs.locust.io/`).

# End-to-end tests

An end-to-end test will check that the whole system works as expected from the end-user point of view. The test needs to behave like a real client, and call the system through the same **User Interface (UI)**.

Depending on the type of application you are writing, a simple HTTP client might not be enough to simulate a real user. For instance, if the visible part of the system through which users are interacting is a web application with HTML pages that gets rendered on a client-side, you will need to use a tool like **Selenium** (http://docs.seleniumhq.org/). It will automate your browser in order to make sure that the client requests every CSS and JavaScript files and then renders correctly every page.

JavaScript frameworks are now doing a lot of work on the client side to produce pages. Some of them have completely removed server-side rendering of templates, and just grab data from the server to generate the HTML page by manipulating the **Document Object Model** (**DOM**) through the browser APIs. Calls to the server, in that case, consist of getting all the static JavaScript files needed for rendering a given URL, plus the data.

 Writing end-to-end tests is outside the scope of this book, but you can refer to *Selenium Testing Tools Cookbook* from the same editor to learn how to write some.

The following points summarize what we've learned in this section:

- Functional tests are the most important tests to write, and it's easy to do it in Flask by instantiating the app in the tests and interacting with it
- Unit tests are a good complement, but don't abuse mocks
- Integration tests are like functional tests, but against a real deployment
- Load tests are useful to learn about your microservice bottlenecks and plan for the next steps
- End-to-end tests require using the same UI that the client would normally use

Knowing when you will need to write integration, load, or end-to-end tests depends on how your project is managed--but both unit and functional tests should be written every time you change something. Ideally, each change you make in your code should include a new test or modify an existing test.

Unit tests can be written using vanilla Python, thanks to the excellent `unittest` package included in the standard library--and we will see later how the **pytest** (http://docs.pytest.org) library adds awesomeness on the top of it.

For functional tests, we'll look in the next section at WebTest.

# Using WebTest

**WebTest** (http://webtest.readthedocs.io) has been around for a long time. It was written by Ian Bicking back in the days of the **Paste** project, and is based on the **WebOb** (http://docs.webob.org) project, which provides a Request and Response class similar (but not compatible) to Flask's.

WebTest wraps call to a WSGI application like FlaskTest does, and lets you interact with it. WebTest is somewhat similar to FlaskTest, with a few extra helpers when dealing with JSON, and a neat feature to call non-WSGI applications.

To use it with Flask, you can install the flask-webtest package (https://flask-webtest.readthedocs.io/), and you will get a similar integration level as Flask's native tool:

```python
import unittest
from flask_basic import app as tested_app
from flask_webtest import TestApp

class TestMyApp(unittest.TestCase):
    def test_help(self):
        # creating a client to interact with the app
        app = TestApp(tested_app)

        # calling /api/ endpoint
        hello = app.get('/api')

        # asserting the body
        self.assertEqual(hello.json['Hello'], 'World!')

if __name__ == '__main__':
    unittest.main()
```

We've said earlier that integration tests were similar to functional tests except that they called a real server instead of instantiating a local WSGI app.

WebTest leverages the WSGIProxy2 library (https://pypi.python.org/pypi/WSGIProxy2), which converts calls that are made to the Python application to HTTP requests made to a real HTTP application.

The previous script can be slightly modified to become an integration test if you set an HTTP_SERVER variable in the environ function, as follows:

```python
import unittest
import os
class TestMyApp(unittest.TestCase):
```

```
def setUp(self):
    # if HTPP_SERVER is set, we use it as an endpoint
    http_server = os.environ.get('HTTP_SERVER')
    if http_server is not None:
        from webtest import TestApp
        self.app = TestApp(http_server)
    else:
        # fallbacks to the wsgi app
        from flask_basic import app
        from flask_webtest import TestApp
        self.app = TestApp(app)

def test_help(self):
    # calling /api/ endpoint
    hello = self.app.get('/api')

    # asserting the body
    self.assertEqual(hello.json['Hello'], 'World!')

if __name__ == '__main__':
    unittest.main()
```

When this last test is executed with `HTTP_SERVER=http://myservice/`, it performs all its calls to that service.

That trick is pretty handy to turn some of your functional tests into integration tests without having to write two distinct tests. As we said earlier, it has some limitations, since you can't interact locally with the application instance. But it's extremely useful to validate that a deployed service works as expected directly from your test suite, just by flipping an option.

# Using pytest and Tox

So far, all the tests we have written used `unittest.TestCase` classes and `unittest.main()` to run them. As your project grows, you will have more and more tests modules around.

To automatically discover and run all the tests in a project, the `unittest` package has introduced a *Test Discovery* feature in Python 3.2, which finds and runs tests given a few options. This feature has been around for a while in projects like **Nose** (`https://nose.read thedocs.io`) and **pytest**, and that's what inspired the `unittest` package in the standard library.

Which runner to use is a matter of taste, and as long as you stick to writing your tests in `TestCase` classes, your tests will be compatible with all of them.

That said, the pytest project is very popular in the Python community, and since it offers extensions, people have started to write useful tools around it. Its runner is also quite efficient, as it starts to run the tests while they are still discovered in the background, making it a little faster than the others. Its output in the console is also beautiful and bright.

To use it in your project, you can simply install the `pytest` package with `pip`, and use the provided `pytest` command line. In the following example, the `pytest` command runs all the modules that start with `test_`:

```
$ pytest test_*
============== test session starts ===============================
platform darwin -- Python 3.5.2, pytest-3.0.5, py-1.4.32, pluggy-0.4.0
rootdir: /Users/tarek/Dev/github.com/microbook/code, inifile:
collected 7 items

test_app.py .
test_app_webtest.py .
test_bugzilla.py ...
test_error.py ..

============== 7 passed in 0.55 seconds ==============================
```

The `pytest` package comes with a lot of extensions, which are listed at http://plugincompat.herokuapp.com/.

Two useful extensions are **pytest-cov** and **pytest-flake8**. The first one uses the **coverage** tool (https://coverage.readthedocs.io) to display the test coverage of your project, and the second one runs the **Flake8** (https://gitlab.com/pycqa/flake8) linter to make sure that your code is following the PEP8 style, and has no unused imports.

Here's an invocation example with some style issues left on purpose:

```
$ pytest --cov=flask_basic --flake8 test_*
============== test session starts ===============================
platform darwin -- Python 3.5.2, pytest-3.0.5, py-1.4.32, pluggy-0.4.0
rootdir: /Users/tarek/Dev/github.com/microbook/code, inifile:
plugins: flake8-0.8.1, cov-2.4.0
collected 11 items

test_app.py F.
test_app_webtest.py F.
test_bugzilla.py F...
```

```
----------- coverage: platform darwin, python 3.5.2-final-0 -----------
Name                Stmts   Miss  Cover
----------------------------------------
flask_basic.py          6      1    83%
============= FAILURES =======================================
_____ FLAKE8-check _____
test_app.py:18:1: E305 expected 2 blank lines after class or function
definition, found 1
test_app.py:21:1: W391 blank line at end of file


_____ FLAKE8-check _____
test_app_webtest.py:29:1: W391 blank line at end of file


_____ FLAKE8-check _____
test_bugzilla.py:26:80: E501 line too long (80 > 79 characters)
test_bugzilla.py:28:80: E501 line too long (82 > 79 characters)
test_bugzilla.py:40:1: W391 blank line at end of file


============== 3 failed, 7 passed, 0 skipped in 2.19 seconds =============
```

Another useful tool that can be used in conjunction with pytest is **Tox** (`http://tox.readth edocs.io`).

If your projects need to run on several version of Python, or if you only want to make sure that your code can work on the latest Python 2 and Python 3 versions, Tox can automate the creation of separate environments to run your tests.

Telling Tox to run your project on Python 2.7 and Python 3.5 is done by installing Tox (using the `pip installs tox` command), and then creating a `tox.ini` configuration file in the root of your project. Tox makes the assumption that your project is a Python package, and therefore, has a `setup.py` file in the root directory alongside the `tox.ini` file, but that's the only requirement.

The `tox.ini` file contains the command lines to run the tests along with the Python versions it should be run against:

```
[tox]
envlist = py27,py35

[testenv]
deps = pytest
    pytest-cov
    pytest-flake8

commands =  pytest --cov=flask_basic --flake8 test_*
```

When Tox is executed by calling the `tox` command, it will create a separate environment for each Python version, deploy your package and its dependencies in it, and run the tests in it using the `pytest` command.

You can run a single environment with `tox -e`, which is very handy when you want to run the tests quickly. For instance, `tox -e py35` will just run `pytest` under Python 3.5.

Even if you support a single Python version, using Tox will ensure that your project can be installed in a current Python environment, and that you've correctly described all the dependencies.

Using this tool is highly recommended.

 *Chapter 9, Packaging Runnerly*, covers in detail how to package microservices, and will use Tox to do so among other instruments.

# Developer documentation

So far, we've looked at the different kinds of tests a microservice can have, and we've mentioned that the documentation should evolve with the code.

We're talking here about developer documentation. This includes everything a developer should know about your microservices project, things such as:

- How it's designed
- How to install it
- How to run the tests
- What are the exposed APIs and what data comes in and out, and so on

The **Sphinx** tool (`http://www.sphinx-doc.org/`), which was developed by Georg Brandl to document Python itself, became the standard in the Python community.

Sphinx treats documents like source code by separating the content from the layout. The usual way to use Sphinx is to have a `docs` directory in the project that contains the documentation content, and then call Sphinx's command-line utility to generate the documentation using an output format like HTML.

Producing an HTML output with Sphinx makes an excellent static website, which can be published on the web, as the tool adds index pages, a small JavaScript-based search engine, and navigation features.

The content of the documentation must be written in **reStructuredText (reST)** (`http://docu tils.sourceforge.net/rst.html`), which is the standard markup language in the Python community. A reST file is a simple text file with a non-intrusive syntax to mark section headers, links, text styles, and so on. Sphinx adds a few extensions and summarizes reST usage in this document, which should be your go-to page for learning how to write docs (`h ttp://www.sphinx-doc.org/en/latest/rest.html`).

 **Markdown** (`https://daringfireball.net/projects/markdown/`) is another popular markup language, which is used in the open source community. Unfortunately, Sphinx relies on some reST extensions, and has limited support to Markdown via the **recommonmark** package. The good news is that if you are familiar with Markdown, reST is not that different.

When you start a project with Sphinx using `sphinx-quickstart`, it generates a source tree with an `index.rst` file, which is the landing page of your documentation. From there, calling `sphinx-build` on it will create your documentation.

For example, if you want to generate an HTML documentation, you can add a `docs` environment in your `tox.ini` file, and let the tool build the documentation for you, as follows:

```
[tox]
envlist = py35,docs
...

[testenv:docs]
basepython=python
deps =
    -rrequirements.txt
    sphinx
commands=
    sphinx-build -W -b html docs/source docs/build
```

Running `tox -e docs` will generate your documentation.

Showing code examples in Sphinx can be done by pasting your code in a literal block prefixed by a :: marker or a `code-block` directive. In HTML, Sphinx will render it using the **Pygments** (`http://pygments.org/`) syntax highlighter:

```
Flask Application
=================

Below is the first example of a **Flask** app in the Flask official doc:

.. code-block:: python

    from flask import Flask
    app = Flask(__name__)

    @app.route("/")
    def hello():
        return "Hello World!"
    if __name__ == "__main__":
        app.run()

That snippet is a fully working app!
```

But adding code snippets in your documentation means that they might get deprecated as soon as you change your code. To avoid deprecation, one method is to have every code snippet displayed in your documentation extracted from the code itself.

To do this, you can document your modules, classes, and functions with their docstrings, and use the **Autodoc** Sphinx extension (`http://www.sphinx-doc.org/en/latest/ext/autodoc.html`), which grabs docstrings to inject them in the documentation.

This is how Python documents its standard library at `https://docs.python.org/3/library/index.html`. In the following example, the `autofunction` directive will catch the docstring from the `index` function that's located in the `myservice/views/home.py` module:

```
APIS
====

**myservice** includes one view that's linked to the root path:

.. autofunction :: myservice.views.home.index
```

When rendered in HTML, the page will look like this:

---

# APIS

**myservice** includes one view that's linked to the root path:

`myservice.views.home.index()`
    Home view.

    This view will return an empty JSON mapping.

©2017, joe. | Powered by Sphinx 1.5.1 & Alabaster 0.7.9 | Page source

---

The other option is to use a `literalinclude` directive, which will let you point a file and offer some options to highlight sections of that file. And when the file is a Python module, it can be included in the test suite to make sure it works.

The following is a full example of a project documentation using Sphinx:

```
Myservice
=========


**myservice** is a simple JSON Flask application that uses **Flakon**.

The application is created with :func:`flakon.create_app`:
.. literalinclude:: ../../myservice/app.py


The :file:`settings.ini` file which is passed to :func:`create_app`
contains options for running the Flask app, like the DEBUG flag:
.. literalinclude:: ../../myservice/settings.ini
   :language: ini


Blueprint are imported from :mod:`myservice.views` and one
Blueprint and view example was provided in :file:`myservice/views/home.py`:

.. literalinclude:: ../../myservice/views/home.py
   :name: home.py
   :emphasize-lines: 13
```

Views can return simple mappings (as highlighted in the example above), in that case, they will be converted into a JSON response.

When rendered in HTML the page will look like this:

# Myservice

**myservice** is a simple JSON Flask application that uses **Flakon**.

The application is created with **flakon.create_app()**:

```
import os
from flakon import create_app
from myservice.views import blueprints


_HERE = os.path.dirname(__file__)
_SETTINGS = os.path.join(_HERE, 'settings.ini')

app = create_app(blueprints=blueprints, settings=_SETTINGS)
```

The `settings.ini` file which is passed to **create_app()** contains options for running the Flask app, like the DEBUG flag:

```
[flask]
DEBUG = true
```

Blueprint are imported from **myservice.views** and one Blueprint and view example was provided in `myservice/views/home.py`:

```
from flask import Blueprint


home = Blueprint('home', __name__)


@home.route('/')
def index():
    """Home view.

    This view will return an empty JSON mapping.
    """
    return {}
```

Views can return simple mappings (as highlighted in the example above), in tha case they will be converted into a JSON response.

©2017, joe. | Powered by Sphinx 1.5.1 & Alabaster 0.7.9 | Page source

Of course, using Autodoc and `literalinclude` will not fix your narratives or design documents--maintaining a proper documentation up to date is hard, and requires more work than what developers want to put in it.

So anything that can be done to automate part of this documentation work is great.

 In `Chapter 4`, *Designing Runnerly*, we will see how we can document, in Sphinx, the microservice HTTP APIs by using `Swagger` and the `sphinx-swagger` extension.

The following points summarize this section:

- Sphinx is a powerful tool to document your project
- Treating your documentation as source code will facilitate its maintenance
- Tox can be used to rebuild the documentation when something changes
- If your documentation points to your code, it will be easier to maintain

# Continuous Integration

Tox can automate every step you are doing when you change something in your project: running tests on various Python interpreters, verifying coverage and PEP 8 conformance, building documentation, and so on.

But running all the checks on every change can be time and resource consuming, in particular, if you support several interpreters.

A **Continuous Integration** (CI) system solves this issue by taking care of this work every time something changes in your project.

Pushing your project in a shared repository under a **Distributed Version Control System** (**DVCS**) like Git or Mercurial, on a server will let you trigger a CI every time someone pushes a change on the server.

If you work on an open source software, and don't want to maintain your code server, GitHub (`http://github.com`), GitLab (`http://gitlab.com`), and Bitbucket (`https://bitbucket.org/`) are the most popular services. They will host your project for free if it's public, and offer social features, which will make it very easy for anyone to contribute to your project. They all provide integration points to run whatever needs to run when some changes are made in the project.

For example, on GitHub, if you see a typo in a reST document, you can change it directly from your browser, preview the result, and send a **Pull Request** (**PR**) to the project maintainer with a few clicks. The project will automatically get rebuilt, and a build status might even be displayed directly on your PR once it's done.

A lot of open source projects use these services to create a prosperous community of contributors. Mozilla uses GitHub for its **Rust** project (`https://github.com/rust-lang`), and there's no doubt that it helped lower the bar for attracting contributors.

# Travis-CI

GitHub integrates directly with some CIs. A very popular one is **Travis-CI** (`https://travis-ci.org/`), which runs for free for open source projects. Once you have an account on Travis-CI, a settings page will let you directly activate it for some of your GitHub projects.

Travis-CI relies on a `.travis.yml` YAML file, which needs to be located in the root of your repository, and describes what should be done with your project when something changes.

The YAML file has an `env` section, which can be used to describe a *matrix* of builds. A matrix is a collection of builds, which runs in parallel every time you change something in your project.

That matrix can be matched with your Tox environments by running each one of them separately via `tox -e`. By doing this, you will be able to know when a change breaks a particular environment:

```
language: python
python: 3.5
env:
  - TOX_ENV=py27
  - TOX_ENV=py35
  - TOX_ENV=docs
  - TOX_ENV=flake8
install:
  - pip install tox
script:
  - tox -e $TOX_ENV
```

Travis-CI includes everything needed to work with Python projects, so here, in the `install` section, the `pip` command can be used to install Tox and get started.

 The **tox-travis** project is an interesting one, which extends Tox to simply Travis integration. It provides features like an environment detection, which simplifies the writing of `tox.ini` files.

In case you have system-level dependencies, you can install them via the YAML file, and even run bash commands. The default environment runs Linux Debian, and you can type `apt-get` commands directly in the YAML file in the `before_install` section.

Travis also has support for setting up specific services like databases (refer to `https://docs .travis-ci.com/user/database-setup/`), which can get deployed for your projects via the `services` section.

If your microservice uses PosgtreSQL, MySQL, or any other popular open source databases, the chances are that it's available. If not, you can always compile it and run it on your build. The Travis documentation (`https://docs.travis-ci.com/`) is a good place to start when you work with Travis-CI.

 Travis can trigger builds on Linux agents, and also has some limited support for macOS X. Unfortunately, there's no support for Windows yet.

# ReadTheDocs

In the same vein as Travis, another service that can be hooked from within your GitHub repository is **ReadTheDocs** (**RTD**) (`https://docs.readthedocs.io`).

It generates and hosts the project documentation for you. There's nothing concrete to do in your repository. You just configure RTD, so it creates the documentation out of a **Sphinx HtmlDir**, and the service finds the elements automatically.

For non-trivial integration, RTD can be configured via a YAML file. Once the documentation is ready, it will be accessible at `https://<yourprojectname>.readthedocs.io`.

RTD comes with versions support, which is useful when you release a new version of your service. That feature scans Git tags, and lets you build and publish your documentation per each tag, and decide which one is the default.

Like versions, RTD offers internationalization (i18n) support in case you want to write your documentation in several languages.

# Coveralls

Another popular service you can hook in your repository if you use Travis-CI and GitHub or Bitbucket is **Coveralls** (`https://coveralls.io/`). This service displays your test code coverage in a nice web UI.

Once you've added your repository in your Coveralls account, you can trigger a call to `http://coveralls.io` directly from Travis-CI by instructing Tox to ping to `http://coveralls.io` after the tests are run.

The changes in the `tox.ini` file are done in the `[testenv]` section in bold.

```
[testenv]
passenv = TRAVIS TRAVIS_JOB_ID TRAVIS_BRANCH
deps = pytest
    pytest-cov
    coveralls
    -rrequirements.txt

commands =.
    pytest --cov-config .coveragerc --cov myservice myservice/tests
    - coveralls
```

The `coveralls-python` package (called Coveralls in PyPI) is used to send the payload to `coveralls.io` via its `coveralls` command after the `pytest` call is done.

Notice that the call is prefixed with a hyphen (-). Like in Makefiles, this prefix will ignore any failure, and will prevent Tox from failing when you run it locally. Running coveralls locally will always fail unless you set up a special `.coveralls.yml` file that contains an authentication token. When coveralls is running from Travis-CI, there's no need to have it, thanks to the magic of tokens passed from GitHub to the various services.

For Coveralls to work from Travis, there are a few environment variables that need to be passed via `passenv`; everything else should work automatically.

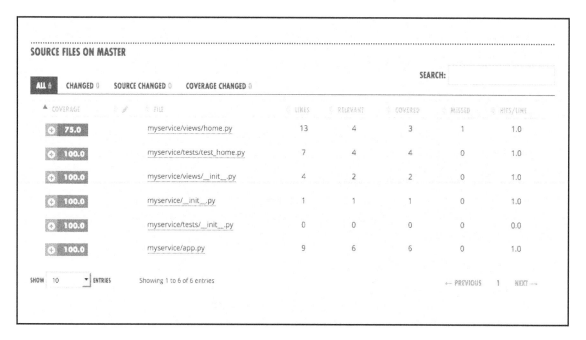

Every time you change your project and Travis-CI triggers a build, it will, in turn, trigger Coveralls to display an excellent summary of the coverage and how it evolves over time, like in the preceding screenshot.

Many other services can be hooked on GitHub or Travis-CI, Coveralls being one example.

Once you start to add services to your project, it's good practice to use badges in your project's README so the community can see in one glance the status for each one of them with links to the service.

For example, add this README.rst file in your repository:

```
microservice
==========

This project is a template for building microservices with Flask.

.. image::
https://coveralls.io/repos/github/tarekziade/microservice/badge.svg?branch=
master
    :target:
https://coveralls.io/github/tarekziade/microservice?branch=master

.. image:: https://travis-ci.org/tarekziade/microservice.svg?branch=master
    :target: https://travis-ci.org/tarekziade/microservice

.. image::
https://readthedocs.org/projects/microservice/badge/?version=latest
    :target: https://microservice.readthedocs.io
```

The preceding file be displayed like this on GitHub on your project's landing page:

# Summary

In this chapter, we went through the different tests that can be written for your microservices projects. Functional tests are the tests you will write more often, and WebTest is a great tool to write them. To run the tests, `pytest` combined with Tox will make your life easier.

Last, but not the least, if you host your project on GitHub, you can sct up a whole continuous integration system for free, thanks to Travis-CI. From there, numerous free services can be hooked to complement Travis, like Coveralls. You can also automatically build and publish your documentation on ReadTheDocs.

 If you want to look at how everything fits together, the microservice project published on GitHub at `https://github.com/Runnerly/microser vice`uses Travis-CI, RTD, and coveralls.io.

Now that we've covered how a Flask project can be continuously developed, tested, and documented, we can look at how to design a full microservices-based project. The next chapter will go through the design of such an application.

# 4
# Designing Runnerly

In Chapter 1, *Understanding Microservices*, we said that the natural way to build a microservices-based app is to start with a monolithic version that implements all the features, and then to split it into microservices where it makes sense. Trying to come up with a perfect design based on several microservices on day one is a recipe for disaster. It's very hard to know how the application is going to be organized and how it will evolve when it matures.

In this chapter, we will go through this process by building a monolithic application where we're implementing the required features. Then we'll look at where the app can be decomposed into smaller services. By the end of the chapter, we'll end up with a microservices-based design.

The chapter is organized into three main sections:

- Presentation of our Runnerly application and its user stories
- How Runnerly can be built as a monolithic application
- How a monolith can evolve into microservices

Of course, in real life, the splitting process happens over time once the monolithic app design matures for a bit. But for the purpose of this book, we'll make the assumption that the first version of the application was used for a while and offered us some insights to split it the right way, thanks to our time machine.

# The Runnerly application

**Runnerly** is a toy application for runners that was created for this book. Don't look for it in the Apple Store or the Play Store, as it's not released or deployed for real users.

However, the application is working for real, and you can find and study its different components on GitHub in the Runnerly organization at `https://github.com/Runnerly`.

Runnerly offers a web view where users can see their runs, races, and training plans, all in one glimpse. The view is responsive so the users can display the app on their phones or their desktop browser. Runnerly also sends monthly reports about the user activity.

A user who is registered into Runnerly needs to hook his/her account to **Strava** (`https://www.strava.com`), thanks to its standard **OAuth2** (`https://oauth.net/2/`) mechanism.

 The OAuth2 standard is based on the idea of authorizing a third-party application to call a service with an access token that is unique to the user. The token is generated by the service and usually has a limited scope in what calls can be performed on the service. Strava has a full set of APIs that can be used that way, documented at `https://strava.github.io/api/v3/`.

After it has been authorized by the user, Runnerly pulls runs out of Strava to feed its database. This flow simplifies a lot of the integration work to make the application compatible with most running devices out there. If your device works with Strava, it will work with Runnerly.

Once the database starts to get some content from Strava, the dashboard will display the last 10 runs and will let the users use Runnerly's extra features: races, training plans, and monthly reports.

Let's dive into Runnerly's features through its user stories.

# User stories

The best way to describe an application is through its *user stories*. User stories are very simple descriptions of all the interactions a user can have with an application and is the first high-level document that is usually written when a project starts.

The level of detail for each interaction is at first very simple, then gets revisited every time a new particular case appears. User stories are also helpful to detect when it's worth splitting a feature into its microservice: a story that stands on its own could be a good candidate.

For Runnerly, we can start with this small set:

- As a user, I can create an account on Runnerly with my email and activate it through a confirmation link I receive in my mailbox.
- As a user, I can connect to Runnerly and link my profile to my Strava account.
- As a connected user, I can see my last 10 runs appear in the dashboard.
- As a connected user, I can add a race I want to participate in. Other users can see the race as well in their dashboard.
- As a registered user, I receive a monthly report by email that describes how I am doing.
- As a connected user, I can select a training plan for a race I am planning to do, and see a training schedule on the dashboard. A training plan is a simple list of runs that are not done yet.

There are already a few components emerging from this set of user stories. In no particular order, these are:

- The app needs a *registration mechanism* that will add the user to our database and make sure they own the email used for registration.
- The app will *authenticate users* with a password.
- To pull data out of Strava, *a strava user token needs to be stored* in the user profile and used to call the service.
- Besides runs, *the database needs to store races and training plans*.
- Training programs are a list of runs to be performed at specific dates to be as performant as possible for a given race. Creating a good training plan requires information about the user, such as their age, sex, weight, and fitness level.
- Monthly reports are built by *querying the database and generating a summary sent by email*.

These descriptions are enough to get us started. The next section describes how the application can be designed and coded.

# Monolithic design

This section presents extracts from the source code of the monolithic version of Runnerly. The whole application can be found at `https://github.com/Runnerly/monolith`, if you want to study it in detail.

A design pattern that is often referred to when building applications is the **Model-View-Controller** (**MVC**), which separates the code into three parts:

- **Model**: This manages the data
- **View**: This displays the Model for a particular context (web view, PDF view, and so on)
- **Controller**: This manipulates the Model to change its state

While it's clear that SQLAlchemy can be the *Model* part, the *View* and *Controller* distinction can be a bit vague when it comes to Flask because what is called a view is a function that receives a request and sends back a response. And that function can both display and manipulate the data. So it can act as a *View* and as a *Controller*.

The Django project uses the **Model-View-Template** (**MVT**) acronym to describe that pattern, where *View* is the Python callable, and *Template* is the template engine, or whatever is in charge of producing a response in a particular format, given some data.

For instance, in a JSON view, `json.dumps()` is the *Template*. When you render an HTML page with Jinja, the template is the HTML template that's called via `render_template()`.

In any case, the first step of designing our application is to define the Model part.

# Model

In a Flask application based on SQLAlchemy, the model is described through classes, which represent the database schema.

For Runnerly, the database tables are:

- **User**: This contains info about each user, including their credentials
- **Run**: This is a list of runs with all the info extracted from Strava, and runs for a training plan
- **Race**: This is a list of races added by users, with date, location, and distance
- **Plan**: This is a training plan that is defined by a collection of runs to be done

Using the **Flask-SQLAlchemy** (`http://flask-sqlalchemy.pocoo.org/`) extension, you can specify the tables using the `Model` class as a base class. The following is the definition for the `User` table with the `SQLAlchemy` class:

```
from flask_sqlalchemy import SQLAlchemy

db = SQLAlchemy()

class User(db.Model):
    __tablename__ = 'user'
    id = db.Column(db.Integer, primary_key=True, autoincrement=True)
    email = db.Column(db.Unicode(128), nullable=False)
    firstname = db.Column(db.Unicode(128))
    lastname = db.Column(db.Unicode(128))
    password = db.Column(db.Unicode(128))
    strava_token = db.Column(db.String(128))
    age = db.Column(db.Integer)
    weight = db.Column(db.Numeric(4, 1))
    max_hr = db.Column(db.Integer)
    rest_hr = db.Column(db.Integer)
    vo2max = db.Column(db.Numeric(4, 2))
```

When used in a Flask app, Flask-SQLAlchemy will take care of wrapping all the calls to SQLAlchemy and exposing a session object to your Flask app views to manipulate your model.

# View and Template

When a request is received, and a view is invoked, Flask-SQLAlchemy will set up a database session object inside an application context. The following is a fully functional Flask app that uses the schema described earlier in a View that can be queried from `/users`:

```
from flask import Flask, render_template

app = Flask(__name__)

@app.route('/users')
def users():
    users = db.session.query(User)
    return render_template("users.html", users=users)

if __name__ == '__main__':
    db.init_app(app)
    db.create_all(app=app)
    app.run()
```

When the `db.session.query()` method is called, it performs a query on the database and turns every result from the User table into `User` objects that are passed to the `users.html` Jinja template for rendering.

In the previous example, Jinja is called to produce an HTML page, which can display the user info with a template that could look like this:

```
<html>
  <body>
    <h1>User List</h1>
    <ul>
      {% for user in users: %}
      <li>
      {{user.firstname}} {{user.lastname}}
      </li>
      {% endfor %}
    </ul>
  </body>
</html>
```

For editing data through the web, **WTForms** (`http://wtforms.readthedocs.io`) can be used to generate forms for each model. WTForms is a library that generates HTML forms with Python definitions and takes care of extracting data from incoming requests and validating them before you update your model.

The **Flask-WTF** (`https://flask-wtf.readthedocs.io/`) project wraps **WTForms** for Flask and adds some useful integration, such as securing forms with **Cross-Site Request Forgery** (**CSRF**) tokens.

 CSRF tokens will ensure that a malicious third-party website can't send valid forms to your app when you are logged in. Chapter 7, *Securing Your Services*, will explain in detail how CSRF works and why it's important for your app security.

The following module implements a form for the `User` table, using `FlaskForm` as its basis:

```
from flask_wtf import FlaskForm
import wtforms as f
from wtforms.validators import DataRequired

class UserForm(FlaskForm):
    email = f.StringField('email', validators=[DataRequired()])
    firstname = f.StringField('firstname')
    lastname = f.StringField('lastname')
    password = f.PasswordField('password')
    age = f.IntegerField('age')
```

```
weight = f.FloatField('weight')
max_hr = f.IntegerField('max_hr')
rest_hr = f.IntegerField('rest_hr')
vo2max = f.FloatField('vo2max')

display = ['email', 'firstname', 'lastname', 'password',
           'age', 'weight', 'max_hr', 'rest_hr', 'vo2max']
```

The display attribute is just a helper to help the template iterate into a particular ordered list of fields when rendering the form. Everything else is using WTForms basic fields classes to create a form for the user table. The WTForm's *Fields* documentation provides the full list at `http://wtforms.readthedocs.io/en/latest/fields.html`.

Once created, `UserForm` can be used in a view that has two goals. The first one is to display the form on `GET` calls, and the second one is to update the database on `POST` calls when the user submits the form:

```
@app.route('/create_user', methods=['GET', 'POST'])
def create_user():
    form = UserForm()
    if request.method == 'POST':
        if form.validate_on_submit():
            new_user = User()
            form.populate_obj(new_user)
            db.session.add(new_user)
            db.session.commit()
            return redirect('/users')
    return render_template('create_user.html', form=form)
```

The `UserForm` class has a method to validate the incoming `POST` data, as well as a method to serialize the values into a `User` object. When some data is invalid, the form instance will keep the list of errors in `field.errors` in case the template wants to display them for the user.

The `create_user.html` template iterates through the form field list and WTForm takes care of rendering the proper HTML tags :

```
<html>
 <body>
  <form action="" method="POST">
    {{ form.hidden_tag() }}
    <dl>
     {% for field in form.display %}
     <dt>{{ form[field].label }}</dt>
     <dd>{{ form[field]() }}</dd>
       {% if form[field].errors %}
```

```
      {% for e in form[field].errors %} <p>{{ e }}</p> {% endfor %}
    {% endif %}
  {% endfor %}
</dl>
<p>
<input type=submit value="Publish">
  </form>
 </body>
</html>
```

The `form.hidden_tag()` method will render all hidden field, such as the CSRF token. Once this form is working, it's easy to reuse the same pattern for every form needed in the app.

For Runnerly, we'll need to reproduce this pattern to create forms for adding training plans and races. The form part of the template can be reused for all forms and placed in a Jinja macro since it's generic, and most of the work will consist of writing a `form` class per SQLAlchemy model.

There's a project called **WTForms-Alchemy** (`https://wtforms-alchemy.readthedocs.io/`) that can be used to create forms out of SQLAlchemy models automatically. The same `UserForm` that we've manually created earlier would be much simpler with WTForms-Alchemy since the only step required is to point the SQLAlchemy model:

```
from wtforms_alchemy import ModelForm

class UserForm(ModelForm):
    class Meta:
        model = User
```

But in practice, forms are often tweaked to a point where it's easier to write them explicitly. But starting with WTForms-Alchemy and seeing how the forms evolve along the way can be a solution.

Let's summarize what has been done so far to build the app:

- We've created the database model using SQLAlchemy (Model)
- We've created views and forms that are interacting with the database via the Model (View and Template)

There are two things missing to build our complete monolithic solution. They are:

- **Background tasks**: This involves implementing the code that regularly retrieves Strava runs and generates monthly reports
- **Authentication and authorization**: This lets our users log in and restrict editing to just their information

# Background tasks

The code that fetches new runs from Strava to add them in the Runnerly database can poll Strava regularly, like every hour. The monthly report can also be called once per month to generate a report and send it to the user by email. Both features are part of the Flask application and use the SQLAlchemy models to do their work.

But unlike user requests, they are background tasks, and they need to run on their own outside the HTTP request/response cycle.

If not using simple cron jobs, a popular way to run repetitive background tasks in Python web apps is to use **Celery** (http://docs.celeryproject.org), a distributed task queue that can execute some work in a standalone process.

To do this, an intermediate called a *message broker* is in charge of passing messages back and forth between the application and Celery. For instance, if the app wants Celery to run something, it will add a message in the broker. Celery will poll it and do the job.

A message broker can be any service that can store messages and provide a way to retrieve them. The Celery project works out of the box with **Redis** (http://redis.io), **RabbitMQ** (http://www.rabbitmq.com), and **Amazon SQS** (https://aws.amazon.com/sqs/) and provides an abstraction for a Python app to work on both sides of it: to send and run jobs.

The part that runs the job is called a worker, and Celery provides a `Celery` class to start one. To use celery from a Flask application, you can create a `background.py` module that instantiates a `Celery` object and marks your background tasks with a `@celery.task` decorator.

In the following example, we're using the **stravalib** (http://pythonhosted.org/stravalib) library to grab runs from Strava for each user in Runnerly that has a Strava token:

```
from celery import Celery
from stravalib import Client
from monolith.database import db, User, Run

BACKEND = BROKER = 'redis://localhost:6379'
```

```python
    celery = Celery(__name__, backend=BACKEND, broker=BROKER)
_APP = None

    def activity2run(user, activity):
        """"Used by fetch_runs to convert a strava run into a DB entry.
        """
        run = Run()
        run.runner = user
        run.strava_id = activity.id
        run.name = activity.name
        run.distance = activity.distance
        run.elapsed_time = activity.elapsed_time.total_seconds()
        run.average_speed = activity.average_speed
        run.average_heartrate = activity.average_heartrate
        run.total_elevation_gain = activity.total_elevation_gain
        run.start_date = activity.start_date
        return run

    @celery.task
    def fetch_all_runs():
        global _APP
        # lazy init
        if _APP is None:
            from monolith.app import app
            db.init_app(app)
            _APP = app
        else:
            app = _APP

        runs_fetched = {}

        with app.app_context():
            q = db.session.query(User)
            for user in q:
                if user.strava_token is None:
                    continue
                runs_fetched[user.id] = fetch_runs(user)

        return runs_fetched

    def fetch_runs(user):
        client = Client(access_token=user.strava_token)
        runs = 0
        for activity in client.get_activities(limit=10):
            if activity.type != 'Run':
                continue
            q = db.session.query(Run).filter(Run.strava_id == activity.id)
            run = q.first()
```

```
        if run is None:
            db.session.add(activity2run(activity)
            runs += 1

    db.session.commit()
    return runs
```

In this example, the task looks for each user that has a Strava token, then imports their most recent 10 run activities into Runnerly.

This module is a fully working Celery application that can accept jobs from a Redis broker. After we've used the `pip-install` command for `celery` and `redis` Python packages, we can run this module with the `celery -A background worker` command, assuming a Redis instance is running on the machine.

This command will run a Celery worker server that will register the `fetch_all_runs()` function as being an invokable task and listen for incoming messages in Redis.

From there, in your Flask app, you can import the same `background.py` module and call that decorated function directly. You will get a future-like object that will call the Celery worker via Redis to run the function in a separate process:

```
from flask import Flask, jsonify

app = Flask(__name__)

@app.route('/fetch')

def fetch_runs():
    from monolith.background import fetch_all_runs
    res = fetch_all_runs.delay()
    res.wait()
    return jsonify(res.result)
```

In this example, we're waiting for the task to complete and the call to `/fetch` just sits there until the job is done. Of course, in Runnerly, we want to fire-and-forget the task and not call `.wait()` because it's going to take several seconds per user.

In a sense, since the Celery service is invoked by the Flask application by passing messages via Redis, it could be considered as a microservice itself. That's also interesting in terms of deployment since both the Redis server and the Celery app can be deployed on another server. But since the code that's executed lives in the same code base, this is still considered as a monolithic design.

Another aspect of running background workers is when you want your jobs to be executed periodically. Instead of having the Flask app trigger the job every hour, we can use Celery's *Periodic Task* feature (http://docs.celeryproject.org/en/latest/userguide/periodic-tasks.html), which acts as a scheduler.

The Flask app, in that case, would schedule the periodic task the same way it triggered the single task.

# Strava token

The missing part of the puzzle to make those Strava imports work is to get a Strava token for each user and store it in our user table.

As said earlier, this can be done via an OAuth2 dance where the connected user is redirected to Strava to authorize Runnerly, then redirected back to Runnerly with an OAuth2 code that can be converted into a token we can store.

The stravalib library provides some helpers to perform that dance. The first one is the authorization_url() method, which returns a full URL that can be presented to the users to initiate the OAuth2 dance:

```
app.config['STRAVA_CLIENT_ID'] = 'runnerly-strava-id'
app.config['STRAVA_CLIENT_SECRET'] = 'runnerly-strava-secret'

def get_strava_auth_url():
    client = Client()
    client_id = app.config['STRAVA_CLIENT_ID']
    redirect = 'http://127.0.0.1:5000/strava_auth'
    url = client.authorization_url(client_id=client_id,
                                   redirect_uri=redirect)
    return url
```

In the example, redirect is the URL Strava that will redirect once the application is granted access. In this example, it's the app running locally. The get_strava_auth_url() method can be used to present a link to a connected Runnerly user.

Once the user authorizes Runnerly on the Strava site, the /strava_auth view will get a code that can be exchanged for a token that will stay valid for future Strava requests on behalf of that user. The stravalib library's Client class has an exchange_code_for_token() method to do the conversion.

The view then simply copies the token into the user database entry:

```
@app.route('/strava_auth')
@login_required
def _strava_auth():
    code = request.args.get('code')
    client = Client()
    xc = client.exchange_code_for_token
    access_token = xc(client_id=app.config['STRAVA_CLIENT_ID'],
        client_secret=app.config['STRAVA_CLIENT_SECRET'], code=code)
    current_user.strava_token = access_token
    db.session.add(current_user)
    db.session.commit()
    return redirect('/')
```

In that view, `@login_required` and `current_user` are part of the authentication and authorization processes presented in the next section.

# Authentication and authorization

Our monolithic application is almost ready.

One last thing that we need to add is a way for users to authenticate. Runnerly needs to know who's connected since the dashboard will display user-specific data. Forms also need to be secured. For instance, we don't want users to be able to edit other users' information.

For our monolithic solution, we'll implement a very simple basic authentication (`https://en.wikipedia.org/wiki/Basic_access_authentication`) scheme where the user sends its credentials in the Authorization header. From a security point of view, using basic authentication is fine as long as the server uses SSL. When websites are called through HTTPS, the entire request is encrypted (including the query part of the URL), so the transport is secured.

As far as passwords are concerned, the simplest form of protection is to make sure you don't store them in the clear in the database, but instead store them in a hashed form that can't be converted back to the original password. That will minimize the risk of leaking passwords if your server is compromised. For the authentication process, it just means that when the user logs in, you need to hash the incoming password to compare it to the stored hash.

The transport layer is usually not the weak spot for an application security. What happens to the service once the request is received is what matters the most. When the authentication process happens, there's a window during which an attacker can intercept the password (in clear or hashed form). In Chapter 7, *Securing Your Services*, we'll talk about ways to reduce this attack surface.

Werkzeug provides a few helpers to deal with password hashes, generate_password_hash() and check_password_hash(), which can be integrated into our User class.

By default, Werkzeug uses **PBKDF2** (https://en.wikipedia.org/wiki/PBKDF2) with **SHA-1**, which is a secure way to hash a value with salt.

Let's extend our User class with methods to set and verify a password:

```
from werkzeug.security import generate_password_hash,
check_password_hash
class User(db.Model):
    __tablename__ = 'user'
    # ... all the Columns ...

    def __init__(self, *args, **kw):
        super(User, self).__init__(*args, **kw)
        self._authenticated = False

    def set_password(self, password):
        self.password = generate_password_hash(password)

    @property
    def is_authenticated(self):
        return self._authenticated

    def authenticate(self, password):
        checked = check_password_hash(self.password, password)
        self._authenticated = checked
        return self._authenticated
```

When creating new users in the database, the set_password() method can be used to hash and store a password in the User model. Any attempt to verify the password can be made with authenticate(), which will compare hashes.

Once we have that mechanism in place, the **Flask-Login**
(`https://flask-login.readthedocs.io/`) extension provides everything needed to log in
and log out users, and to keep track of who's connected so you can change how your app
works.

Flask-Login provides two functions to set a user in the current Flask session: *login_user()*
and `logout_user()`. When the `login_user()` method is called, the user ID is stored in
the Flask session, and a cookie is set on the client side. The user will be remembered for the
next requests until they log out.

To have this mechanism in place, a `LoginManager` instance needs to be created on your
application at startup.

Here's the implementation of the login and logout views, along with the `LoginManager`
creation:

```python
from flask_login import LoginManager, login_user, logout_user

@app.route('/login', methods=['GET', 'POST'])
def login():
    form = LoginForm()
    if form.validate_on_submit():
        email, password = form.data['email'], form.data['password']
        q = db.session.query(User).filter(User.email == email)
        user = q.first()
        if user is not None and user.authenticate(password):
            login_user(user)
            return redirect('/')
    return render_template('login.html', form=form)

@app.route("/logout")
def logout():
    logout_user()
    return redirect('/')

login_manager = LoginManager()
login_manager.init_app(app)

@login_manager.user_loader
def load_user(user_id):
    user = User.query.get(user_id)
    if user is not None:
        user._authenticated = True
    return user
```

The `@login_manager.user_loader` decorated function is used every time Flask-Login needs to convert a stored user ID to an actual user instance.

The authentication part is done in the login view by calling `user.authenticate()`, and then set in the session with `login_user(user)`.

The last thing to do is to protect some of our views from unauthorized access. For instance, the user edition form should not be accessible if you are not logged in. The `@login_required` decorator will reject any attempt to access a view if you are not logged in with a `401 Unauthorized` error.

It needs to be placed after the `@app.route()` call:

```
@app.route('/create_user', methods=['GET', 'POST'])
@login_required
def create_user():
    # ... code
```

In the code, `@login_required` will ensure that you are a valid user and that you've authenticated.

However, this decorator does not deal with permissions. Permissions handling is out of scope for the Flask-Login project, and an extension such as Flask-Principal (`https://pythonhosted.org/Flask-Principal/`) can be used to handle this on the top of Flask-Login.

However, for our very simple use case, it might be overkill. One specific role Runnerly users have is *admin*. Admins have super powers across the app, while simple users can only change their info.

If we add an `is_admin` Boolean flag in the User model, we can create a similar decorator such as `@login_required`, which will also check this flag:

```
def admin_required(func):
    @functools.wraps(func)
    def _admin_required(*args, **kw):
        admin = current_user.is_authenticated and current_user.is_admin
        if not admin:
            return app.login_manager.unauthorized()
        return func(*args, **kw)
    return _admin_required
```

In the same vein, more granular permission verifications can be done by looking at the `current_user` variable Flask-Login sets in the application context. For example, you could use this to allow a user to change their data, but prevent the user from changing other users' data.

# Putting together the monolithic design

This monolithic design is excellent and should be the kind of result you would aim for in your first development iteration. Everything should be built of course through TDD, as explained in `Chapter 3`, *Coding, Testing, and Documenting - The Virtuous Cycle*.

It's a short and clean implementation on the top of a relational database that can be deployed with a PostgreSQL or MySQLServer. Thanks to the SQLAlchemy abstractions, a local version can run with SQLite 3 and facilitate your day-to-day work and your tests.

To build this app, we've used the following extensions and library:

- **Flask-SQLAlchemy and SQLAlchemy**: These are used for the Model
- **Flask-WTF and WTForms**: These are used for all the forms
- **Celery and Redis**: These are used for background processes and periodic tasks
- **Flask-Login**: This is used for managing authentication and authorization

The overall design looks like the following diagram:

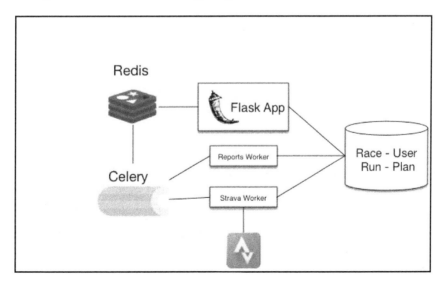

A typical deployment will group the Flask app with one Redis and one Celery instance on the same server and serve requests through a web server such as Apache or nginx. The database can be located on the same server, or on a dedicated server.

The server can spawn several Flask processes and Celery processes to raise the number of requests and users it can handle.

When this deployment is not sufficient to serve the load, the first change that comes to mind is to add other application servers and dedicated servers for the database server and the Redis broker.

The third step, if needed, will be to have more Redis and PostgreSQL instances, and some thoughts will be required on the best approach because you will need to set up replication and maybe sharding strategies.

 When an application reaches that third step, solutions out of the box, such as **Amazon SQS** and **Amazon RDS**, might be a good fit, as we'll see in `Chapter 11`, *Deploying on AWS*.

# Splitting the monolith

Let's project into the world where Runnerly, as implemented previously, starts to be used by a lot of people. Features are added, bugs are fixed, and the database is steadily growing.

The first problem that we're facing is the background process that creates reports and calls Strava. Since we're having thousands of users, these tasks take most of the server resources, and users are experiencing slowdowns on the frontend.

It's getting obvious that we need to have them running on separate servers. With the monolithic application using Celery and Redis, it's not an issue. We can dedicate a couple of new servers for the background jobs.

But the biggest concern if we do this is that the Celery worker code needs to import the Flask application code to operate. So the deployment dedicated to the background workers needs to include the whole Flask app. That also means that every time something changes in the app, we'll need to update the Celery workers as well to avoid regression.

That also means we'll have to install on a server where the only role is to pump data out of Strava, all the dependencies the Flask application has. If we use Bootstrap in our templates, we'll have to deploy it on the Celery worker server!

This dependency issue begs the question: "Why does the Celery worker need to be in the Flask application in the first place?" That design was excellent when we started to code Runnerly, but it became obvious that it's fragile.

The interactions Celery has with the application are very specific. The Strava worker needs to:

- Get the Strava tokens
- Add new runs

Instead of using the Flask app code, the Celery worker code could be entirely independent and just interacts with the database directly.

Having the Celery worker acting as a separate microservice is a great first step to split our monolithic app--let's call it the **Strava Service**. The worker that's in charge of building reports can be split the same way to run, on its own, the **Reports Service**. Each one of these Celery workers can focus on performing one single task.

The biggest design decision when doing this is whether these new microservices call the database directly or whether they call it via an HTTP API that acts as an intermediate between the services and the database.

Direct database calls seem like the simplest solution, but this introduces another problem. Since the original Flask app, the Strava service and the Reports Service will all share the same database; every time something changes in it, they all get impacted.

If there's an intermediate layer that exposes to the different services just the info they need to do their jobs, it reduces the database dependency problem. If well designed, an HTTP API contract compatibility can be maintained when changes are made in the database schema.

As far as the Strava and Report microservices are concerned, they are Celery workers, so we don't have to design any HTTP API for them. They get some work from the Redis broker and then interact with the service wrapping database calls. Let's call this new intermediate the **Data Service**.

# Data Service

The following diagram describes our new application organization. Both the **Reports** and **Strava** service get some work from Redis and interact with the **Data Service**, as shown in the following diagram:

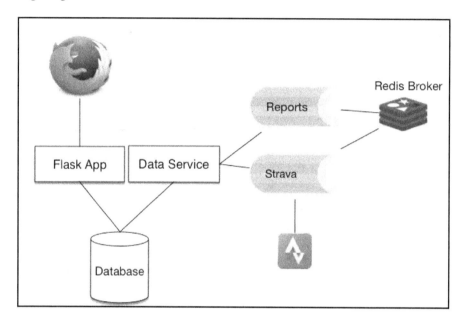

The Data Service is an HTTP API that wraps the database containing all the users and runs data. The dashboard is the frontend that implements the HTML user interface.

 When you have any doubt about whether it's a good idea to split out a new microservice out of your main app, don't do it.

Some of the information required by the Celery workers can be passed through the Redis broker, such as the Strava tokens for the Strava service.

For the Reports service, however, it's not practical to send all the info through Redis because the amount of data can be significant. If a runner is doing 30 runs per month, it's simpler to let the Reports service pull them directly from the Data Service.

The Data service view needs to implement the following APIs:

- For the Strava service--a POST endpoint to add runs
- For the Reports service
- A GET endpoint to retrieve a list of user IDs
- A GET endpoint to get a list of runs given a user ID and a month

As you can see, the HTTP API is minimal--we want to expose as few entry points as possible. Although the structure of a run is going to be shared across all services, we need to expose as a few number of fields as possible.

For our service implementation, we will rely on the Open API 2.0 standard.

# Using Open API 2.0

The Open API 2.0 specification, also known as Swagger (`https://www.openapis.org/`) is a simple description language that comes as a JSON or YAML file, that lists all your HTTP API endpoints, how they are used, and the structure of the data that comes in and out. It makes the assumption that your service sends and receives JSON documents.

Swagger has the same goal that **WSDL** (`https://en.wikipedia.org/wiki/Web_Services_Description_Language`) had back in the XML web services era, but it's much lighter and straight to the point.

The following example is a minimal Open API description file which defines one single `/apis/users_ids` endpoint and supports the `GET` method to retrieve the list of user IDs:

```
swagger: "2.0"
info:
  title: Runnerly Data Service
  description: returns info about Runnerly
  license:
    name: APLv2
    url: https://www.apache.org/licenses/LICENSE-2.0.html
  version: 0.1.0
basePath: /api
paths:
  /user_ids:
    get:
      operationId: getUserIds
      description: Returns a list of ids
      produces:
      - application/json
```

```
responses:
  '200':
    description: List of Ids
    schema:
        type: array
        items:
            type: integer
```

The full Open API 2.0 specification can be found at `http://swagger.io/specification/`. It's very detailed and will let you describe metadata about the API, its endpoints, and the data types it uses.

The data types described in the schema sections are following the **JSON-Schema** specification (`http://json-schema.org/latest/json-schema-core.html`). Here, we're describing that the `/get_ids` endpoint returns an array of integers.

You can provide a lot of details about your API in that spec--things such as what headers should be present in your requests, or what will be the content-type of some responses, can be added to it.

Describing your HTTP endpoints with Swagger offers some excellent possibilities:

- There are a plethora of Open API 2.0 clients that can consume your description and do something useful with it, such as building functional tests against your service or validating data that's sent to it
- It provides a standard, language-agnostic documentation for your API
- The server can check that the requests and responses follow the spec

Some web frameworks even use the Swagger spec to create all the routing and I/O data checks for your microservices--for instance, **Connexion** (`https://github.com/zalando/connexion`), does this for Flask.

There are two schools of thought when people are building HTTP APIs with Swagger.

- The *specification-first* one, where you create a Swagger spec file and then create your app on the top of it, using all the info provided in the spec. That's the principle behind Connexion.
- The *specification-extracted* one, where it's your code that generates the Swagger spec file. Some toolkits out there will do this by reading your view docstrings, for instance.

The biggest advantage of the first approach is that your Swagger specification is guaranteed to be up-to-date since it drives the app. The second approach is still valuable, for example, when you want to introduce Swagger in an existing project.

For implementing a Flask app that uses the first approach, a framework such as Connexion will give you excellent high-level helpers. All you have to do is pass the spec file and your functions, and Connexion, will generate a Flask app. Connexion uses the `operationId` field to resolve which function will be called for each operation.

A small caveat of this approach is that the Swagger file will include implementation details (the full path to the Python functions), which is a bit intrusive for a language-agnostic specification. There's also an automatic resolver, that will look for the Python function given the path and method of each operation. In that case, the implementation of `GET` `/api/users_ids` will need to be located at `api.users_ids.get()`.

Flakon (presented in `Chapter 2`, *Discovering Flask*) has a different approach. The project has a special Blueprint class called `SwaggerBlueprint`, which won't require you to add the Python functions in the spec or try to guess where it should be given the operation.

This custom Blueprint takes a Swagger spec file and provides an `@api.operation` decorator that is similar to `@api.route`. This decorator takes an operationId name instead of a route--so the Blueprint can link the view to the right route explicitly.

In the following example, we're creating a Swagger Blueprint and implementing the **getUserIds** operation:

```
from flakon import SwaggerBlueprint

api = SwaggerBlueprint('swagger', spec='api.yml')

@api.operation('getUserIds')
def get_user_ids():
    # .. do the work ..
```

The Python implementation can be renamed and moved around without having to change the Swagger spec.

The rest of the Data Service API is implemented as described, and can be found in the Runnerly repository (`https://github.com/Runnerly`).

# More splitting

So far, we've split out of our monolith everything related to background tasks, and we've added a few HTTP API views for the new microservices to interact with the main application.

Since the new API allows us to add runs, there's another part we can split out of the monolith--the Training feature.

This feature can run on its own as long as it's able to generate new runs. When a user wants to start a new training plan, the main app can interact with the Training microservice and ask it to generate new runs.

Alternatively, the design could be reversed for better data isolation: the Training microservice publishes an API that returns a list of runs with their specific structure, exactly like the Strava API that returns activities. The main Flask app can then convert them into Runnerly runs. The Training plan can work without any specific knowledge about the Runnerly users: it gets asked to generate a plan given a few params.

But doing this new split should happen for a good reason. "Is the code behind the training algorithm CPU consuming?", "Is it growing into a full expert system that's being used by other applications?", "Will the Training feature need other data in the future to work?"

 Every time you make the decision to split out a new microservice, there's a risk of ending up with a bloated app.

In the same vein, the Race feature could probably be a standalone microservice at some point, since a list of races could be completely independent of the Runnerly database.

The following diagram shows the final Runnerly design, featuring four microservices and the main Flask app. In `Chapter 8`, *Deploying on AWS*, we'll see how we can even get rid of that main application, turn the Data Service as a full microservice, and build a JavaScript application that integrates everything:

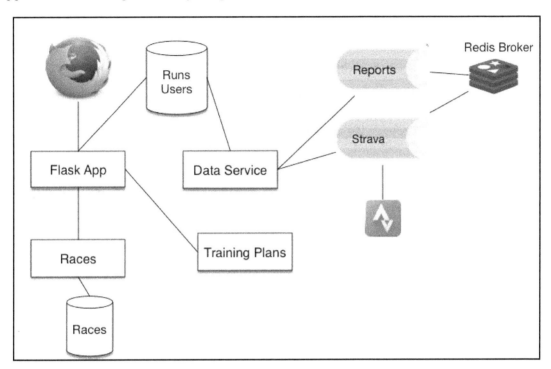

# Summary

The Runnerly app is a typical web app that interacts with a database and a few backend services. And building it as a monolithic application is the way to go for the first few iterations.

In this chapter, we've demonstrated how the monolith could be gradually split into microservices, and how tools such as Celery can help in that process. Each background process that can be split in an independent Celery task is a potential microservice.

We've also looked at Swagger, which is a great tool to help define APIs between microservices.

This splitting process should be conservative and progressive because it's quite easy to end up with a system where the overhead for building and maintaining microservices outweighs the benefits to splitting those things out.

If you like software architecture, the last version of the app is pretty appealing. It offers a lot of options for deploying and scaling Runnerly.

However, we've moved from a single application to many applications that need to interact with each other. Every link in the preceding diagram can be a weak point for your application. What happens, for instance, if Redis goes down? Or if there's a network split between the Data Service and the Strava Service in the middle of a process?

The same question goes for every new network link that was added in our architecture. We need to be resilient when something goes wrong. We need to know where we're at and what to do when a service that was out gets back online.

All of these problems are addressed in the next chapter.

# 5
# Interacting with Other Services

In the previous chapter, the Runnerly monolithic app was split into several microservices, and more network interactions between the different parts were consequently added.

When a user looks at the main web view, the application needs to fetch the list of runs and races from the database and the races. The network calls that are triggered by that request are *synchronous* because we want to display the results immediately.

On the other hand, the Celery workers are doing their duty in the background, and they receive their order via a Redis broker *asynchronously*.

There are also cases where a mix of synchronous and asynchronous calls are useful. For instance, letting the user pick a new training plan can trigger the creation of a series of new runs in the background while displaying some info about the plan itself.

In future versions of Runnerly, we could also have more service-to-service interactions, where an event in a service triggers a series of reactions in other services. Having the ability to loosely couple different parts of the system via some asynchronous messaging is quite useful to prevent interdependencies.

In any case, the bottom line is that we need to interact with other services through the network synchronously and asynchronously. These interactions need to be efficient, and when something goes wrong, we need to have a plan.

The other problem introduced by adding more network connections is **testing**: how do we test in isolation a microservice that needs to call other microservices to function?

In this chapter, we'll explain:

- How a service can call another service in a synchronous way, and make these calls as efficient as possible
- How a service can make asynchronous calls and communicate with other services via events
- Some techniques to test services that have network dependencies

# Synchronous calls

As we've seen in the previous chapters, synchronous interactions between microservices can be done via RESTful HTTP APIs using JSON payloads.

That's by far the most used pattern, because both HTTP and JSON are the golden standards. If your web service implements an HTTP API that accepts JSON, any developer using any programming language will happily use it.

Following a RESTful scheme, on the other hand, is not a requirement and is prone to interpretation. Countless blog posts are debating the virtue of using POST versus PUT response on the internet.

Some projects implement **Remote Procedure Call** (**RPC**) APIs over HTTP rather than REST APIs. In RPC, the focus is on the action, which is part of the endpoint URL. In REST, the focus is on the resource, and actions are defined by HTTP methods.

Some projects are a mix of both and don't strictly follow a given standard. The most important thing is that your service behavior should be consistent and well-documented.

 This book leans on REST rather than RPC, but is not strict about it, and does not have a strong opinion about all the PUT versus POST debates.

Sending and receiving JSON payloads is the simplest way for a microservice to interact with the others, and only requires microservices to know the entry points and parameters to pass using HTTP requests.

To do this, you just need to use an HTTP client. Python has one built-in in the http.client module, but the Requests library (https://docs.python-requests.org) has a better API to work with and offers built-in features that will make your life easier.

HTTP requests in the `requests` library are built around the concept of session, and the best way to use it is to create a `Session` object that is reused every time you interact with any service.

A `Session` object can hold, among other things, authentication information and some default headers you want to set for all requests your application will make. In the following example, the `Session` object will automatically create the right `Authorization` and `Content-Type` headers:

```
from requests import Session

s = Session()
s.headers['Content-Type'] = 'application/json'
s.auth = 'tarek', 'password'

# doing some calls, auth and headers are all set!
s.get('http://localhost:5000/api').json()
s.get('http://localhost:5000/api2').json()
```

Let's see how we can generalize this pattern in a Flask app that needs to interact with other services.

# Using Session in a Flask app

Flask's `Application` object has an `extensions` mapping that can be used to store utilities such as connectors. In our case, we want to store a `Session` object. We can create a function that will initialize a placeholder in the `app.extensions` mapping and add a `Session` object in it:

```
from requests import Session

def setup_connector(app, name='default', **options):
    if not hasattr(app, 'extensions'):
        app.extensions = {}

    if 'connectors' not in app.extensions:
        app.extensions['connectors'] = {}
    session = Session()

    if 'auth' in options:
        session.auth = options['auth']
    headers = options.get('headers', {})
    if 'Content-Type' not in headers:
        headers['Content-Type'] = 'application/json'
```

```
            session.headers.update(headers)

            app.extensions['connectors'][name] = session
            return session


        def get_connector(app, name='default'):
            return app.extensions['connectors'][name]
```

In this example, the `setup_connector()` function will create a `Session` object and store it in the app's extensions mapping. The created `Session` will set the `Content-Type` header to `application/json` by default, so it's suitable for sending data to JSON-based microservices.

Using the session from a view can then be done with the `get_connector()` function once it has been set up on the app. In the following example, a Flask app running on port `5001` will synchronously call a microservice running on `5000` to serve its content:

```
        from flask import Flask, jsonify

        app = Flask(__name__)
        setup_connector(app)

        @app.route('/api', methods=['GET', 'POST'])
        def my_microservice():
            with get_connector(app) as conn:
                sub_result = conn.get('http://localhost:5000/api').json()
            return jsonify({'result': sub_result, 'Hello': 'World!'})

        if __name__ == '__main__':
            app.run(port=5001)
```

A call to the service will propagate a call to the other service:

```
    $ curl http://127.0.0.1:5001/api
    {
      "Hello": "World!",
      "result": {
        "Hello": "World!",
        "result": "OK"
      }
    }
```

This naive implementation is based on the hypothesis that everything will go smoothly. But what will happen if the microservice that's called lags and takes 30 seconds to return?

By default, requests will hang indefinitely until the answer is ready, which is not a behavior we'd want when calling microservices. The `timeout` option is useful in this case. Used when making a request, it will raise a `ReadTimeout` in case the remote server fails to answer promptly.

In the following example, we drop the call if it's hanging for more than 2 seconds:

```
from requests.exceptions import ReadTimeout

@app.route('/api', methods=['GET', 'POST'])
def my_microservice():
    with get_connector(app) as conn:
        try:
            result =
 conn.get('http://localhost:5000/api',timeout=2.0).json()
        except ReadTimeout:
            result = {}
    return jsonify({'result': result, 'Hello': 'World!'})
```

Of course, what should be done when a timeout happens depends on your service logic. In this example, we silently ignore the problem and send back an empty result. But maybe in other cases, you will need to raise an error. In any case, handling timeouts is mandatory if you want to build a robust service-to-service link.

The other error that can happen is when the connection completely drops, or the remote server is not reachable at all. Requests will retry several times and eventually will raise a `ConnectionError` you need to catch:

```
from requests.exceptions import ReadTimeout, ConnectionError

@app.route('/api', methods=['GET', 'POST'])
def my_microservice():
    with get_connector(app) as conn:
        try:
            result = conn.get('http://localhost:5000/api',
                              timeout=2.).json()
        except (ReadTimeout, ConnectionError):
            result = {}
    return jsonify({'result': result, 'Hello': 'World!'})
```

Since it's good practice to always use the timeout option, a better way would be to set a default one at the session level, so we don't have to provide it on every request call.

To do this, the requests library has a way to set up custom *transport adapters,* where you can define a behavior for a given host the session will call. It can be used to create a general timeout, but also to offer a retries option in case you want to tweak how many retries should be done when the service is not responsive.

Back to our setup_connector() function. Using an adapter, we can add timeout and retries options that will be used by default for all requests:

```python
from requests.adapters import HTTPAdapter

class HTTPTimeoutAdapter(HTTPAdapter):
    def __init__(self, *args, **kw):
        self.timeout = kw.pop('timeout', 30.)
        super().__init__(*args, **kw)

    def send(self, request, **kw):
        timeout = kw.get('timeout')
        if timeout is None:
            kw['timeout'] = self.timeout
        return super().send(request, **kw)

def setup_connector(app, name='default', **options):
    if not hasattr(app, 'extensions'):
        app.extensions = {}

    if 'connectors' not in app.extensions:
        app.extensions['connectors'] = {}
    session = Session()

    if 'auth' in options:
        session.auth = options['auth']

    headers = options.get('headers', {})
    if 'Content-Type' not in headers:
        headers['Content-Type'] = 'application/json'
    session.headers.update(headers)

    retries = options.get('retries', 3)
    timeout = options.get('timeout', 30)
    adapter = HTTPTimeoutAdapter(max_retries=retries, timeout=timeout)
    session.mount('http://', adapter)
    app.extensions['connectors'][name] = session

    return session
```

The `session.mount(host, adapter)` call will tell requests to use the
`HTTPTimeoutAdapter` every time a request for any HTTP service is made. The `http://`
value for the host is a catch-all in this case.

The beautiful thing about the `mount()` function is that the session behavior can be tweaked
on a service-per-service basis depending on your app logic. For instance, you can mount
another instance on the adapter for a particular host if you need to set up some custom
timeouts and retries values:

```
adapter2 = HTTPTimeoutAdapter(max_retries=1, timeout=1.)
session.mount('http://myspecial.service', adapter2)
```

Thanks to this pattern, a single request `Session` object can be instantiated into your
application to interact with many other HTTP services.

# Connection pooling

Requests use `urllib3` under the hood, which will create one pool of connectors per host
you are calling and reuse them when the code calls a host.

In other words, if your service calls several other services, you don't need to worry about
recycling connections made to those services; requests should handle it for you.

Flask is a synchronous framework, so if you are running with a single thread, which is the
default behavior, then the `requests` library's connection pooling doesn't help you much.
Every call will happen one after the other. Requests should only keep one connector open
per remote host.

But if you run your Flask application with several threads and have a lot of concurrent
connections, these pools can play a vital role in making sure you're controlling how many
connections are made to other services. You don't want your app to open an unlimited
number of simultaneous connections to another service. It's a recipe for disaster.

Our `HTTPTimeoutAdapter` class can be used to control the growth of our pools. The class
inherits from `HTTPAdapter`, which surfaces `urllib3` pool options.

You can pass these options to the constructor:

- `pool_connections`: This helps you figure out how many simultaneous
  connections are kept open.

- `pool_maxsize`: This helps you figure out the maximum number of connections the pool handles.
- `max_retries`: This helps you figure out the maximum number of retries per connection.
- `pool_block`: This helps you figure out whether the connection pool should block connections and when the `pool_maxsize` is reached. If set to `False`, it will create new connections even if the pool is full, but not add them in the pool. If set to `True`, it will not create new connections when the pool is full and wait. This is useful to maximize the number of connections open to a host.

For example, our adapter could hold 25 simultaneous connections if the app is executed with a web server that allows multiple threads:

```
adapter = HTTPTimeoutAdapter(max_retries=retries,
                             timeout=timeout, pool_connections=25)
```

Allowing multiple threads can be a great way to improve your service performances, but it comes with most significant risks. With its thread-local mechanism, Flask will ensure that each thread gets its version of `flask.g` (the global), `flask.request` or `flask.response`, so you don't have to deal with thread-safety, but your views will be visited concurrently by several threads, so you need to be careful about what's happening in them.

If you don't share any states outside `flask.g` and just calling the `Request` session, it should work. Request's session is not thread-safe you should have one session per thread.

But if you are changing any shared state and don't do the proper locking work to avoid race conditions, you will be in trouble. If your views get too complicated to make sure it is thread-safe, it's best to run with a single thread and spawn multiple processes. In that case, each process will execute a `Request` session that has a single connection to the external service, and that will serialize the calls.

This serialization is a limiting factor synchronous frameworks have, and it forces us to make deployments that consume more memory to spawn all the processes or use implicit asynchronous tools such as **Gevent**.

In any case, if the single-threaded application is fast to respond, it mitigates this limitation a lot.

One way to speed up your application for calls to other services, is to make sure it uses HTTP cache headers.

# HTTP cache headers

In the HTTP protocol, there are a few cache mechanisms that can be used to indicate to a client that a page it's trying to fetch has not changed since their last visit. Caching is something we can do in our microservices on all the read-only API endpoints such as GETs and HEADs.

The simplest way to implement it is to return along with a result an **ETag** header in the response. An ETag value is a string that can be considered as a version for the resource the client is trying to get. It can be a timestamp, an incremental version, or a hash. It's up to the server to decide what to put in it. But the idea is that it should be unique to the value of the response.

Like web browsers, when the client fetches a response that contains such a header, it can build a local dictionary cache that stores the response bodies and ETags as its values, and the URLs as its keys.

When making a new request, the client can look up the dictionary and pass along a stored ETag value in the `If-Modified-Since` header. If the server sends back a 304 response, it means that the response has not changed and the client can use the previously stored one.

This mechanism greatly reduces, the response times from the server since it can immediately return an empty 304 response when the content has not changed. The 304 response is also smaller data for the network, since it has no body.

There's a project called `CacheControl` (`http://cachecontrol.readthedocs.io`) that can be used with the `Request` session, which implements this behavior for you fairly transparently.

In our previous example, having the `HTTPTimeoutAdapter` class derives from `cachecontrol.CacheControlAdapter` instead of `request.adapters.HTTPAdapter` is the only thing you need to do to activate the cache.

Of course, this means the services that you are calling should implement this caching behavior by adding the proper ETag support.

It's not possible to implement a generic solution for this because the cache logic depends on the nature of the data your service is managing.

The rule of thumb is to version each resource and change that version every time the data changes. In the following example, the Flask app uses the current server time to create ETag values associated with users' entries. The ETag value is the current time since the epoch in milliseconds and is stored in the modified field.

The `get_user()` method returns a user entry from `_USERS` and sets the ETag value with `response.set_etag`. When the view gets some calls, it also looks for the `If-None-Match` header to compare it to the user's modified field, and returns a 304 response if it matches:

```python
import time
from flask import Flask, jsonify, request, Response, abort

app = Flask(__name__)

def _time2etag(stamp=None):
    if stamp is None:
        stamp = time.time()
    return str(int(stamp * 1000))

_USERS = {'1': {'name': 'Tarek', 'modified': _time2etag()}}

@app.route('/api/user/<user_id>', methods=['POST'])
def change_user(user_id):
    user = request.json
    # setting a new timestamp
    user['modified'] = _time2etag()
    _USERS[user_id] = user
    resp = jsonify(user)
    resp.set_etag(user['modified'])
    return resp

@app.route('/api/user/<user_id>')
def get_user(user_id):
    if user_id not in _USERS:
        return abort(404)
    user = _USERS[user_id]

    # returning 304 if If-None-Match matches
    if user['modified'] in request.if_none_match:
        return Response(status=304)

    resp = jsonify(user)

    # setting the ETag
    resp.set_etag(user['modified'])
    return resp
```

```
if __name__ == '__main__':
    app.run()
```

The `change_user()` view sets a new modified value when the client `POST` a user. In the following client session, we're changing the user and making sure we get a 304 response when providing the new ETag value:

```
$ curl http://127.0.0.1:5000/api/user/1
{
  "modified": "1486894514360",
  "name": "Tarek"
}

$ curl -H "Content-Type: application/json" -X POST -d
'{"name":"Tarek","age":40}' http://127.0.0.1:5000/api/user/1
{
  "age": 40,
  "modified": "1486894532705",
  "name": "Tarek"
}

$ curl http://127.0.0.1:5000/api/user/1
{
  "age": 40,
  "modified": "1486894532705",
  "name": "Tarek"
}

$ curl -v -H 'If-None-Match: 1486894532705'
http://127.0.0.1:5000/api/user/1
< HTTP/1.0 304 NOT MODIFIED
```

This demonstration is a toy implementation that might not work well in production because relying on a server clock to store ETag values means you are sure that the clock is never set back in time and that if you have several servers, their clocks are all synchronized with a service such as **ntpdate**.

There's also the problem of race conditions if two requests change the same entry within the same millisecond. Depending on your app, maybe it's not an issue, but maybe it's a big one. A cleaner option is to have the modified field handled by your database system directly and make sure its changes are done in serialized transactions.

Some developers use hash functions for their ETag value because it's easy to compute in a distributed architecture and it doesn't introduce any of the problems timestamps have. But calculating a hash has a CPU cost, and it means you need to pull the whole entry to do it--so it might be as slow as if you were sending back the actual data. That said, with a dedicated table in your database for all your hashes, you can probably come up with a solution that makes your 304 response very fast to return.

As we said earlier, there's no generic solution to implement an efficient HTTP cache logic-- but it's worth performing it if your client is doing a lot of reads on your service.

When you have no choice but to send some data back, there are several ways to make it as efficient as possible, as we'll see in the next section.

# Improving data transfer

JSON is quite verbose. Verbosity is great when you need to interact with your data. Everything comes as clear text and is as easy to read as plain Python dictionary and lists.

But sending HTTP requests and responses with JSON payloads can add some bandwidth overhead in the long run. Serializing and deserializing data from Python objects to JSON structures also adds a bit of CPU overhead.

You can reduce the size of data transfers and speed up processing times using *compression* or switching to *binary payloads*.

# GZIP compression

The first simple thing you can do to reduce the bandwidth is to use GZIP compression, so everything that is sent over the wire gets smaller. Web servers such as Apache or nginx provide native support to compress responses *on the fly*, and it's better to avoid implementing your ad hoc compression at the Python level.

For example, this nginx configuration will enable GZIP compression for any response produced by the Flask app on port 5000, with an `application/json` content type:

```
http {
    gzip  on;
    gzip_types application/json;
    gzip_proxied      any;
    gzip_vary on;

    server {
```

```
listen          80;
server_name    localhost;
location / {
     proxy_pass http://localhost:5000;
}
}
```

From the client-side, making an HTTP request to the nginx server at `localhost:8080` proxying for the application at `localhost:5000` with an `Accept-Encoding: gzip` header will trigger the compression:

```
$ curl http://localhost:8080/api -H "Accept-Encoding: gzip"
<some binary output>
```

In Python, request responses will automatically decompress responses that are `gzip` encoded, so you don't have to worry about doing it when your service is calling another service. Unzipping the data adds some processing, but Python's `gzip` module relies on the `zlib` (http://www.zlib.net/), which is very fast (and massively spiffy).

```
>>> import requests
>>> requests.get('http://localhost:8080/api', headers={'Accept-Encoding':
'gzip'}).json()
{'Hello': 'World!', u'result': 'OK'}
```

To compress the data you're sending to the server, you can use the `gzip` module and specify a `Content-Encoding` header:

```
>>> import gzip, json, requests
>>> data = {'Hello': 'World!', 'result': 'OK'}
>>> data = bytes(json.dumps(data), 'utf8')
>>> data = gzip.compress(data)
>>> headers = {'Content-Encoding': 'gzip'}
>>> requests.post('http://localhost:8080/api',
...                 headers=headers,
...                 data=data)

<Response [200]>
```

In that case, however, you will get the zipped content in your Flask application, and you will need to decompress it in your Python code unless you implement something in nginx with Lua to handle it. Apache, on the other hand, can decompress it for you with the `mode_deflate` module and its `SetInputFilter` option.

To summarize, setting up GZIP compression for all your service responses is a no-brainer with nginx or Apache, and your Python client can benefit from it by setting the right header. Handling GZIP compression in HTTP requests is a little trickier because if you don't use Apache, you need to implement decompression of incoming data in Python code or somewhere else.

If you want to further reduce the size on HTTP request/response payloads, another option is to switch to binary payloads rather than JSON payloads compressed with `gzip`. That way, you don't have to deal with unzipping the data and will get a speedup. But we'll see that the compression is not as good.

# Binary payloads

While it's usually not relevant, if your microservice deals with a lot of data, using an alternative format can be an attractive option to increase performances and decrease the required network bandwidth without having to rely on GZIP.

The two widely used binary formats out there are **Protocol Buffers** (**protobuf**) and **MessagePack.**

**Protocol buffers** (`https://developers.google.com/protocol-buffers`) requires you to describe the data that's being exchanged into some schema that will be used to index the binary content.

It adds quite some work because all data that's transferred will need to be described in a schema and you will need to learn a new **Domain Specific Language** (DSL).

The following example is taken from the protobuf documentation:

```
package tutorial;

message Person {
  required string name = 1;
  required int32 id = 2;
  optional string email = 3;

  enum PhoneType {
    MOBILE = 0;
    HOME = 1;
    WORK = 2;
  }

  message PhoneNumber {
    required string number = 1;
```

```
        optional PhoneType type = 2 [default = HOME];
    }

    repeated PhoneNumber phones = 4;
}

message AddressBook {
    repeated Person people = 1;
}
```

Needless to say, it's not very *Pythonic* and looks more like a database schema. We could argue that describing the data that gets transferred is good practice, but it could become a bit redundant with the Swagger definition if the microservice uses that.

MessagePack (http://msgpack.org/), on the other hand, is schemaless and can compress and uncompress your data by just calling a function.

It's a simple alternative to JSON, and has implementations in most languages. The msgpack python library (installed using the pip install msgpack-python command) offers the same level of integration as JSON:

```
>>> import msgpack
>>> data = {"this": "is", "some": "data", 1: 2}
>>> msgpack.dumps(data)
b'x83x01x02xa4thisxa2isxa4somexa4data'
>>> msgpack.loads(msgpack.dumps(data))
{1: 2, b'this': b'is', b'some': b'data'}
```

 Notice that the strings are converted into binaries when the data is serialized then deserialized back with the default serializer. This is something to take into account if you need to keep the original types.

Clearly, using MessagePack is quite simple compared to Protobuf--but which one is the faster and provides the best compression ratio depends a lot on your data. In some rare cases, plain JSON might be even quicker to serialize than a binary format.

In terms of compression, you can expect a 10% to 20% compression with MessagePack, but if your JSON contains a lot of strings--which is often the case in microservices--GZIP will do a much better job.

In the following example, a huge JSON payload of 87k containing a lot of strings, is converted using `MessagePack` and then gzipped in both cases:

```
>>> import json, msgpack
>>> with open('data.json') as f:
...     data = f.read()
...
>>> python_data = json.loads(data)
>>> len(json.dumps(python_data))
88983
>>> len(msgpack.dumps(python_data))
60874
>>> len(gzip.compress(bytes(json.dumps(data), 'utf8')))
5925
>>> len(gzip.compress(msgpack.dumps(data)))
5892
```

Using `MessagePack` reduces the size of the payload by quite a lot, but GZIP is crushing it by making it 15 times smaller with both JSON and `MessagePack` payloads!

It's clear that whatever format you are using, the best way to reduce the payload sizes is to use GZIP--and if your web server does not deal with decompression, it's straightforward in Python thanks to `gzip.uncompress()`.

Now, between using `MessagePack` and JSON, the binary format is usually faster and is more Python friendly. For instance, if you pass a Python dictionary with integer keys, JSON will convert them into strings while `MessagePack` will do the right thing:

```
>>> import msgpack, json
>>> json.loads(json.dumps({1: 2}))
{'1': 2}
>>> msgpack.loads(msgpack.dumps({1: 2}))
{1: 2}
```

But there's also the problem of date representations: `DateTime` objects are not directly serializable in JSON and `MessagePack`, so you need to make sure you convert them.

In any case, in a world of microservices where JSON is the most accepted standard, sticking with string keys and taking care of dates are minor annoyances to stick with a universally adopted standard.

 Unless all your services are in Python with well-defined structures, and you need to speed up the serialization steps as much as possible, it's probably simpler to stick with JSON.

# Putting it together

We will quickly recall what we covered in this section about performing synchronous calls:

- Requests can be used as the HTTP client to call other services. It offers all the features necessary to deal with timeouts, errors, and has its pool of connectors.
- Going multithread can improve your microservice's performance when it's calling other services, since Flask is a synchronous framework, but it's dangerous. Solutions such as Gevent can be investigated.
- Implementing HTTP cache headers is a great way to speed up repeated requests for data.
- GZIP compression is an efficient way to lessen the size of requests and responses and is easy to set up.
- Binary protocols are an attractive alternative to plain JSON, but might not be that useful.

The next section will focus on asynchronous calls; everything your microservice can do that goes beyond the request-response pattern.

# Asynchronous calls

In microservice architectures, asynchronous calls play a fundamental role when a process that used to be performed in a single application now implicates several microservices.

Asynchronous calls can be as simple as a separate thread or process within a microservice app, that's getting some work to be done and perform it without interfering with the HTTP request-responses round trips that are happening at the same time.

But doing everything directly from the same Python process is not very robust. What happens if the process crashes and gets restarted? How do we scale background tasks if they are built like that?

It's much more reliable to send a message that gets picked by another program, and let the microservice focus on its primary goal, which is to serve responses to clients.

In the previous chapter, we looked at how Celery could be used to build a microservice that gets some work from a message broker like Redis or RabbitMQ. In that design, the Celery worker blocks until a new message is added to the Redis queue.

But there are other ways to exchange messages between services that are not necessarily a worker blocking on a queue.

# Task queues

The pattern used by Celery workers is a **push-pull** tasks queue. One service pushes messages into a specific queue, and some workers pick them up from the other end and perform an action on them. Each task goes to a single worker. Consider the following diagram:

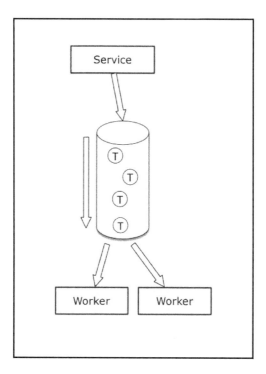

There's no bidirectional communication. The sender just deposits a message in the queue and leaves. The next available worker gets the next message.

This blind, unidirectional message passing is perfect when you want to perform some asynchronous parallel tasks, and that makes it easy to scale.

Plus, once the sender has confirmed that the message was added in the broker, we can have message brokers such as RabbitMQ offer some message persistence. In other words, if all workers go offline, we don't loose the messages that are in the queue.

# Topic queues

A variation of the task queue pattern is the topic pattern. In that case, instead of having workers blindly picking every message that is added to one or several queues, they *subscribe* to specific topics. A topic is just a label on a message, and workers can decide to filter the messages they pick from the queue so that they match the topic.

In our microservices, this means we can have specialized workers that all register to the same messaging broker and get a subset of the messages that are added to it.

Celery is an excellent tool for building tasks queues, however, for more complex messaging, we need to use another tool:

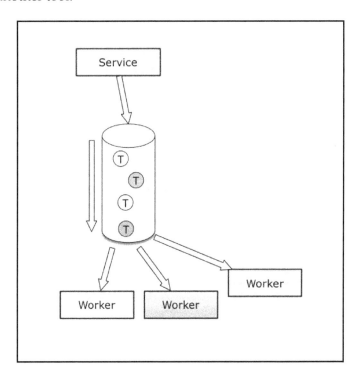

To implement complex messaging pattern, the good news is that we can use a Rabbit MQ message broker who still works with Celery and interacts with another library.

To install a RabbitMQ broker, you can look at the download page at `http://www.rabbitmq` `.com/download.html`and get started from there. A RabbitMQ broker is a TCP server that manages queues internally and dispatches messages from publishers to subscribers via RPC calls. Using it with Celery is just a small portion of what this system can offer.

RabbitMQ implements the **Advanced Message Queuing Protocol** (**AMQP**). This protocol, described in `http://www.amqp.org/` is a complete standard that has been developed for years by majority of the companies in the industry.

AMQP is organized into three concepts: queues, exchanges, and bindings:

- A *queue* is a recipient that holds messages and waits for consumers to pick them
- An *exchange* is an entry point for publishers to add new messages to the system
- A *binding* defines how messages are routed from exchanges to queues

For our topic queue, we need to set one *exchange*, so RabbitMQ accepts new messages, and all the *queues* we want for workers to pick messages. In the middle, we want to route the messages to the different queues depending on the topics, using a *binding*.

Let's say we have two workers, one that wants to receive messages about races and another one about training plans.

Every time a message is about a race, it gets labeled `race.id`, where `race` is a fixed prefix, and `id` is a unique ID for the race. Similarly, for training plans, it is `training.id`.

Using the `rabbitmqadmin` command line that gets installed with RabbitMQ, we can create all the necessary parts:

```
$ rabbitmqadmin declare exchange name=incoming type=topic
exchange declared

$ rabbitmqadmin declare queue name=race
queue declared

$ rabbitmqadmin declare queue name=training
queue declared

$ rabbitmqadmin declare binding source="incoming" destination_type="queue"
destination="race" routing_key="race.*"
binding declared

$ rabbitmqadmin declare binding source="incoming" destination_type="queue"
destination="training" routing_key="training.*"
binding declared
```

In this setup, every message is sent to RabbitMQ, wherein, if the topic starts with `race.`, it will be pushed into the *race* queue, and the `training.` ones will end up in the *training* queue.

To interact with RabbitMQ in the code, we can use **Pika** (`https://pika.readthedocs.io`) a Python RPC client that implements all the RPC endpoints a Rabbit service publishes.

 Everything we do with Pika can be done on the command line using **rabbitmqadmin**. You can directly get the status of all parts of the system, send and receive messages, and check what's in a queue. It's an excellent way to experiment with your messaging setup.

The following script shows how to publish two messages in RabbitMQ in the incoming exchange. One about `Race 34` and one about `Training 12`:

```
from pika import BlockingConnection, BasicProperties

# assuming there's a working local RabbitMQ server with a working
  guest/guest account
def message(topic, message):
    connection = BlockingConnection()
    try:
        channel = connection.channel()
        props = BasicProperties(content_type='text/plain',
                                delivery_mode=1)
        channel.basic_publish('incoming', topic, message, props)
    finally:
        connection.close()
# sending a message about race 34
message('race.34', 'We have some results!')

# training 12
message('training.12', "It's time to do your long run")
```

These RPC calls will end up adding one message respectively in the *race* and *training* queues. A Race worker script that waits for news about races would look like this:

```
import pika

def on_message(channel, method_frame, header_frame, body):
    race_id = method_frame.routing_key.split('.')[-1]
    print('Race #%s: %s' % (race_id, body))
    channel.basic_ack(delivery_tag=method_frame.delivery_tag)

print("Race NEWS!")
connection = pika.BlockingConnection()
channel = connection.channel()
```

```
channel.basic_consume(on_message, queue='race')
try:
    channel.start_consuming()
except KeyboardInterrupt:
    channel.stop_consuming()

connection.close()
```

Notice that Pika is sends back an ACK to RabbitMQ about the message, so it can be safely removed from the queue once the worker has succeeded.

An example of the output is as follows:

```
$ bin/python pika_worker.py
Race NEWS!
Race #34: b'We have some results!'
```

AMQP offers many patterns you can investigate to exchange messages. The tutorial page at `http://www.rabbitmq.com/getstarted.html`has many examples, and they are all implemented using Python and Pika.

To integrate these examples in our microservices, the publisher part is straightforward. Your Flask application can create a synchronous connection to RabbitMQ using `pika.BlockingConnection` and send messages through it. Projects such as **pika-pool** (`https://github.com/bninja/pika-pool`) implement simple connection pools so you can manage RabbitMQ channels without having to connect/disconnect every time you are sending something through RPC.

The consumers, on the other hand, are trickier to integrate into microservices.

Pika can be embedded into an event loop running in the same process as the Flask application, and trigger a function when a message is received. That would be okay in an asynchronous framework, but for a Flask application, you will need to execute the code that uses the Pika client in a separate thread or process. The reason for this is that the event loop would be blocked every time a request is received in Flask.

The most reliable way to use a Pika client in order to interact with RabbitMQ is to have a standalone Python application that consumes messages on behalf of your Flask microservice and performs synchronous HTTP calls. It adds yet another intermediary, but with the ability to acknowledge that a message was successfully received, and with all the Requests tricks we learned earlier in this chapter, we can build a reliable bridge:

```
import pika
import requests
from requests.exceptions import ReadTimeout, ConnectionError
```

```
FLASK_ENDPOINT = 'http://localhost:5000/event'

def on_message(channel, method_frame, header_frame, body):
    message = {'delivery_tag': method_frame.delivery_tag,
               'message': body}
    try:
        res = requests.post(FLASK_ENDPOINT, json=message,
                            timeout=1.)
    except (ReadTimeout, ConnectionError):
        print('Failed to connect to %s.' % FLASK_ENDPOINT)
        # need to implement a retry here
        return

    if res.status_code == 200:
        print('Message forwarded to Flask')
        channel.basic_ack(delivery_tag=method_frame.delivery_tag)

connection = pika.BlockingConnection()
channel = connection.channel()
channel.basic_consume(on_message, queue='race')
try:
    channel.start_consuming()
except KeyboardInterrupt:
    channel.stop_consuming()

connection.close()
```

This script will perform HTTP calls on Flask with the messages delivered in the queue.

There's also a RabbitMQ plugin that does something similar by pushing messages to HTTP endpoints, but isolating this bridge into our little script offers more potential if we need to add logic-specific code. From a robustness and performance point of view, it's also probably better to avoid integrating HTTP pushes inside RabbitMQ.

In Flask, the /event endpoint can be a classical view:

```
from flask import Flask, jsonify, request

app = Flask(__name__)

@app.route('/event', methods=['POST'])
def event_received():
    message = request.json['message']
    # do something...
    return jsonify({'status': 'OK'})
```

```
if __name__ == '__main__':
    app.run()
```

# Publish/subscribe

The previous pattern has workers that handle specific topics of messages, and the messages consumed by a worker are completely gone from the queue. We even added code to acknowledge that the message was consumed.

When you want a message to be published to several workers, the **Publish/Subscribe** (**pubsub**) pattern needs to be used.

This pattern is the basis for building a general event system and is implemented exactly like the previous one where there is one exchange and several queues. The difference is that the exchange part has a `fanout` type.

In that setup, every queue that you bind to a fanout exchange will receive the same message.

With a pubsub in place, you can broadcast messages to all your microservices if you need to.

# RPC over AMQP

AMQP also implements a synchronous request/response pattern, which means that we could use RabbitMQ instead of the usual HTTP JSON calls to have our microservice directly interact.

This pattern is a very appealing way to have two microservices communicate directly with each other. Some frameworks, such as **Nameko** (`http://nameko.readthedocs.io`) are using it to build microservices.

But the benefits of using RPC over AMQP rather than REST or RPC over HTTP are not that obvious unless the communication channel you want to set up is specific and maybe not part of the published API. Sticking with a single API is probably better to keep your microservices as simple as possible.

# Putting it together

In this section, we learned the following about asynchronous section:

- Asynchronous calls should be used every time a microservice can execute some work out of band. There's no good reason to block a request if what you are doing is not utilized in the response.
- Celery is a nice way to do some background processing.
- Service-to-service communication is not always limited to task queues.
- Sending events around is a good way to prevent services inter-dependencies.
- We can build a full event system around a broker such as Rabbit MQ to make our microservices interact with each other via messages.
- Pika can be used to coordinate all the message passing.

# Testing

As we learned in Chapter 3, *Coding, Testing and Documenting - the Virtuous Cycle*, the biggest challenge when writing functional tests for a service that calls other services is to isolate all network calls.

In this section, we'll see how we can mock synchronous calls made with Requests, and asynchronous calls for Celery workers and other asynchronous processes.

# Mocking synchronous calls

If you are using Requests to perform all the calls--or you are using a library that is based on Requests and that does not customize it too much, this isolation work is easier to do, thanks to the transport adapters we saw earlier in this chapter.

The **requests-mock** project (https://requests-mock.readthedocs.io) implements an adapter that will let you mock network calls in your tests.

Earlier in this chapter, we saw an example of a Flask app that was an HTTP endpoint to serve some content on its /api endpoint.

That application used a Request session that was created by a setup_connector() function and retrieved in a view by a get_connector() function.

In the following test, we're mounting the `requests_mock` adapter into that session by calling `session.mount()` with a fresh `requests_mock.Adapter()` instance:

```python
import json
import unittest
from flask_application import app, get_connector
from flask_webtest import TestApp
import requests_mock

class TestAPI(unittest.TestCase):
    def setUp(self):
        self.app = TestApp(app)
        # mocking the request calls
        session = get_connector(app)
        self.adapter = requests_mock.Adapter()
        session.mount('http://', self.adapter)

    def test_api(self):
        mocked_value = json.dumps({'some': 'data'})
        self.adapter.register_uri('GET', 'http://127.0.0.1:5000
                                  /api', text=mocked_value)
        res = self.app.get('/api')
        self.assertEqual(res.json['result']['some'], 'data')
```

Using this adapter offers the ability to manually register responses through `register_uri` for some given endpoints on the remote service (here `http://127.0.0.1:5000/api`). The adapter will intercept the call and immediately return the mocked value.

In the `test_api()` test, it will let us try out the application view and make sure it uses the provided JSON data when it calls the external service.

The `requests-mock` will also let you match requests using regular expressions, so it's a pretty powerful adapter to use in your tests to avoid a network dependency when they run.

That said, mocking responses from other services is still a fair amount of work and quite painful to maintain. It also means you need to keep an eye on how the other services are evolving over time, so your tests are not based on a mock that's not a reflection of the real API anymore.

Using mocks is encouraged to build good functional tests coverage, but make sure you are doing integration tests as well, where the service is tested in a deployment where it calls other services for real.

# Mocking asynchronous calls

If your application sends or receives calls asynchronously, setting up some testing is a little bit harder than for synchronous calls.

Asynchronous calls mean that the application is sending something somewhere and don't expect a result immediately--or just forgets about it altogether.

It can also means that the application may react to an event that is sent to it, as in the different patterns we've looked at based around Pika.

## Mocking Celery

If you are building tests for Celery workers, the simplest way to run your tests is to use a real Redis server. A Redis server is straightforward to run on any platform. Even Travis-CI will let you run one. So, instead of adding a lot of work to mock all the interactions, your Flask code will have with Redis to send some jobs to workers, and post them for real.

Using a real broker means that you can run your Celery worker in your test, just to validate that the app sent the proper job payloads. Celery provides a pytest test fixture that will run for you in a separate thread and shut it down once the test is over.

This is done by implementing a few fixtures to configure Celery to use Redis and to point your tests's tasks. The first step is to create a `tasks.py` file inside your tests directory which contains your Celery tasks.

The following is an example of such a file. Notice that we don't create a Celery instance--but use the `@shared_tasks` decorator to mark functions as being celery tasks:

```
from celery import shared_task
import unittest

@shared_task(bind=True, name='echo')
def echo(app, msg):
    return msg
```

This module implements a Celery task named `echo` that will echo back a string. To configure `pytest` to use it, you need to implement the `celery_config` and `celery_includes` fixtures:

```
import pytest

@pytest.fixture(scope='session')
def celery_config():
    return {
        'broker_url': 'redis://localhost:6379',
        'result_backend': 'redis://localhost:6379'
    }

@pytest.fixture(scope='session')
def celery_includes():
    return ['myproject.tests.tasks']
```

The `celery_config` function is used to pass all the options to create a Celery worker, and `celery_includes` will just import the list of modules it returns. In our case, it will register the echo task in the Celery tasks registry.

From there, your tests can use the `echo` task, and have the worker get called for real:

```
from celery.execute import send_task

class TestCelery(unittest.TestCase):
    @pytest.fixture(autouse=True)
    def init_worker(self, celery_worker):
        self.worker = celery_worker

    def test_api(self):
        async_result = send_task('echo', ['yeah'], {})
        self.assertEqual(async_result.get(), 'yeah')
```

Notice that, here, we've used `send_task()` to trigger the execution of the task.

This function can run any task that was registered as a broker by Celery, as long as the task has a unique name.

It's good practice to name all your tasks and to make sure these names are unique throughout all your microservices.

The reason is that when a microservice wants to run a task from a worker that is its microservice, we don't want to have to import that worker code just to get the task function.

In the following example, the *echo* task is running in a standalone microservice and we can trigger it via a `send_task()` call just by knowing the task name--no need to import the code; every interaction happens through Redis:

```
>>> import celery
>>> redis = 'redis://localhost:6379'
>>> app = Celery(__name__, backend=redis, broker=redis)
>>> f = app.send_task('echo', ['meh'])
>>> f.get()
'meh'
```

Back to your testing, if your tests are mocking some Celery workers, make sure the remote application that implements the tasks has a name for each one of them, and make sure that the application you are testing uses `send_task()` throughout its code.

That way, your Celery fixtures will magically mock the workers for your app.

Lastly, the application will probably not wait for the Celery worker to return the result synchronously--so you will need to inspect what the test worker has done after the API call.

# Mocking other asynchronous calls

If you do some messaging with Pika and RabbitMQ, the Pika library directly uses the socket module to interact with the server, and that makes it painful to mock because we would need to track what data is sent and received over the wire.

Like for Celery, you could just run a local RabbitMQ server for your tests--Travis-CI also making it available (`https://docs.travis-ci.com/user/database-setup/`).

Sending messages, in that case, is done as usual, and you can create a script that picks them in the Rabbit queues to verify them.

When you need to test a process where an event is received from RabbitMQ, if that happens via an HTTP call, as in our little `AMQP-to-HTTP` bridge, you can simply manually trigger the events from the tests.

What's important is to make sure you can run your tests without depending on other microservices. But dependencies on messaging servers such as Redis or RabbitMQ are not a problem as long as you can run them in a dedicated testing environment.

# Summary

In this chapter, we've looked at how a service can interact with other services synchronously, by using a `Requests` session, and asynchronously, by using Celery workers or more advanced messaging patterns based on RabbitMQ.

We've also looked at ways to test a service in isolation by mocking other services, but without mocking the message brokers themselves.

Testing each service in isolation is useful, but when something goes wrong, it's hard to know what happened, in particular, if the bug happens in a series of asynchronous calls.

In that case, tracking what's going with a centralized logging system helps a lot. The next chapter will explain how we can tool our microservices to follow their activities.

# 6
# Monitoring Your Services

In the previous chapter, we tested services that are interacting with each other in isolation. But when something bad happens in a real deployment, we need to have a global overview of what's going on. For example, when a microservice calls another one which in turn calls a third one, it can be hard to understand which one failed. We need to be able to track down all the interactions that a particular user had with the system that led to a problem.

Python applications can emit logs to help you debug issues, but jumping from one server to another to gather all the information you need to understand the problem can be hard. Thankfully, we can centralize all the logs to monitor a distributed deployment.

Continuously monitoring services are also important to assert the health of the whole system and follow how everything behaves. This involves answering questions such as, Is there a service that's dangerously approaching 100% of RAM usage?, How many requests per minute is that particular microservice doing? Do we have too many servers deployed for that API, can we remove a few boxes to reduce the price? Did a change we just deploy affect performance adversely?

To be able to answer questions like these continuously, every microservice we're deploying needs to be tooled to report primary metrics to a monitoring system.

This chapter is organized into two main sections:

- Centralizing logs
- Performance metrics

By the end of the chapter, you will have a full understanding of how to set up your microservices to monitor them.

# Centralizing logs

Python comes with the `logging` package, which lets you stream logs to a variety of places including standard out, rotating log files, syslog, or a TCP or UDP socket.

There's even an SMTP backend. In the following example, the `email_errors` decorator will send an email every time an exception is happening in the decorated function. Note that the handler is doing a telnet session with the SMTP server to send the email, so if there's any issue during that session, you might get a second exception when the `logger.exception()` function is called:

```python
import logging
from logging.handlers import SMTPHandler

host = "smtp.example.com", 25
handler = SMTPHandler(mailhost=host, fromaddr="tarek@ziade.org",
                      toaddrs=["tarek@ziade.org"],
                      subject="Service Exception")

logger = logging.getLogger('theapp')
logger.setLevel(logging.INFO)
logger.addHandler(handler)

def email_errors(func):
    def _email_errors(*args, **kw):
        try:
            return func(*args, **kw)
        except Exception:
            logger.exception('A problem has occured')
            raise
    return _email_errors

@email_errors
def function_that_raises():
    print(i_dont_exist)

function_that_raises()
```

If the call works, an email will be received with the full traceback enclosed.

 Python has a lot of handlers built-in the logging package; refer to `https://docs.python.org/3/library/logging.handlers.html`.

Logging to the standard output or a log file is fine when you are developing your service, but as we said earlier, that won't scale in a distributed system.

Sending emails on errors is an improvement, but with high-traffic microservices, it's common to get the same exception a thousand times an hour. If you are spamming an email box with a lot of emails, your server IP will get blacklisted by the SMTP server and your service will be unresponsive because it will be busy sending out lots of emails.

We need something better for a distributed system. A way to collect logs from all microservices with the least overhead possible, and some user interface to visualize them.

There are several existing systems to centralize logs generated by Python applications. Most of them can receive logs in HTTP or UDP payloads, with a preference for the latter because it reduces the overhead when your app sends them.

**Sentry** (`https://sentry.io/`) is a well-known tool in the Python community for centralizing error logs and provides a nice UI to deal with tracebacks. When a problem occurs in a service, Sentry can detect and aggregate the errors. The UI has a little resolution workflow that will let people deal with the problem.

But Sentry is focused on errors and is not well suited for general logging. If you want to get logs other than errors, you need to use something else.

Another open-source solution is **Graylog** (`http://graylog.org`), which is a general logging application that comes with a powerful search engine based on **Elasticsearch** (`https://www.elastic.co/`) where the logs are stored. **MongoDB** (`https://www.mongodb.com/`) is also used to store application data.

Graylog can receive any logs via its custom logging format or alternative formats, such as plain JSON. It has a built-in collector or can be configured to work with collectors such as **fluentd** (`http://www.fluentd.org/`).

# Setting up Graylog

A Graylog server is a Java application that uses MongoDB as its database, and stores all the logs it receives into **Elasticsearch**. Needless to say, a Graylog stack has quite a lot of moving parts that are hard to set up and administrate, and you will need some dedicated people if you deploy it yourself.

A typical production setup will use a dedicated Elastic Search cluster and several Graylog nodes with a MondoDB instance on each. You can have a look at Graylog architecture documentation (`http://docs.graylog.org/en/latest/pages/architecture.html`) for more details.

An excellent way to try out Graylog is to use its Docker (`https://docs.docker.com`) image, as described here in `http://docs.graylog.org/en/latest/pages/installation/docker.html`.

Chapter 10, *Containerized Services*, explains how to use Docker for deploying microservices, and gives the basic knowledge you need to build and run Docker images.

Like Sentry, Graylog is backed by a commercial company, which offers some hosting solutions. Depending on your project's nature and size, it can be a good solution to avoid maintaining this infrastructure yourself. For instance, if you run a commercial project that has a **Service-Level Agreement** (**SLA**), operating an Elasticsearch cluster smoothly is not a small task and will require some attention.

But for projects that don't generate a lot of logs, or if having the log management down for a bit is not the end of the world, then running your Graylog stack can be a good solution.

For this chapter, we'll just use the Docker image and docker-compose (a tool that can run and bind several docker images from one call) and a minimal set up to demonstrate how our microservices can interact with Graylog.

To run a Graylog service locally, you need to have Docker installed (see `Chapter 10`, *Dockerizing your service*) and use the following Docker compose configuration (taken from Graylog documentation):

```
version: '2'
services:
  some-mongo:
    image: "mongo:3"
  some-elasticsearch:
    image: "elasticsearch:2"
    command: "elasticsearch -Des.cluster.name='graylog'"
  graylog:
    image: graylog2/server:2.1.1-1
    environment:
      GRAYLOG_PASSWORD_SECRET: somepasswordpepper
      GRAYLOG_ROOT_PASSWORD_SHA2:
8c6976e5b5410415bde908bd4dee15dfb167a9c873fc4bb8a81f6f2ab448a918
      GRAYLOG_WEB_ENDPOINT_URI: http://127.0.0.1:9000/api
    links:
      - some-mongo:mongo
      - some-elasticsearch:elasticsearch
    ports:
      - "9000:9000"
      - "12201/udp:12201/udp"
```

If you save that file in a `docker-compose.yml` file and run `docker-compose up` in the directory containing it, Docker will pull the MongoDB, Elasticsearch and Graylog images and run them.

Once it's running, you can reach the Graylog dashboard at `http://localhost:9000` in your browser, and access it with `admin` as the user and password.

The next step is to go to **System** | **Inputs** to add a new UDP input so Graylog can receive our microservices logs.

This is done by launching a new GELF UDP input on port `12012`, as shown in the following screenshot:

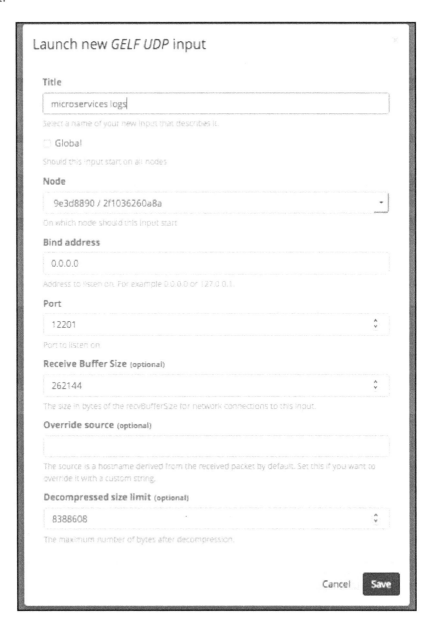

Once the new input is in place, Graylog will bind the UDP port `12201` and will be ready to receive data. The `docker-compose.yml` file has that port exposed for the Graylog image, so your Flask applications can send data via the localhost.

If you click on **Show Received Messages** for the new input, you will get a search result displaying all the collected logs:

Congratulations! You are now ready to receive logs in a centralized place and watch them live in the Graylog dashboards.

# Sending logs to Graylog

To send logs to Graylog from Python, you can use **Graypy** (`https://github.com/severb/graypy`), which converts Python logs to the **Graylog Extended Log Format** (**GELF**) (`http://docs.graylog.org/en/latest/pages/gelf.html`).

Graypy will send the logs via UDP by default, but can also send them via AMQP if you need to be 100% sure that every log makes it to Graylog.

> In most cases, UDP is good enough for centralizing logs. But unlike TCP, some packets may be dropped, and you won't know it. If your logging strategy needs more guarantee, a RabbitMQ-based transport will be more reliable.

Plugging graypy consists of using the provided handler in place of one of the built-in handlers:

```
handler = graypy.GELFHandler('localhost', 12201)
logger = logging.getLogger('theapp')
logger.setLevel(logging.INFO)
logger.addHandler(handler)
```

The `graypy.GELFHandler` class will convert the log into a UDP payload and send it to a GELF UDP Input. In the previous example, the input is listening on localhost, port `12201`.

It's unlikely that the code that sends the UDP payload will raise an error, and the overhead will be minimal since it's sending UDP datagrams without acknowledging that the other end has read it.

To integrate Graypy into your Flask application, you can add the handler directly on `app.logger`. You can also automatically log exceptions in an error handler registered every time Flask aborts because of an exception (intended or unintended):

```
import logging
import graypy
import json
from flask import Flask, jsonify
from werkzeug.exceptions import HTTPException, default_exceptions

app = Flask(__name__)

def error_handling(error):
    if isinstance(error, HTTPException):
        result = {'code': error.code, 'description':
                    error.description}
    else:
        description = default_exceptions[500].description
        result = {'code': 500, 'description': description}

    app.logger.exception(str(error), extra=result)
    result['message'] = str(error)
    resp = jsonify(result)
    resp.status_code = result['code']
    return resp


for code in default_exceptions.keys():
    app.register_error_handler(code, error_handling)

@app.route('/api', methods=['GET', 'POST'])
def my_microservice():
```

```
      app.logger.info("Logged into Graylog")
      resp = jsonify({'result': 'OK', 'Hello': 'World!'})
      # this will also be logged
      raise Exception('BAHM')
      return resp

if __name__ == '__main__':
      handler = graypy.GELFHandler('localhost', 12201)
      app.logger.addHandler(handler)
      app.run()
```

When calling /api, this application will send a simple log to Graylog, then the exception with its full traceback. In the following screenshot, we can see the traceback generated by this example:

The user will get the error as well, in a JSON response.

# Adding extra fields

Graypy adds some metadata fields to each log such as the following:

- The remote address
- The PID, process, and thread names
- The name of the function from which the call was made

Graylog itself will add the hostname from which each log is received, as the **source** field, and a few other fields.

For a distributed system, we need to add more contextual information to be able to search efficiently in our logs. For example, knowing the username is useful to search for a sequence of calls that was made in the stack in the same user session.

This information is usually stored inside app.session in our microservices, and we can use a logging.Filter class to add it in each logging record sent to Graylog:

```
from flask import session
import logging

class InfoFilter(logging.Filter):
    def filter(self, record):
        record.username = session.get('username', 'Anonymous')
        return True

app.logger.addFilter(InfoFilter())
```

By adding this filter, we will have a username field added in each Graylog entry.

Any contextual information you may think of that can be useful for understanding what's going on should go there. Although, keep in mind that adding more data in your logs can have an opposite effect. If the logs have too many details, it might become hard to search them efficiently, in particular, if a single request generates several log entries.

To conclude this part about log centralization, we've looked at how microservices can send all its logs to a centralized service with minimal overhead via UDP. Once the logs are stored, the centralized service should offer efficient search features.

Keeping all the logs is extremely useful to investigate microservices issues, but this should not happen that often, hopefully.

On the other hand, being able to monitor your applications continuously and server performances will let you be proactive when one of the servers is on its knees.

 Graylog Enterprise is a hosted version of Graylog with extra features, like archiving older logs — https://www.graylog.org/enterprise/feature/archiving

# Performance metrics

When a microservice eats 100% of server memory, bad things will happen. Some Linux distributions will just kill the greedy process using the infamous **out-of-memory killer** (**oomkiller**).

Using too much RAM can happen for several reasons:

- The microservice has a memory leak and steadily grows, sometimes at a very fast pace. It's very common in Python C extensions to forget to dereference an object and leak it on every call.
- The code uses memory without care. For example, a dictionary that's used as an ad hoc memory cache can grow indefinitely over the days unless there's an upper limit by design.
- There's simply not enough memory allocated to the service--the server is getting too many requests or is too weak for the job.

It's important to be able to track memory usage over time to find out about these issues before it impacts users.

Reaching 100% of the CPU in production is also problematic. While it's desirable to maximize the CPU usage, if the server is too busy when new requests are coming in, the service will not be responsive.

Lastly, knowing that the server disk is almost full will prevent a service to crash when it's out of space.

Hopefully, most of these problems can be discovered with a load test before the project goes to production. A load test is a good way to determine how much load a server can hold during the test and over time, and tweak the CPU/RAM resources depending on the expected load.

To do this, let's tool our service to monitor the system resources continuously.

# System metrics

A Linux-based system makes it simple to monitor the CPU, memory, and disk. There are system files that get continuously updated with this information and numerous tools to read them. Commands such as `top` will let you follow all the running processes and sort them by RAM or CPU usage.

In Python, the **psutil** (https://pythonhosted.org/psutil) project is a cross-platform library you can use to get all this info programmatically.

Combined with the graypy package, you can write a small script to send system metrics to Graylog continuously.

In the following example, an asyncio loop sends the CPU usage in percent every second to Graylog:

```python
import psutil
import asyncio
import signal
import graypy
import logging
import json

loop = asyncio.get_event_loop()
logger = logging.getLogger('sysmetrics')
def _exit():
    loop.stop()

def _probe():
    info = {'cpu_percent': psutil.cpu_percent(interval=None)}
    logger.info(json.dumps(info))
    loop.call_later(1., _probe)

loop.add_signal_handler(signal.SIGINT, _exit)
loop.add_signal_handler(signal.SIGTERM, _exit)
handler = graypy.GELFHandler('localhost', 12201)
logger.addHandler(handler)
logger.setLevel(logging.INFO)
loop.call_later(1., _probe)

try:
    loop.run_forever()
finally:
    loop.close()
```

Running this script as a daemon on your server will let you track its CPU usage.

The **system-metrics** (https://github.com/tarekziade/system-metrics/) project is roughly the same script but adds info about memory, disks, and network. If you use the pip install command, a command-line script will be available to probe your system.

Once the script runs, you can create a dashboard with a few widgets in the Graylog web app, as described in `http://docs.graylog.org/en/latest/pages/dashboards.html` and create an alert that will send you an email on specific conditions. *Alerts* in Graylog are configured on *Streams*, which are processing incoming messages in real-time.

To send an email when the CPU gets over 70%, you can create a stream that will collect the `cpu_percent` field sent by our `psutil` script using a stream rule:

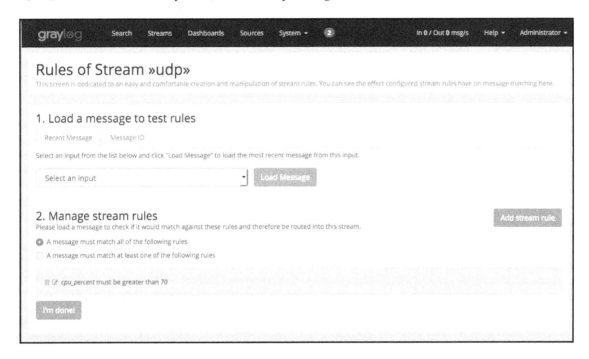

From there, you can manage alerts for the stream and add an email one that will get triggered when the condition is met for some time.

Like we did for sending logs, we can also add custom performance metrics inside our microservice code depending on our needs.

# Code metrics

For some microservices, it can also be useful to get performance metrics inside the code.

New Relic, for instance, will track Jinja2 and database call performances by wrapping some calls inside Flask to measure how long it takes to generate a template or perform a database call.

But adding your instrumentation inside the code needs to be done carefully if that instrumentation ships in production. Slowing down the service is easy. For instance, it's unthinkable to use Python built-in profilers because they add a significant overhead.

A simple pattern is to measure the time taken by some of your functions explicitly.

In the following example, the `@timeit` decorator will collect execution times for the `fast_stuff()` and `some_slow_stuff()` functions and a message will be sent to Graylog at the end of the request with the duration for each call:

```python
import functools
import logging
import graypy
import json
import time
import random
from collections import defaultdict, deque
from flask import Flask, jsonify, g

app = Flask(__name__)

class Encoder(json.JSONEncoder):
    def default(self, obj):
        base = super(Encoder, self).default
        # specific encoder for the timed functions
        if isinstance(obj, deque):
            calls = list(obj)
            return {'num_calls': len(calls), 'min': min(calls),
                    'max': max(calls), 'values': calls}
        return base(obj)

def timeit(func):
    @functools.wraps(func)
    def _timeit(*args, **kw):
        start = time.time()
        try:
            return func(*args, **kw)
        finally:
            if 'timers' not in g:
```

```
                g.timers = defaultdict(functools.partial(deque,
maxlen=5))
            g.timers[func.__name__].append(time.time() - start)
        return _timeit

    @timeit
    def fast_stuff():
        time.sleep(.001)

    @timeit
    def some_slow_stuff():
        time.sleep(random.randint(1, 100) / 100.)

    def set_view_metrics(view_func):
        @functools.wraps(view_func)
        def _set_view_metrics(*args, **kw):
            try:
                return view_func(*args, **kw)
            finally:
                app.logger.info(json.dumps(dict(g.timers), cls=Encoder))
        return _set_view_metrics

    def set_app_metrics(app):
        for endpoint, func in app.view_functions.items():
            app.view_functions[endpoint] = set_view_metrics(func)

    @app.route('/api', methods=['GET', 'POST'])
    def my_microservice():
        some_slow_stuff()
        for i in range(12):
            fast_stuff()
        resp = jsonify({'result': 'OK', 'Hello': 'World!'})
        fast_stuff()
        return resp


    if __name__ == '__main__':
        handler = graypy.GELFHandler('localhost', 12201)
        app.logger.addHandler(handler)
        app.logger.setLevel(logging.INFO)
        set_app_metrics(app)
        app.run()
```

Using such instrumentation, you will be able to track down each call duration in Graylog:

# Web server metrics

The last metrics that we want to have in our centralized logger is everything related to the HTTP requests and responses performance. We could add those metrics inside the Flask application alongside our timers, but it's better to do it at the web server level to reduce the overhead and to make metrics compatible with content that's not generated by Flask.

For instance, if nginx serves static files directly, we still want to track that. Graylog has a marketplace (https://marketplace.graylog.org) for extending the system with *content packs*, and there's an **nginx content pack** (https://github.com/Graylog2/graylog-content pack-nginx) that will parse nginx's access and error logs to push them in Graylog.

The pack comes with a default dashboard, and its input is using the nginx ability to send logs through UDP using **syslog** (http://nginx.org/en/docs/syslog.html).

Using this configuration, you will be able to track valuable information such as:

- The average response time
- The number of requests per minute
- The remote address
- The endpoint and verb of the request
- The status code and size of the response

Combined with app-specific metrics and system metrics, all these logs will let you build live dashboards you can use to follow what's going on in your deployments:

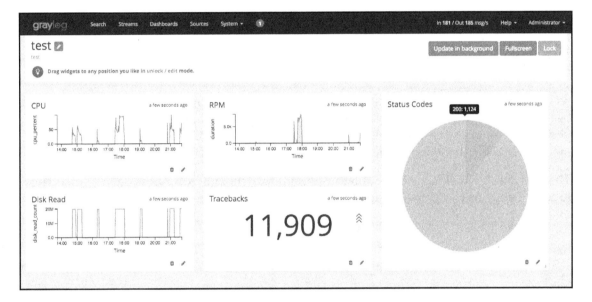

# Summary

In this chapter, we've seen how to add some instrumentation in our microservices and at the web server level. We've also learned how to set up Graylog to centralize and use all the generated logs and performance metrics.

Graylog uses Elasticsearch to store all the data, and that choice offers fantastic search features that will make your life easier to look for what's going on. The ability to add alerts is also useful for being notified when something's wrong. But deploying Graylog should be considered carefully. An Elastic Search cluster is heavy to run and maintain once it has a lot of data.

For your metrics, time-series based systems such as **InfluxDB** (open source) from **InfluxData** (`https://www.influxdata.com/`) is a faster and lightweight alternative. But it's not meant to store raw logs and exceptions.

So if you just care about performance metrics and exceptions, maybe a good solution would be to use a combination of tools: **Sentry** for your exceptions and **InfluxDB** for tracking performances. In any case, as long as your applications and web servers generate logs and metrics via UDP, it makes it easier to move from one tool to another.

The next chapter will focus on another important aspect of microservices development: how to secure your APIs, offer some authentication solutions, and avoid fraud and abuse.

# 7
# Securing Your Services

So far in this book, all the interactions between services were done without any form of authentication or authorization. Each HTTP request would happily return a result. This can't happen in production for two simple reasons: we need to know who is calling the service (authentication) and we need to make sure that the caller is allowed to perform the call (authorization). For instance, we probably don't want an anonymous caller to delete entries in a database.

In a monolithic web application, authentication happens with a login form, and once the user is identified, a cookie is set and used for all subsequent requests.

In a microservice-based architecture, we can't use that scheme everywhere because services are not users and won't use web forms to authenticate. We need a way to allow or reject a call between each service automatically.

The OAuth2 authorization protocol (`https://oauth.net/2/`) gives us the flexibility to add authentication and authorization in our microservices, that can be used to authenticate both users and services. In this chapter, we'll discover some aspects of OAuth2 and how to implement an authentication microservice. This service will be used to secure service-to-service interactions.

Securing services also means we want to avoid any fraud and abuse of the system. For instance, if a client starts to hammer one of our endpoints, whether it's malicious or an unintended bug, we need to detect that behavior and try to protect the system. There's not much we can do in case of a massive **Distributed Denial Of Service (DDoS)** attack, but setting up a basic web application firewall is easy to do and a great way to protect the system from basic attacks.

Lastly, a few things can be done at the code level to protect your services, such as controlling system calls or making sure HTTP redirects are not ending up in hostile web pages. The last part of the chapter will enumerate some of them and demonstrate how you can continuously scan your code for potential security issues.

In this chapter, we will cover the following topics:

- An overview of the Oauth2 protocol
- How token-based authentication works in practice
- What is the JWT standard and how to use it in a "token dealer" for securing microservices
- How to implement a web application firewall
- Some best practices to secure your microservice code

# The OAuth2 protocol

OAuth2 is a widely adopted standard that secures web applications and their interactions with users and other web applications, and yet it's hard to understand because it's based on many RFCs that are quite complicated to grasp fully.

The core idea of OAuth2 is that a centralized service is in charge of authenticating a caller, and can grant some access in the form of codes or tokens; let's call them keys. Those keys can be used by users or services to access a resource, as long as the service providing that resource accepts that key.

That's what we've used in `Chapter 4`, *Designing Runnerly*, to build the Strava microservice. The service interacts with the Strava API on behalf of the users after it was granted access via Strava's authentication service. This grant is called an **Authorization Code Grant** and is the most commonly used grant. It's known as **three-legged OAuth** because it involves the user, the authentication service, and a third-party application. Strava generates a code that can be used to call their APIs, and the Strava Celery worker we've created uses it in every call.

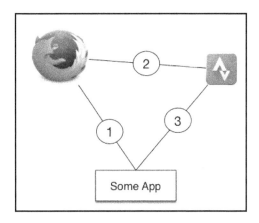

In the preceding diagram, the typical flow is to have the user interact with an application that wants to access a service like Strava. When the user calls app (**1**), they get redirected to the Strava service to grant access to the Strava API by app (**2**). Once it's done, **Some App** gets an authorization code through an HTTP callback and can use the Strava API on behalf of user (**3**).

For a service-to-service authentication that doesn't necessarily involve a particular user, there's another grant type called **Client Credentials Grant** (**CCG**), where *service A* can authenticate to the authentication microservice and ask for a token that it can use to call *service B*.

 For more information you can refer to the CCG scenario described in the **OAuth2** Authorization Framework section 4.4
(https://tools.ietf.org/html/rfc6749#section-4.4).

It works like the authorization code, but the service is not redirected to a web page like a user. Instead, it's implicitly authorized with a secret key that can be traded for a token.

For a microservices-based architecture, using these two type of grants will let us centralize every aspect of authentication and authorization of the system. Building a microservice that implements part of the OAuth2 protocol to authenticate services and keep track of how they interact with each other is a good solution to reduce security issues; everything is centralized in a single place.

The CCG flow is by far the most interesting part to look at in this chapter because it allows us to secure our microservices interactions independently from the users. It also simplifies permission management since we can issue tokens with different scopes depending on the context.

The three-legged flow is something that can be added if some of our microservices are used by third-party on behalf of specific users, but we will focus on CCG.

 If you don't want to implement and maintain the authentication part of your application and you can trust a third party to manage this process, then **Auth0** is an excellent commercial solution that provides all the APIs needed for a microservice-based application (`https://auth0.com/`).

Before we go ahead and implement our authentication microservice, let's look at how token-based authentication works from the ground. If you understand the next section correctly, everything else in OAuth2 should be easier to grasp.

# Token-based authentication

As we said earlier, when a service wants to get access to another service without any user intervention, we can use a CCG flow.

The idea behind CCG is that a service can authenticate to an authentication service exactly like a user would do, and ask for a token that it can then use to authenticate against other services.

A token is a like a password. It's proof that you are allowed to access a particular resource. Whether you are a user or a microservice, if you own a token that the resource recognizes, it's your key to access that resource.

Tokens can hold any information that is useful for the authentication and authorization process. Some of them can be:

- The user name or ID, if it's pertinent to the context
- The scope, which indicates what the caller is allowed to do (read, write, and so on)
- A *timestamp* indicating when the token was issued
- An *expiration* timestamp, indicating how long the token is valid

A token is usually built as a *self-contained* proof that you can use a service. Self-contained means that the service will be able to validate the token without having to call an external resource, which is an excellent way to avoid adding dependencies between services. Depending on the implementation, a token can also be used to access different microservices.

OAuth2 uses the JWT standard for its tokens.

> There's nothing in OAuth2 that requires the use of JWT — they just happen to be a good fit for what OAuth2 wants to do.

# The JWT standard

The **JSON Web Token** (**JWT**) described in RFC 7519 (`https://tools.ietf.org/html/rfc 7519`) is a standard that is commonly used to represent tokens.

Tokens are, in that case, a long string composed of three dot-separated parts:

- **Header**: This provides info on the token, such as which hashing algorithm is used
- **Payload**: This is the actual data
- **Signature**: This is a signed hash of the token to check that it's legitimate

JWT tokens are base64 encoded so they can be used in query strings.

Here's a JWT token in its encoded form:

```
eyJhbGciOiJIUzI1NiIsInR5cCI6IkpXVCJ9
.
eyJ1c2VyIjoidGFyZWsifQ
.
OeMWz6ahNsf-TKg8LQNdNMnFHNtReb0x3NMs0eY64WA
```

> Each part in the token above is separated by a line break for display purpose. The original token is a single line.

And if we use Python to decode it:

```
>>> import base64
>>> def decode(data):
...     # adding extra = for padding if needed
...     pad = len(data) % 4
...     if pad > 0:
...         data += '=' * (4 - pad)
...     return base64.urlsafe_b64decode(data)
...
>>> decode('eyJhbGciOiJIUzI1NiIsInR5cCI6IkpXVCJ9')
```

```
b'{"alg":"HS256","typ":"JWT"}'
>>> decode('eyJ1c2VyIjoidGFyZWsifQ')
b'{"user":"tarek"}'
>>> decode('0eMWz6ahNsf-TKg8LQNdNMnFHNtReb0x3NMs0eY64WA')
b'9\xe3\x16\xcf\xa6\xa16\xc7\xfeL\xa8<-
\x03]4\xc9\xc5\x1c\xdbQy\xbd1\xdc\xd3,\xd1\xe6:\xe1'
```

Every part of the JWT token is a JSON mapping except the signature. The header usually contains just the `typ` and the `alg` keys. The `typ` key says it's a JWT token, and the `alg` key indicates which hashing algorithm is used.

In the following header example, we have **HS256**, which stands for **HMAC-SHA256**:

```
{"typ": "JWT",  "alg": "HS256"}
```

The payload contains whatever you need, and each field is called a **JWT Claim** in the RFC 7519 jargon.

The RFC has a predefined list of claims that a token may contain, called **Registered Claim Names**. Here's a subset of them:

- `iss`: This is the issuer, which is the name of the entity that generated the token. It's typically the fully-qualified hostname, so the client can use it to discover its public keys by requesting `/.well-known/jwks.json`.
- `exp`: This is the **Expiration Time**, which is a timestamp after which the token is invalid
- `nbf`: This stands for **Not Before Time**, which is a timestamp before which the token is invalid
- `aud`: This is the **Audience**, which is the recipient for whom the token was issued
- `iat`: This stands for **Issued At**, which is a timestamp for when the token was issued

In the following payload example, we're providing the custom `user_id` value along with timestamps that make the token valid `24h` after it was issued. Once valid, that token can be used for `24h`:

```
{
  "iss": "https://tokendealer.example.com",
  "aud": "runnerly.io",
  "iat": 1488796717,
  "nbt": 1488883117,
  "exp": 1488969517,
  "user_id": 1234
}
```

These headers gives us a lot of flexibility to control how long our tokens will stay valid.

Depending on the nature of the microservice, the token **Time-To-Live** (**TTL**) can be very short or infinite. For instance, a microservice that interacts with other microservices within your system should probably rely on tokens that are valid for a while to avoid having to regenerate tokens all the time. On the other hand, if your tokens are distributed in the wild, it's a good idea to make them short lived.

The last part of a JWT token is the signature. It contains a signed hash of the header and the payload. There are several algorithms used to sign and hash. Some are based on a secret key, and some are based on public and private key pair.

Let's see how we can deal with JWT tokens in Python.

# PyJWT

In Python, the **PyJWT** (`https://pyjwt.readthedocs.io/`) library provides all the tools you need to generate and read back JWT tokens.

Once you've pip-installed pyjwt (and cryptography), you can use the `encode()` function and the `decode()` functions to create tokens.

In the following example, we're creating a JWT token using HMAC-SHA256 and reading it back. The signature is verified when the token is read, by providing the secret:

```
>>> import jwt

>>> def create_token(alg='HS256', secret='secret', **data):
...     return jwt.encode(data, secret, algorithm=alg)
...
>>> def read_token(token, secret='secret', algs=['HS256']):
...     return jwt.decode(token, secret)
...
>>> token = create_token(some='data', inthe='token')
>>> print(token)
b'eyJ0eXA1Oi1JKV1Q1LCJhbGci0iJIUzI1NiJ9.eyJpbnRoZSI6InRva2VuIiwic29tZSI6ImRh
dGEifQ.oKmFaNV-C2wHb_WaMAfIGDqBPnOCyOzVf-JWvh-6bRQ'
>>> read = read_token(token)
>>> print(read)
    {'inthe': 'token', 'some': 'data'}
```

The **create_token()** function calls **jwt.decode()** with the algorithms argument to make sure the token is verified with the right algorithm. This is good practice to prevent attacks where a malicious token can trick the server into using an unexpected algorithm, as noted in

`https://auth0.com/blog/critical-vulnerabilities-in-json-web-token-libraries`

When executing this code, the token is displayed in its compressed and uncompressed form.

If you use one of the registered claims, PyJWT will control them. For instance, if the `exp` field is provided and the token is outdated, the library will raise an error.

Using a secret for signing and verifying the signature is great when you have a few services running, but it can soon become a problem because it means you need to share the secret among all services that need to verify the signature. And when the secret needs to be changed, it can be a challenge to change it across your stack securely.

Basing your authentication on a secret that you are sharing around is also a weakness. If a single service is compromised and the secret is stolen, your whole authentication system is compromised.

A better technique is to use an asymmetric key composed of a public key and a private key. The private key is used by the token issuer to sign the tokens, and the public key can be utilized by anyone to verify that the signature was signed by that issuer.

Of course, if an attacker has access to the private key, or can convince clients that a forged public key is the legitimate one, you would still be in trouble.

But using a public/private key pair reduces the attack surface of your authentication process by a lot. And, since the authentication microservice will be the only place that has the private key, you can focus on adding extra security to it. For instance, such sensible services are often deployed in a *firewalled* environment where all accesses are strictly controlled.

Let's see how we can create asymmetric keys in practice.

# X.509 certificate-based authentication

The **X.509** standard (`https://en.wikipedia.org/wiki/X.509`) is used to secure the Web. Every website using SSL out there (serving pages on HTTPS), have an X.509 certificate on their web server and use it to encrypt and decrypt data on-the-fly.

These certificates are issued by a **Certificate Authority** (**CA**), and when your browser opens a page that presents a certificate, it has to be published from one of the CAs supported by the browser.

The reason why CA exists is to limit the risk of compromised certificates by having a limited number of trusted entities that generates and manages them, independently from the companies that use them.

Since anyone can create a self-signed certificate in a shell, it would be quite easy to end up in a world where you don't know if you can trust a certificate. If the certificate is issued by one of the CAs trusted by the browser, like **Let's Encrypt** (https://letsencrypt.org/), it should be legitimate.

For our microservices, using a self-signed certificate can be good enough if we own every part of the architecture, and that's what we'll demonstrate in the section. However, if your microservices are exposed to other third parties, or vice versa, it's better to rely on a trusted CA. Let's Encrypt is free and is a pretty good one. This project aims at securing the Web, but by using extend you can also use it to secure your microservices as long as you own a domain name.

For now, let's create our self-signed certificate and see how it can be used to sign JWT tokens.

In a shell, you can use the openssl command to create a certificate and extract a public and private key pair out of a certificate.

If you are under the latest macOS operating system, you might need to install openssl from brew since it was removed from macOS.

```
$ openssl req -x509 -newkey rsa:4096 -keyout key.pem -out cert.pem -days
365
Generating a 4096 bit RSA private key
........................++
........................++
writing new private key to 'key.pem'
Enter PEM pass phrase:
Verifying - Enter PEM pass phrase:
-----
You are about to be asked to enter information that will be incorporated
into your certificate request.
What you are about to enter is what is called a Distinguished Name or a DN.
There are quite a few fields, but you can leave some blank
```

```
For some fields, there will be a default value,

 If you enter '.', the field will be left blank.
-----
Country Name (2 letter code) [AU]:FR
State or Province Name (full name) [Some-State]:
Locality Name (eg, city) []:
Organization Name (e.g., company) [Internet Widgits Pty Ltd]:Runnerly

 Organizational Unit Name (eg, section) []:
Common Name (e.g. server FQDN or YOUR name) []:Tarek
Email Address []:tarek@ziade.org

$ openssl x509 -pubkey -noout -in cert.pem > pubkey.pem

$ openssl rsa -in key.pem -out privkey.pem
Enter pass phrase for key.pem:
writing RSA key
```

These three calls generate four files:

- The `cert.pem` file has the certificate
- The `pubkey.pem` file has the public key extracted from the certificate
- The `key.pem` file has the RSA private key, encrypted
- The `privkey.pem` file has the RSA private key, in clear

 **RSA** stands for **Rivest, Shamir, and Adleman**, the three authors. The RSA encryption algorithm generates crypto keys that can go up to 4,096 bytes and are considered secure.

From there, we can use `pubkey.pem` and `privkey.pem` in our PyJWT script to sign and verify the signature of the token, using `RSASSA-PKCS1-v1_5` signature algorithm and the `SHA-512` hash algorithm:

```
import jwt

with open('pubkey.pem') as f:
    PUBKEY = f.read()

with open('privkey.pem') as f:
    PRIVKEY = f.read()

def create_token(**data):
    return jwt.encode(data, PRIVKEY, algorithm='RS512')
```

```
def read_token(token):
    return jwt.decode(token, PUBKEY)

token = create_token(some='data', inthe='token')
print(token)

read = read_token(token)
print(read)
```

The result is similar to the previous run, except that we get a much bigger token:

b'eyJ0eXAiOiJKV1QiLCJhbGciOiJSUzUxMiJ9.eyJzb21lIjoiZGF0YSIsImludGhlIjoidG9r
ZW4ifQ.VHKP2yO1dCUrS5YAOCZsGXF_mesMJNNYcnBHe4mFiPpBDCbMhrI8h10vr1BaCiN8rVEM
cUXQ4Gc7183w6ga3spyEzONg3-Sv-eId4rPbTqbbmPErrnWPRIH9hQMHsMebVOlI91OvNmV-
J3DIEmV4riqRluJMIFYuy_A7fB2r8IqeHBfrsEPWmvw2_tIZ3V3dJGU4ZBkn8zdzgfbou_LHc28
_dyC32kR2Ec1nsRV3zRffEjx60cjzmNNFqB9kYZHun0IIzBqdh0IiRxPF4rgYG3oBKJXP3u2uyf
BifNy3Bz4bMPJ8iRRmQleciyFdzDkm7J4SAyz5I0TKHSPOZA-9x6dgacQ9w_JAtmElH7u8_ES_2
TxmvbBLqsXIzghAhG10CL79UeSKeXMTjc8DOQrIbWmaRCIbPy9AdlIJQxqul4UnCoUhUQ6PZwD6
CEuaZTjKdPvql7n_-u1Tjrw7e339WC9QZS5DFCzMe2F0TY-kI52-AaNEoRaO8oSCwW3E7u-
NcSt-
bD019MdX3bxN0FdNvL62BUDqqxind7TFF7YFX3zTxTu15Pex2F64YvnhG1CDk337htROt8B9vH8
CIUWo_2ujkair8zCdd9sfIdssOGFDnawIX2NPGd4vZ1dpw0DwHBaXw0gP8zzcRAsuZ7rfNMZeJT
H6gB-kMc5UKf26nAc'
{'some': 'data', 'inthe': 'token'}

Notice that adding over 700 bytes of data to each request can add up over time, so the secret-based JWT token technique is an option to keep in mind if you need to reduce the network overhead.

Now that we've learned how to deal with JWT tokens, let start to implement our authentication microservice; we'll call it the TokenDealer.

# The TokenDealer microservice

Our first step to building the authentication microservice will be to implement everything needed to perform a CCG flow. For that flow, the app receives requests from services that want a token and generates them on-demand. The generated tokens will have a lifespan of one day.

This service will be the only service to possess the private key that is used to sign the tokens and will expose the public key for other services that want to verify tokens. This service will also be the only place where all the client IDs and secret keys are kept.

We will greatly simplify the implementation by stating that once a service gets a token, it can access any other service in our ecosystem. When a service is accessed with a token, it can verify that token locally or call the TokenDealer to perform the verification. The first option, where checks happen locally, will remove one network roundtrip, but the tradeoff is that it will add some CPU overhead when working with JWT tokens, which can be problematic in some context. For example, if your microservice is doing some CPU-intensive work, adding the work required for checking the token might require to use a server with bigger CPUs, which might add some extra costs.

That's the reason why it's good to have the two options.

To implement everything we've described, three endpoints will be created in this microservice:

- `GET /.well-known/jwks.json`: This is the public key published in the **JSON Web Key** (**JWK**) format as described in **RFC 7517** (`https://tools.ietf.org/html/rfc7517`), when other microservices want to verify tokens on their own.
- `POST /oauth/token`: This returns a token, given some credentials. Adding the `/oauth` prefix is a convention widely adopted since it's used in the OAuth RFC.
- `POST /verify_token`: This returns the token payload, given a token. If the token is not valid, it returns a 400.

Using the microservice skeleton at `https://github.com/Runnerly/microservice`, we can create a very simple Flask blueprint that implements these three views.

Let's look at the most important one, `POST /oauth/token`.

# The POST/oauth/token implementation

For the CCG flow, the service that wants a token sends a POST request with an URL-encoded body that contains the following fields:

- `client_id`: This is a unique string identifying the requester.
- `client_secret`: This is a secret key that authenticates the requester. It should be a random string generated up-front and registered with the auth service.
- `grant_type`: This is the grant type, must be `client_credentials`.

We'll make a few assumptions to simplify the implementation:

- We're keeping the list of secrets in a Python mapping
- `client_id` is the name of the microservice
- The secret is generated with `binascii.hexlify(os.urandom(16))`

The authentication part will just ensure that the secret is valid, then the service will create a token and return it:

```python
import time
from flask import request, current_app, abort, jsonify
from werkzeug.exceptions import HTTPException
from flakon import JsonBlueprint
from flakon.util import error_handling
import jwt


home = JsonBlueprint('home', __name__)


def _400(desc):
    exc = HTTPException()
    exc.code = 400
    exc.description = desc
    return error_handling(exc)


_SECRETS = {'strava': 'f0fdeb1f1584fd5431c4250b2e859457'}


def is_authorized_app(client_id, client_secret):
    return compare_digest(_SECRETS.get(client_id), client_secret)


@home.route('/oauth/token', methods=['POST'])
def create_token():
    key = current_app.config['priv_key']
    try:
        data = request.form
        if data.get('grant_type') != 'client_credentials':
            return _400('Wrong grant_type')

        client_id = data.get('client_id')
        client_secret = data.get('client_secret')
        aud = data.get('audience', '')

        if not is_authorized_app(client_id, client_secret):
            return abort(401)

        now = int(time.time())

        token = {'iss': 'https://tokendealer.example.com',
```

```
                      'aud': aud,
                      'iat': now,
                      'exp': now + 3600 * 24}

        token = jwt.encode(token, key, algorithm='RS512')
        return {'access_token': token.decode('utf8')}
    except Exception as e:
        return _400(str(e))
```

The `create_token()` view uses the private key found in the application configuration under the `priv_key` key.

The `hmac.compare_digest()` function is used to compare the two secrets to avoid a timing attack by a client which would try to guess the `client_secret` one character at a time. It's equivalent to the "==" operator.

From the documentation: *This function uses an approach designed to prevent timing analysis by avoiding content-based short circuiting behavior, making it appropriate for cryptography*

This blueprint is all we need with a pair of keys to run a microservice that will take care of generating self-contained JWT tokens for all our microservices that require authentication.

The whole source code of the TokenDealer microservice can be found at `ht tps://github.com/Runnerly/tokendealer`where you can look at how the two other views are implemented.

The microservice could offer more features around token generation. For instance, the ability to manage scopes and make sure *microservice A* is not allowed to generate a token that can be used in *microservice B* or managing a whitelist of services that are authorized to ask for some tokens.

But the pattern we've implemented is the basis for an efficient token-based authentication system in a microservice environment, you can develop on your own, and is good enough for our Runnerly app.

In the following diagram, training plans, data service, and races can use JWT tokens to restrict access to their respective endpoints:

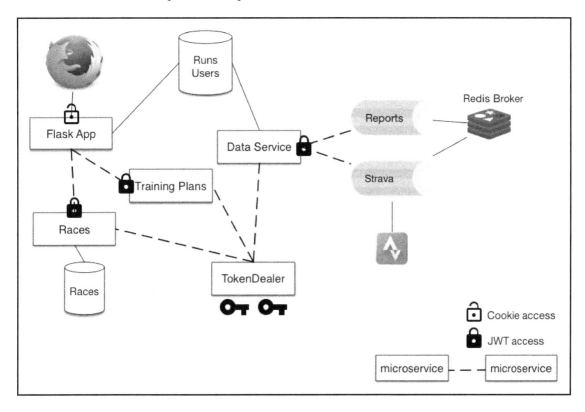

JWT access in this diagram means that the service requires a JWT token. Those services may validate the token by calling the TokenDealer. The Flask app in this diagram needs to obtain tokens from the TokenDealer on behalf of its users (link not shown in the diagram).

Now that we have a TokenDealer service that implements CCG, let's see in practice how it can be used by our services the next section.

# Using TokenDealer

In Runnerly, the **Data Service** | **Strava** worker link (**3**) is a good example of a place where authentication is required. Adding runs via the **Data Service** needs to be restricted to authorized services:

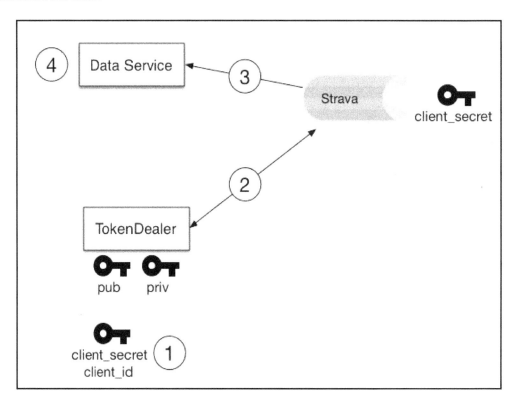

Adding authentication for that link is done in four steps:

1. The **TokenDealer** keeps a `client_id` and `client_secret` pair for the **Strava** worker and shares it with the **Strava** worker developers (**1**).
2. The **Strava** worker uses `client_id` and `client_secret` to ask a token to the **TokenDealer** (**2**).
3. The **Strava** worker adds the token in each request against to the **Data Service** (**3**).
4. The **Data Service** verifies the token by calling the **TokenDealer**, or by performing a local JWT verification (**4**)

In a full implementation, the first step is semiautomated. Generating a client secret is usually done through some web admin panel in the authentication service. That secret is then provided to the Strava microservice developers.

From there, the service can get a new token every time it needs it (because it's the first time or because the token is outdated) and add that token in the Authorization header when calling **Data Service**.

The following is an example of such a call using the `requests` library--we have in that example a TokenDealer running on `localhost:5000` and a Data Service running on `localhost:5001`.

```
import requests

server = 'http://localhost:5000'
secret = 'f0fdeb1f1584fd5431c4250b2e859457'

data = [('client_id', 'strava'),
        ('client_secret', secret),
        ('audience', 'runnerly.io'),
        ('grant_type', 'client_credentials')]

def get_token():
    headers = {'Content-Type': 'application/x-www-form-urlencoded'}
    url = server + '/oauth/token'
    resp = requests.post(url, data=data, headers=headers)
    return resp.json()['access_token']
```

 Notice that the `/oauth/token` is accepting form encoded data rather than a JSON payload, since this is the standard implementation.

The `get_token()` function retrieves a token, which can then be used in the `Authorization` header, when the code calls the Data Service:

```
_TOKEN = None

def get_auth_header(new=False):
    global _TOKEN
    if _TOKEN is None or new:
        _TOKEN = get_token()
    return 'Bearer ' + _TOKEN

_dataservice = 'http://localhost:5001'
```

```
def _call_service(endpoint, token):
    # not using session etc, to simplify the reading  :)
    return requests.get(_dataservice + '/' + endpoint,
                        headers={'Authorization': token})
def call_data_service(endpoint):
    token = get_auth_header()
    resp = _call_service(endpoint, token)
    if resp.status_code == 401:
        # the token might be revoked, let's try with a fresh one
        token = get_auth_header(new=True)
        resp = _call_service(endpoint, token)
    return resp
```

The `call_data_service()` function will try to get a new token if the call to the Data Service leads to a 401 response.

This refresh-token-on-401 pattern can be used in all your microservices to automate token generation.

This covers service-to-service authentication. You can find the full implementation in the Runnerly's GitHub repository to play with this JWT-based authentication scheme and use it as a basis for building your authentication process.

The next section of this chapter looks at another important aspect of securing your web services, that is, adding a web application firewall.

# Web application firewall

When you're exposing HTTP endpoints to others, you are expecting callers to behave as intended. Each HTTP conversation is supposed to follow a scenario that you have programmed in the service.

In the real world, that's not always the case. If the caller has a bug or is just not calling your service correctly, the expected behavior should be to send back a 4xx response and explain to the client why the request was rejected. That's also the case for malicious requests sent by attackers. Any unintended behavior should be dismissed.

The **Open Web Application Security Project (OWASP)** (https://www.owasp.org) is an excellent resource to learn about ways to protect your web apps from bad behaviors. They even provide a set of rules for the **ModSecurity** (https://modsecurity.org/crs/) toolkit's **Web Application Framework (WAF)** that can be used to avoid a lot of attacks.

In microservices-based applications, anything that's published to the web can be attacked, but, unlike monolithic applications, most of the system is not dealing directly with users via HTML user interfaces or public APIs, and that narrows down the spectrum of potential attacks.

We'll see in this section how to provide essential protection for our JSON-based microservices.

But before we do this, let's look at some of the most common attacks:

- **SQL Injection**: The attacker sends raw SQL statements in the request. If your server uses some of the request content (typically the arguments) to build SQL queries, it might perform the attacker's request on the database. In Python, though, if you use SQLAlchemy and avoid raw SQL statements altogether, you will be safe. If you use raw SQL, make sure every variable is correctly quoted. We'll see that later in this chapter.
- **Cross Site Scripting (XSS)**: This attack happens only on web pages that display some HTML. The attacker uses some of the query attributes to try to inject their piece of HTML on the page to trick the user into performing some actions thinking they are on the legitimate website.
- **Cross-Site Request Forgery (XSRF/CSRF)**: This attack is based on attacking a service by reusing the user's credentials from another website. The typical CSRF attack happens with POST requests. For instance, a malicious website displays a link to a user to trick that user to perform the POST request on your site using their existing credentials.

Many other attacks are specifically targeting PHP-based systems because it's widespread and easy to find a PHP app that uses invalidated user input when the server is called. Things such as **Local File Inclusion (LFI)**, **Remote File Inclusion (RFI)**, or **Remote Code Execution (RCE)** are all attacks that trick the server to execute something via client input or reveal server files. They can happen of course in Python applications, but Python frameworks are known to have built-in protections to avoid those attacks.

However, bad requests are not always how a client, whether it's malicious or not, can abuse your system. It can send legitimate requests and just hammer your service with it, leading to a **Denial of Service (DoS)** because all the resources are used to handle requests from the attacker. This problem sometimes happens within distributed systems when clients have replay features that are automatically recalling the same API. If nothing is done on the client side to throttle calls, you might end up with a service overloaded by legitimate clients.

Adding a protection on the server-side to back-off such zealous clients is usually not hard to do and goes a long way to protect your microservice stack.

In this section, we'll focus on creating a basic WAF that will explicitly reject a client that's making too many requests on our service.

 The intent of this section is not to create a full WAF, but rather to give you a good understanding of how WAF are implemented and used. That said, using a fully featured WAF like ModSecurity is probably overkill for JSON-based microservices.

We could build our WAF in a Flask microservice, but it would add a lot of overhead if all the traffic has to go through it. A much better solution is to rely directly on the web server.

# OpenResty - Lua and nginx

**OpenResty** (http://openresty.org/en/) is an nginx distribution that embeds a **Lua** (http://www.lua.org/) interpreter that can be used to script the web server.

Lua is an excellent, dynamically-typed programming language, which has a lightweight interpreter, yet, very fast. The language offers a complete set of features and has built-in async features. You can write coroutines directly in vanilla Lua.

For a Python developer, Lua feels quite *Pythonic*, and you can start to build scripts with it in a matter of hours once you know the basic syntax. It has functions, classes, and a standard library that will make you feel at home.

If you install Lua (refer to http://www.lua.org/start.html), you can play with the language using the Lua **Read Eval Print Loop** (REPL) exactly like how you would do with Python:

```
$ lua
Lua 5.1.5  Copyright (C) 1994-2012 Lua.org, PUC-Rio
> io.write("Hello world\n")
Hello world
> mytable = {}
> mytable["user"] = "tarek"
> = mytable["user"]
tarek
> = string.upper(mytable["user"])
TAREK
```

To discover the Lua language, this is your starting page `http://www.lua.org/docs.html`.

Lua is often a language of choice to get embedded in compiled apps. Its memory footprint is ridiculously small, and it allows to add fast dynamic scripting features. That is what is happening in OpenResty. Instead of building nginx modules that require compiling nginx with them, you can extend the web server using Lua scripts and deploy them directly with OpenResty.

When you invoke some Lua code from your nginx configuration, the **LuaJIT** (`http://luajit.org/`) interpreter that's employed by OpenResty will run them in a very efficient way, and won't be slower than nginx code itself. Some performance benchmarks find that Lua can be faster than C or C++ in some cases (refer to `http://luajit.org/performance.html`).

The functions you can add in nginx that way are *coroutines* that will run asynchronously in nginx, so the overhead is minimal even when your server receives a lot of concurrent requests, which is exactly our need for a WAF.

OpenResty comes as Docker image and a package for some Linux distributions. It can also be compiled from the ground, refer to `http://openresty.org/en/installation.html`. On macOS, you can use Brew and the `brew install openresty` command.

Once OpenResty is installed, you will get an `openresty` command, and you can use it exactly like nginx to serve your apps.

In the following example, the nginx configuration will proxy calls to a Flask application running on port 5000:

```
daemon off;
worker_processes  1;
pid openresty.pid;
error_log /dev/stdout info;
events {
  worker_connections  1024;
}
http {
  include       mime.types;
  default_type  application/octet-stream;
  sendfile         on;
  keepalive_timeout  65;
  access_log /dev/stdout;
  server {
    listen       8888;
```

```
server_name  localhost;
location / {
  proxy_pass http://localhost:5000;
  proxy_set_header Host $host;
  proxy_set_header X-Real-IP $remote_addr;
  proxy_set_header X-Forwarded-For $proxy_add_x_forwarded_for;
}
}
}
```

This configuration can be used with the `openresty` command line and will run in the foreground (daemon off) on port `8888` to proxy pass all requests to the Flask app running on port `5000`.

```
$ openresty -c resty.conf
2017/07/14 12:10:12 [notice] 49704#524185: using the "kqueue" event method
2017/07/14 12:10:12 [notice] 49704#524185: openresty/1.11.2.3
2017/07/14 12:10:12 [notice] 49704#524185: built by clang 8.0.0
(clang-800.0.38)
2017/07/14 12:10:12 [notice] 49704#524185: OS: Darwin 16.6.0
2017/07/14 12:10:12 [notice] 49704#524185: hw.ncpu: 4
2017/07/14 12:10:12 [notice] 49704#524185: net.inet.tcp.sendspace: 1042560
2017/07/14 12:10:12 [notice] 49704#524185: kern.ipc.somaxconn: 2048
2017/07/14 12:10:12 [notice] 49704#524185: getrlimit(RLIMIT_NOFILE):
7168:9223372036854775807
2017/07/14 12:10:12 [notice] 49704#524185: start worker processes
2017/07/14 12:10:12 [notice] 49704#524185: start worker process 49705
```

Note that this configuration can also be used in a plain nginx server, since we're not using any Lua yet. That's what's nice with OpenResty: it's a drop-in replacement for nginx and can run your existing configuration files.

 The code and configuration demonstrated in this section can be found at h ttps://github.com/Runnerly/waf.

Lua can be invoked at different moments when a request comes in, the two that are attractive to this chapter are:

- `access_by_lua_block`: This is called on every incoming request before a response is built. This is where we can build access rules in our WAF.
- `content_by_lua_block`: This uses Lua to generate a response.

Let's see in the next section how we can rate-limit incoming requests.

# Rate and concurrency limiting

Rate limiting consists of counting how many requests a server is accepting in a period of time, and rejecting new ones when a limit is reached.

Concurrency limiting consists of counting how many concurrent requests are being served by the web server to the same remote user and starting to reject new ones when it reaches a defined threshold. Since many requests can reach the server simultaneously, a concurrency limiter needs to have a small allowance in its threshold.

Both are implemented using the same technique. Let's look at how to build a concurrency limiter.

OpenResty ships with a rate limiting library written in Lua called `lua-resty-limit-traffic` (`https://github.com/openresty/lua-resty-limit-traffic`); you can use it in a `acces_by_lua_block` section.

The function uses **Lua Shared Dict**, which is a memory mapping that is shared by all nginx workers within the same process. Using a memory dict means that the rate limiting will work at the process level.

 Since we're typically deploying one nginx per service node, the rate limiting will happen per web server. So, if you are deploying several nodes for the same microservice and doing some load balancing, you will have to take this into account when you set the threshold.

In the following example, we're adding a `lua_shared_dict` definition and a `access_by_lua_block` section to activate the rate limiting. Note that this example is a simplified version of the example from the project's documentation:

```
...
http {
  ...
  lua_shared_dict my_limit_req_store 100m;

  server {
    access_by_lua_block {
      local limit_req = require "resty.limit.req"
      local lim, err = limit_req.new("my_limit_req_store",200, 100)
      local key = ngx.var.binary_remote_addr
      local delay, err = lim:incoming(key, true)
      if not delay then
        if err == "rejected" then
          return ngx.exit(503)
        end
```

```
        end
      if delay >= 0.001 then
        ngx.sleep(delay)
        end
    }
    proxy_pass ...
  }
}
```

The `access_by_lua_block` section can be considered as a Lua function and can use some of the variables and function OpenResty exposes. For instance, `ngx.var` is a table containing all the nginx variables and `ngx.exit()` is a function that can be used to immediately return a response to the user. In our case, a `503` when we need to reject a call because of rate-limiting.

The library uses the `my_limit_req_store` dict that is passed to the `resty.limit.req` function and every time a request reaches the server, it calls the `incoming()` function with the `binary_remote_addr` value, which is the client address.

The incoming function will use the shared dict to maintain the number of active connections per remote address and send back a *rejected* value when that number reaches the threshold, for example, when there are more than 300 concurrent requests.

If the connection is accepted, the `incoming()` function sends back a delay value. Lua will hold the request using that delay and the asynchronous `ngx.sleep()` function. The delay will be 0 when the remote client has not reached the threshold of 200, and a small delay when between 200 and 300, so the server has a chance to unstack all the pending requests.

This elegant design will be quite efficient to avoid a service to get overwhelmed by many requests. Setting up a ceiling like that is also a good way to avoid reaching a point where you know your microservice will start to break.

For instance, if some of your benchmarks concluded that your service could not serve more than 100 simultaneous requests before starting to crash, you can set the rate limiting, so it's nginx that rejects requests instead of letting your Flask microservice pile up error logs and heat the CPU just to handle rejections.

 The key used to calculate the rate in this example is the remote address header of the request. If your nginx server is itself behind a proxy, make sure you are using a header that contains the real remote address. Otherwise, you will rate limit a single remote client, the proxy server. It's usually in the X-Forwarded-For header in that case.

If you want a WAF with more features, the `lua-resty-waf` (`https://github.com/p0pr0c k5/lua-resty-waf`) project works like `lua-resty-limit-traffic`, but offers a lot of other protections. It's also able to read ModSecurity rule files, so you can use the rule files from the OWASP project without having to use ModSecurity itself.

# Other OpenResty features

OpenResty comes with many Lua scripts that can be useful to enhance nginx. Some developers are even using it to serve their data directly.

If you look at the components page at `http://openresty.org/en/components.html`, you will find some useful tools to have nginx interact with databases, cache servers, and so on. There's also a website for the community to publish OpenResty components, refer to `https://opm.openresty.org/`.

If you are using OpenResty in front of your Flask microservices, there will probably be other use cases where you can transfer some code that's in the Flask app to a few lines of Lua in OpenResty. The goal should not be to move the app's logic to OpenResty, but rather to leverage the web server to do anything that can be done before or after your Flask app is called.

For instance, if you are using a Redis or a Memcache server to cache some of your GET resources, you can directly call them from Lua to add or fetch a cached version for a given endpoint. The **srcache-nginx-module** (`https://github.com/openresty/srcache-nginx-m odule`) is an implementation of such a behavior and will reduce the number of GET calls made to your Flask apps if you can cache them.

To conclude this section about web application firewalls, OpenResty is a powerful nginx distribution that can be used to create a simple WAF to protect your microservices. It also offers abilities that go beyond firewalling. In fact, if you adopt OpenResty to run your microservices, it opens a whole new world of possibilities, thanks to Lua.

The next section that ends this chapter will focus on what can be done at the code level to protect your microservices.

# Securing your code

In the previous section, we've looked at how to set up a simple WAF. The rate limiting feature we've added is useful but protects us from just one possible attack. Without being paranoid, as soon as you are exposing your app to the world, there are numerous possible attacks, and your code needs to be designed with that threat in mind.

The idea behind secure code is simple, yet hard to do well in practice. The two fundamental principles are:

- Every request from the outside world should be carefully assessed before it does something in your application and data
- Everything your application is doing on a system should have a well-defined and limited scope

Let's look at how to implement these principles in practice.

# Asserting incoming data

The first principle, assert incoming data, just means that your application should not blindly execute incoming requests without making sure what will be the impact.

For instance, if you have an API that will let a caller delete a line in a database, you need to make sure the caller is allowed to do it. This is why we've added authentication and authorization earlier in this chapter.

But there are other ways to breach in. For example, if you have a Flask view that grabs JSON data from the incoming request and uses it to push data to a database, you should verify that the incoming request has the data you are expecting, and not blindly pass it over to your database backend. That's why it can be interesting to use Swagger to describe your data as schemas and use them to validate incoming data.

Microservices usually use JSON, but if you happen to use templates, that's yet another place where you need to be careful in what the template is doing with variables.

**Server-Side Template Injection (SSTI)** is a possible attack when your templates are blindly executing some Python statements. In 2016, such an injection vulnerability was found on Uber's website (`https://hackerone.com/reports/125980`) on a Jinja2 template because a raw formatting was done before the template was executed.

The code was something similar to this small app:

```python
from flask import Flask, request, render_template_string

app = Flask(__name__)

SECRET = 'oh no!'

_TEMPLATE = """\
Hello %s

Welcome to my API!
"""

class Extra(object):
    def __init__(self, data):
        self.data = data

@app.route('/')
def my_microservice():
    user_id = request.args.get('user_id', 'Anynomous')
    tmpl = _TEMPLATE % user_id
    return render_template_string(tmpl, extra=Extra('something'))
```

By doing this preformatting on the template with a raw %s, the view creates a huge security hole in the app, since it allows attackers to inject what they want in the Jinja script before it gets executed.

In the following example, the user_id variable security hole is exploited to read the value of SECRET global variable from the module:

**http://localhost:5000/?user_id={{extra.__class__.__init__.__globals__["SECR ET"]}}**

That's why it's quite important to avoid doing any manual formatting with incoming data when it's used to display a view.

If you need to evaluate untrusted code in a template, you can use Jinja's sandbox, refer to http://jinja.pocoo.org/docs/latest/sandbox/. This sandbox will reject any access to methods and attributes from the object being evaluated. For instance, if you're passing a callable in your template, you will be sure that its attributes such as __class__ cannot be used.

That said, Python sandboxes are tricky to get right, due to the nature of the language. It's easy to misconfigure a sandbox, or the sandbox itself can be compromised with a new version of the language. The safest bet is to avoid evaluating untrusted code altogether and make sure you're not directly relying on incoming data for templates.

Another common place where injection happens is in SQL statements. If some of your SQL queries are built using raw SQL statements, you are exposing your app to SQL injections exploits.

In the following example, a simple `select` query that takes a user ID can be used to inject extra SQL queries, such as an `insert` query. From there, an attacker can hack a server in no time:

```python
import pymysql

connection = pymysql.connect(host='localhost', db='book')

def get_user(user_id):
    query = 'select * from user where id = %s'
    with connection.cursor() as cursor:
        cursor.execute(query % user_id)
        result = cursor.fetchone()
    return result

extra_query = """\
insert into user(id, firstname, lastname, password)
values (999, 'pnwd', 'yup', 'somehashedpassword')
"""

# this call will get the user, but also add a new user!
get_user("'1'; %s" % extra_query)
```

This can be prevented by quoting any value used to build *raw* SQL queries. In **PyMySQL**, you just need to pass the values to the execute argument to avoid this problem:

```python
def get_user(user_id):
    query = 'select * from user where id = %s'
    with connection.cursor() as cursor:
        cursor.execute(query, (user_id,))
        result = cursor.fetchone()
    return result
```

Every database library has this feature. So as long as you are correctly using these libraries when building raw SQL, you should be okay.

The same precaution goes with redirects. One common mistake is to create a login view that makes the assumption that the caller will be redirected to an internal page and use a plain URL for that redirect:

```
@app.route('/login')
def login():
    from_url = request.args.get('from_url', '/')
    # do some authentication
    return redirect(from_url)
```

This view can redirect the caller to any website, which is a significant threat particularly during the login process. A good practice is to avoid free strings when calling `redirect()`, by using the `url_for()` function, which will create a link about your app domain.

But if you need to redirect to third parties sometimes, you can't use the `url_for()` and the `redirect()` functions as they can potentially send your clients to unwanted places.

One solution is to create a restricted list of third-party domains your application is allowed to redirect to and make sure any redirection done by your application or underlying third-party libraries are checked against that list.

This can be done with the `after_request()` hook that will be called if the response Flask is about to send out. In case the application tries to send back a 302, you can check that its location is safe, given a list of domains and ports:

```
from flask import make_response
from urllib.parse import urlparse

# domain:port
SAFE_DOMAINS = ['github.com:443', 'ziade.org:443']

@app.after_request
def check_redirect(response):
    if response.status_code != 302:
        return response
    url = urlparse(response.location)
    netloc = url.netloc
    if url.scheme == 'http' and not netloc.endswith(':80'):
        netloc += ':80'
    if url.scheme == 'https' and not netloc.endswith(':443'):
        netloc += ':443'

    if netloc not in SAFE_DOMAINS:
        # not using abort() here or it'll break the hook
        return make_response('Forbidden', 403)
    return response
```

To summarize, you should always treat incoming data as a potential threat to injection of attacks in your system.

# Limiting your application scope

Even if you're doing a good job at protecting your application from bad behaviors induced by incoming data, you should also make sure the application itself is not able to do some damage in your microservice ecosystem.

If your microservice is authorized to interact with other microservices, these interactions should be authenticated, as we've seen earlier in this chapter, but also limited to the strict minimum allowed. In other words, if a microservice is performing some read calls on another microservice, it should not be able to do any POST call and restricted to read-only.

That scope limitation can be done with the JWT tokens by defining roles (such as read/write) and adding that information in the token under a *permissions* or *scope* key, for example. The target microservice will then be able to reject a call on a POST that is made with a token that is supposed only to read data.

This is what happens when you grant access to an application on your GitHub account, or on your Android phone. A detailed list of what the app wants to do is displayed, and you can grant or reject access.

If you are controlling all parts of your microservices ecosystem, you can also use strict firewalls rules at the system level to whitelist the IPs that are allowed to interact with each microservice, but that kind of set up depends a lot on where you are deploying your application. In the **Amazon Web Services** (**AWS**) cloud environment, you don't need to configure a Linux firewall. All you have to do is set simple access rules in the AWS console.

Chapter 11, *Deploying on AWS*, covers the basics of deploying your microservices on the Amazon cloud.

Besides network accesses, any other resource your application can access should be limited whenever possible. Running the application as a root user on Linux is not a good idea because, in case of a security issue, you are giving full power to the service.

For instance, if your application is calling the system and that call gets hacked by an injection or another exploit, it's a backdoor for an attacker to own the whole operating system.

Root access to a system has become an indirect threat in modern deployments, since most applications are running in **Virtual Machines** (**VM**), but an unrestricted process can still do a lot of damage even if jailed. If an attacker owns one of your VMs, it's the first step to own the whole system.

To mitigate the problem, there are two rules you should follow:

- A web service process should be run by a non-root user
- Be very cautious when executing processes from your web service and avoid it if you can.

For the first rule, the default behavior for web servers such as NGinx is to run its processes using the `www-data` user and group, and that prevents these processes from being able to execute anything on the system. The same rules apply to your Flask processes. We'll see in `Chapter 9`, *Packaging Runnerly*, the best practices to run a stack in the user space on a Linux system.

For the second rule, any Python call to `os.system()`, `subprocess`, `multiprocessing` should be double-checked to avoid making unwanted calls on the system. This is also true for high-level network modules that send emails or connect to third-party servers via FTP, via the local system.

There's a way to continuously check your code for potential security issues using the **Bandit** linter.

# Using Bandit linter

The OpenStack community (`https://www.openstack.org/`) created a nice little security linter called Bandit to try to catch insecure code (`https://wiki.openstack.org/wiki/Security/Projects/Bandit`).

The tool uses the `ast` module to parse the code such as Flake8 or other linters. Bandit will scan for some known security issues in your code.

Once you've installed it with the `pip install bandit` command, you can run it against your Python module using the `bandit` command.

The following script is an example of three unsafe functions. The first one will let you load YAML content that might instantiate arbitrary objects, and the following ones are prone to injection attacks:

```
import subprocess
from sqlalchemy import create_engine
from sqlalchemy.orm import sessionmaker
import yaml

def read_file(filename):
    with open(filename) as f:
        data = yaml.load(f.read())

def run_command(cmd):
    return subprocess.check_call(cmd, shell=True)

db = create_engine('sqlite:///somedatabase')
Session = sessionmaker(bind=db)

def get_user(uid):
    session = Session()
    query = "select * from user where id='%s'" % uid
    return session.execute(query)
```

Running Bandit over that script will detect the three issues and explain the problems in detail:

```
$ bandit bandit_example.py
...
Run started:2017-03-20 08:47:06.872002

Test results:
>> Issue: [B404:blacklist] Consider possible security implications
associated with subprocess module.
   Severity: Low    Confidence: High
   Location: bandit_example.py:1
1    import subprocess
2    from sqlalchemy import create_engine
3    from sqlalchemy.orm import sessionmaker

--------------------------------------------------
>> Issue: [B506:yaml_load] Use of unsafe yaml load. Allows instantiation of
arbitrary objects. Consider yaml.safe_load().
   Severity: Medium    Confidence: High
   Location: bandit_example.py:9


 bandit_example.py
```

```
8        with open(filename) as f:
9            data = yaml.load(f.read())
10

--------------------------------------------------
>> Issue: [B602:subprocess_popen_with_shell_equals_true] subprocess call
with shell=True identified, security issue.
   Severity: High    Confidence: High
   Location: bandit_example.py:13
12 def run_command(cmd):
13       return subprocess.check_call(cmd, shell=True)
14

--------------------------------------------------
>> Issue: [B608:hardcoded_sql_expressions] Possible SQL injection vector
through string-based query construction.
   Severity: Medium    Confidence: Low
   Location: bandit_example.py:23
22       session = Session()
23       query = "select * from user where id='%s'" % uid
24       return session.execute(query)

--------------------------------------------------

...
Files skipped (0):
```

For this book, we are using the version *Bandit 1.4.0*. It has 64 security checks included, and is very easy to extend if you want to create your own checks. You can also tweak its configuration by creating a configuration file in your project.

One security check, for instance, will emit a security warning in case your are running Flask in debug mode, since this is a security issue in production. Consider the following example:

```
$ bandit flask_app.py
...
Test results:
>> Issue: [B201:flask_debug_true] A Flask app appears to be run with
debug=True, which exposes the Werkzeug debugger and allows the execution of
arbitrary code.
   Severity: High    Confidence: Medium
   Location: flask_app.py:15
14 if __name__ == '__main__':
15     app.run(debug=True)
```

This is a great check when shipping in production, but when developing your application, you will want to turn this one off. Excluding your test's modules for security scanning is also a good idea.

The following configuration file, which can be used with the `ini` option will ignore that issue and exclude tests/ files:

```
[bandit]
skips: B201
exclude: tests
```

 Adding a bandit call in your continuous integration pipeline alongside tools such as coveralls, as described in Chapter 3, *Coding, Testing, and Documenting - The Virtuous Cycle*, is a good way to catch potential security issues in your code.

# Summary

In this chapter, we've looked at how to centralize authentication and authorization in a microservices-based application environment using **OAuth2 and JWT tokens**. Tokens give us the ability to limit *what* and *for how long* a caller can do on one of the microservices.

When used with public/private keys, it also prevents an attacker that breaks into one service to break the whole app, as long as it's not the token issuer that's compromised.

Beyond system-level firewall rules, a Web Application Framework is also a good way to prevent some fraud and abuse on your endpoints and is very easy to do with a tool such as **OpenResty**, thanks to the power of the **Lua** programming language.

OpenResty is also an excellent way to empower and speed up your microservices by doing a few things at the web server level when it does not need to be done within the Flask application.

Lastly, a secure code base is the first step to a secure application. You should follow good coding practices and make sure your code does not do anything stupid when interacting with incoming user data and resources. While a tool like Bandit will not magically make your code safe and secure, it will catch the most obvious potential security issues, so there's no hesitation to continuously run it on your code base.

One part that we did not cover in this chapter is how an end user is securely interacting with our microservices. This is covered in the next chapter, where we will wrap up everything and demonstrate how the Runnerly application can be used through a client-side JavaScript application.

# 8
# Bringing It All Together

Most of the work done so far has focused on building microservices, and making them interact with each other. It is time to bring everything together by creating the tip of the iceberg--the **User Interface** (**UI**) through which our end users use the whole system with a browser.

Modern web applications rely a lot on client-side **JavaScript** (**JS**). Some JS frameworks go all the way to provide a full **Model-View-Controller** (**MVC**) system, which runs in the browser and manipulates the **Document Object Model** (**DOM**), which is the structured representation of the web page that's rendered in your browser.

The web development paradigm has shifted from rendering everything on the server side, to rendering everything on the client side with data collected from the server on demand. The reason is that modern web applications change portions of a loaded web page dynamically instead of calling the server for a full rendering. It is faster, requires less network bandwidth, and offers a richer user experience. One of the biggest examples of this shift is the Gmail app, which pioneered the client-side field circa 2004.

Tools like Facebook's **ReactJS** (`https://facebook.github.io/react/`) provide high-level APIs to avoid manipulating the DOM directly, and offer a level of abstraction, which makes client-side web development as comfortable as building Flask applications.

That said, there is a new JS framework every other week, and it is hard to decide which one should be used. **AngularJS** (`https://angularjs.org/`) used to be the coolest toy, and now it seems many developers have switched to implement most of their application UIs with plain ReactJS. Moreover, maybe later in 2017, another new player will be popular.

This volatility is not a bad sign at all. It simply means much innovation is happening in the JavaScript and browsers ecosystem. Features like **Service Workers** (`https://developer.mo zilla.org/en/docs/Web/API/Service_Worker_API`), for instance, are game changers in web development, because they allow developers to run JS code in the background, natively. A new wave of JS tools will probably emerge from that new feature.

As long as you have a clean separation between your UI and the rest of the system, moving from one JS framework to the other should not be too hard. That means, you should not change how your microservices publish data to make them specific to a JS framework.

For Runnerly, we shall use ReactJS to build our little dashboard, and we will wrap it in a dedicated Flask application, which bridges it to the rest of the system. We will also see how that app can interact with all our microservices.

This chapter is composed of the following three parts:

- Building a ReactJS dashboard--a short introduction to ReactJS with an example
- How to embed ReactJS in a Flask app
- Authentication and authorization

By the end of this chapter, you should have a good understanding of how to build a web UI in Flask, and how to make it interact with microservices whether you choose to use ReactJS or not.

# Building a ReactJS dashboard

The ReactJS framework implements its abstraction of the DOM, and makes all the event machinery fast and efficient. Creating a UI using ReactJS consists of creating some classes with a few methods, which are called by the engine when the page is created or updated.

This approach means that you do not have to worry about what will happen when the DOM changes anymore. All you have to do is implement some methods, and let React take care of the rest.

Implementing classes for React can be done in JavaScript or JSX. We will discuss about it in the next section.

# The JSX syntax

The JSX syntax extension (`https://facebook.github.io/jsx/`) adds XML tags to JS, and can be used by tools like ReactJS when the rendering of the page happens. It is promoted by the ReactJS community as the best way to write React apps.

In the following example, a `<script>` section contains a `div` variable whose value is an XML tree representing a `div`. This syntax is valid JSX. From there, the `ReactDOM.render()` function can render the `div` variable in the DOM.

```
<!DOCTYPE html>
<html>
  <head lang="en">
    <meta charset="UTF-8">
  </head>
  <body>
    <div id="content"></div>
    <script src="/static/react/react.min.js"></script>
    <script src="/static/react-dom.min.js"></script>
    <script src="/static/babel/browser.min.js"></script>

    <script type="text/babel">
      var div =
          <div>
              Hello World
          </div>
      ReactDOM.render(div, document.getElementById('content'));
    </script>
  </body>
</html>
```

The two ReactJS scripts are part of the React distribution. The `browser.min.js` file is part of the Babel distribution, and needs to be loaded before the browser encounters any JSX syntax. Babel converts JSX syntax into JS. This conversion is called **transpilation**.

> Babel (`https://babeljs.io/`) is a *transpiler*, which can convert JSX to JS on-the-fly, among other available conversions. To use it, you simply need to mark a script as being of type `text/babel`.

The JSX syntax is the only very specific thing to know about React, as everything else is done with common JavaScript language. From there, building a ReactJS app consists of creating JS classes--with or without JSX--which is used to render web pages.

Let's now look at the heart of ReactJS, *components*.

# React components

ReactJS is based on the idea that the page can be decomposed into basic components, which are called for rendering parts of the page.

For example, if you want to display a list of runs, you can create a Run class that is in charge of rendering a single run given its values, and a Runs class that iterates through a list of runs, and call the Run class to render each item.

Each class is created with the React.createClass() function, which receives a mapping containing the future class methods. The createClass() function generates a new class, and sets a props attribute to hold some properties alongside the provided methods.

In the following example, in a new JavaScript file we define a Run class with a render() function, which returns a <div> tag, and a Runs class:

```
var Run = React.createClass( {
  render: function()   {
    return (
      <div>{this.props.title} ({this.props.type})</div>
    );
  }
} );

var Runs = React.createClass( {
  render: function()   {
    var runNodes = this.props.data.map(function (run)   {
      return (
        <Run
          title= {run.title}
          type= {run.type}
        />
      );
    } );
    return (
      <div>
        {runNodes}
      </div>
    );
  }
} );
```

The Run class returns in a div this value: {this.props.title} ({this.props.type}), which is rendered by visiting the props attribute in the Run instance.

The `props` array is populated when the `Run` instance is created, and that is what happens in the `render()` method of the `Runs` class. The `runNode` variable iterates through the `Runs.props.data` list, which contains a list of runs.

That is our last piece of the puzzle. We want to instantiate a `Runs` class, and put a list of runs to be rendered by React in its `props.data` list.

In our Runnerly app, this list can be provided by the microservice that publishes runs, and we can create another `React` class, which loads this list asynchronously using an **Asynchronous JavaScript and XML (AJAX)** pattern via an `HxmlHttpRequest` class.

That is what happens in the `loadRunsFromServer()` method in the following example. The code calls the server to get the data by making a `GET` request on the URL set in the props, and sets the value of `props.data` by calling the `setState()` method.

```
var RunsBox = React.createClass( {
  loadRunsFromServer: function()  {
    var xhr = new XMLHttpRequest();
    xhr.open('get', this.props.url, true);
    xhr.onload = function()  {
      var data = JSON.parse(xhr.responseText);
      this.setState( { data: data } );
    } .bind(this);
    xhr.send();
  } ,

  getInitialState: function()  {
    return  {data: []} ;
  } ,

  componentDidMount: function()  {
    this.loadRunsFromServer();
  } ,

  render: function()  {
    return (
      <div>
        <h2>Runs</h2>
        <Runs data= {this.state.data}  />
      </div>
    );
  }
} );

// this will expose RunsBox globally
window.RunsBox = RunsBox;
```

When the state changes, it triggers the `React` class to update the DOM with the new data. The framework calls the `render()` method, which displays the `<div>` containing `Runs`. The `Runs` instance, and then each `Run` instance, are handed down in a cascade.

To trigger the `loadRunsFromServer()` method, the class implements the `componentDidMount()` method, which gets called once the class instance is created and mounted in React, ready to be displayed. Last, but not the least, the `getInitialState()` method is called on instantiation, and can be used to initialize the instance of the `props` attribute with an empty `data` array.

This whole process of decomposition and chaining may seem complicated, but once in place, it is quite powerful, because it allows you to focus on rendering each component and letting React deal with how to do it in the most efficient way in the browser.

Each component has a state, and when something changes, React first updates its own internal representation of the DOM--the *virtual DOM*. Once that virtual DOM is changed, React can apply the required changes efficiently on the actual DOM.

All the JSX code we've seen in this section can be saved in a JSX module, and used in an HTML page as follows:

```html
<!DOCTYPE html>
<html>
  <head lang="en">
    <meta charset="UTF-8">
    <title>Runnerly Dashboard</title>
  </head>
  <body>
    <div class="container">
      <h1>Runnerly Dashboard</h1>
      <br>
      <div id="runs"></div>
    </div>
    <script src="/static/react/react.js"></script>
    <script src="/static/react/react-dom.js"></script>
    <script src="/static/babel/browser.min.js"></script>
    <script src="/static/runs.jsx" type="text/babel"></script>
    <script type="text/babel">
    ReactDOM.render(
      <window.RunsBox url="/api/runs.json" />,
      document.getElementById('runs')
    );
    </script>
  </body>
</html>
```

The `RunsBox` class is instantiated with the `/api/runs.json` URL for this demo, and once the page is displayed, React calls that URL, and expects to get back a list of runs, which it passes down to the `Runs` and `Run` instances.

Notice that we have used `window.RunsBox` instead of `RunBox`, because the Babel transpiler does not expose the global variables from the `runs.jsx` file. That is why we had to set the variable as an attribute of the `window` variable so it could be shared between the `<script>` sections.

Using transpiration directly into the browser is a bad idea. It is much better to transpile your JSX files beforehand, as we will see in the next section.

This section described a very basic usage of the ReactJS library, and did not dive into all its possibilities. If you want to get more info on React, you should try the tutorial at `https://facebook.github.io/react/tutorial/tutorial.html`as your first step. This tutorial shows you how your React components can interact with the user through events, which is the next step once you know how to do some basic rendering.

Now that we have the basic layout for building a React-based UI, let's see how we can embed it in our Flask world.

# ReactJS and Flask

People building React apps usually code their server-side parts in **Node.js** (`https://nodejs.org/en/`), because it is simpler to stick with a single language and use its ecosystem for all the tools that are used when working with an application.

However, serving React apps with Flask is not a problem at all. The HTML page can be rendered using Jinja2, and the transpiled JSX files serve as static files like you would do for JavaScript files. Moreover, as we have seen in the previous section, we can get the React distribution as JS files, and just add them into our Flask static directory alongside other files.

Our Flask app, let's name it `dashboard`, will start off with a simple structure like this:

- `setup.py`
- `dashboard/`
  - `__init__.py`
  - `app.py`
  - `templates/`
    - `index.html`
  - `static/`
    - `runs.jsx`

Also, the `app.py` file, a basic Flask application that serves the unique HTML file, will be like this:

```
from flask import Flask, render_template,

app = Flask(__name__)

@app.route('/')
def index():
    return render_template('index.html')

if __name__ == '__main__':
    app.run()
```

Thanks to Flask's convention on static assets, all the files contained inside the `static/` directory is served under the `/static` URL.

The `index.html` template looks like the one described in the previous section, and can grow into something Flask-specific later on.

That is all we need to serve a ReactJS-based app from Flask. However, dropping ReactJS distributions into your Flask static repository is not the best way to maintain your project. We need something better to manage JS dependencies. Moreover, the JavaScript world has great tools to do it as we will see in the next section.

# Using Bower, npm, and Babel

So far, we have used static JavaScript files to build our React UI in a Flask app. However, like the JS community does, it is much better to handle React and any other Javascript library as a package we want to update--like how we do with Python packages regularly.

To do this, we can install the JavaScript package manager on our system **npm** (https://www.npmjs.com/). The npm package manager is installed via Node.js. On macOS, the brew install node command does the trick, or you can go to the Node.js home page (https://nodejs.org/en/), and download it to the system.

Once Node.js and npm are installed, you should be able to call the npm command from the shell as follows:

```
$ npm -v
3.5.2
```

To manage JavaScript dependencies in our Flask project, we will use **Bower** (https://bower.io/), a package manager for web applications, which leverages npm to package all JS dependencies required for a web app--like PIP does for Python packages.

To install Bower, use the npm command like this:

```
$ npm install -g bower
```

The -g switch means that Bower is installed globally in your system's npm, and if the installation worked, you should get a new bower command-line utility.

Once Bower is installed, you can go to the root of your Flask Dashboard app, and run the interactive init command like this:

```
$ bower init
? name dashboard
? description A ReactJS based Dashboard for Runnerly
? authors Tarek Ziade <tarek@ziade.org>
...

{
  name: 'dashboard',
  authors: [
    'Tarek Ziade <tarek@ziade.org>'
  ],
  description: 'A ReactJS based Dashboard for Runnerly',
  main: '',
  license: 'MIT',
  homepage: '',
  ignore: [
    '**/.*',
    'node_modules',
    'bower_components',
    'test',
    'tests'
```

```
        ]
    }

    ? Looks good? Yes
```

After a few questions, the call creates a `bower.json` configuration file, which is used by Bower when grabbing the JavaScript libraries.

Since we want to serve the JavaScript files from our Flask app (and in production from nginx, for instance), we also tell Bower the location of the static directory by adding a `.bowerrc` file with this content:

```
{"directory": "dashboard/static"}
```

Now, if we call Bower's install command to install React and jQuery, the static directory is automatically populated with both libraries.

```
$ bower install --save jquery react
...
jquery#3.2.1 dashboard/static/jquery
react#15.4.2 dashboard/static/react
```

The preceding call will also populate the `bower.json` file with those dependencies. This mechanism is an excellent way to keep track of dependencies when the project gets reinstalled. Think of it as a PIP `requirements.txt` file automatically populated when you call the `pip install` command.

We also need to install the Babel transpiler with npm to transpile the JSX files into JS files and its React preset, as follows:

```
$ npm init
$ npm install -save-dev babel-cli babel-preset-react
```

These preceding calls install the packages locally, and create a `package.json` file, which is similar to the `bower.json` one. Moreover, the babel command line is made available in `node_modules/.bin/`.

From there, running this command converts all our JSX files into a single, plain JS file called `dashboard.js`.

```
$ node_modules/.bin/babel dashboard/static/*.jsx >
dashboard/static/dashboard.js
```

Once this Babel command is called, our Flask template can use the JS version of the React classes by pointing to the JS file instead of the JSX file. In that case, there's no need to do a client-side transpilation on the fly.

It also means that all the global variables we have in our JSX files are now visible everywhere, so, we do not need to hook them on the window variable.

We can also move the `ReactDOM.render()` method call, which we had in a dedicated `<script>` section, into a dedicated `zrender.jsx` file, like this:

```
ReactDOM.render(
  <RunsBox url="/api/runs.json" />,
  document.getElementById('runs')
);
```

Notice that the file starts with a z to ensure that Babel injects it at the end of the `dashboard.js` file when it generates it - since scripts are treated in alphabetical order. This ensures that the `RunBox` class and any other needed variable or JS element are defined before the render call.

 There are other ways to handle inter-module dependencies. Tools like **RequireJS** (`http://www.requirejs.org/`) offer an interesting approach to solve this issue. However, for our little dashboard backed by Flask, which does not have a lot of JS files, what was presented should be good enough.

With all the changes, the final `index.html` file will look like this:

```html
<!DOCTYPE html>
<html>
  <head lang="en">
    <meta charset="UTF-8">
    <title>Runnerly Dashboard</title>
  </head>
  <body>
    <div class="container">
      <h1>Runnerly Dashboard</h1>
      <br>
      <div id="runs"></div>
    </div>
    <script src="/static/react/react.js"></script>
    <script src="/static/react/react-dom.js"></script>
    <script src="/static/dashboard.js"></script>
  </body>
</html>
```

Throughout this section, we have worked with the assumption that the JSON data that React picked was served by the same Flask app at the `/api/runs.json` endpoint.

Doing AJAX calls on the same domain is not an issue, but in case you need to call a microservice that belongs to another domain, there are a few changes required on both the server and the client side.

Let's see how to do cross-domain calls in the next section.

# Cross-origin resource sharing

Allowing client-side JavaScript AJAX to perform cross-domains requests is a potential security risk. If the JS code that's executed in the client page for your domain tries to call another domain that you don't own, it could potentially run malicious JS code and harm your users.

That is why all browsers in the market have a *Same-Origin Policy* when an asynchronous call is made. They ensure that the request is made on the same domain.

Beyond security, it is also a good way to prevent someone from using your bandwidth for their web app. For instance, if you provide a few font files on your website, you might not want another website to use them on their page, and use your bandwidth without any control.

However, there are legitimate use cases for wanting to share your resources to other domains, and you can set up rules on your service to allow other domains to reach your resources.

That is what **Cross-Origin Resource Sharing** (**CORS**) is all about. When the browser sends an AJAX request to your service, an `Origin` header is added, and you can control that it is in the list of authorized domains.

If not, the CORS protocol requires that you send back a few headers listing the allowed domains.

There's also a **preflight** mechanism, where the browser pokes the endpoint via an `OPTIONS` call to know if the request it wants to make is authorized.

On the client side, you do not have to worry about setting up these mechanisms. The browser makes the decisions for you depending on your requests.

However, on the server side, you need to make sure your endpoints answer to the OPTIONS calls, and you need to decide which domains are allowed to reach your resources. If your service is public, you can authorize all domains with a wildcard. However, for a microservice-based application where you control the client side, you should restrict the domains.

In Flask, you can use Flakon's crossdomain() decorator to add CORS support to an API endpoint. In the following Flask app, the /api/runs.json endpoint can be used by any domain:

```
from flask import Flask, jsonify
from flakon import crossdomain

app = Flask(__name__)

@app.route('/api/runs.json')
@crossdomain()
def _runs():
    run1 = {'title': 'Endurance', 'type': 'training'}
    run2 = {'title': '10K de chalon', 'type': 'race'}
    _data = [run1, run2]
    return jsonify(_data)

if __name__ == '__main__':
    app.run(port=5002)
```

When running this app and using cURL to do a GET request, we can see that the Access-Control-Allow-Origin:* header is added:

```
$ curl -v http://localhost:5002/api/runs.json
*   Trying localhost...
* TCP_NODELAY set
* Connected to localhost (127.0.0.1) port 5002 (#0)
> GET /api/runs.json HTTP/1.1
> Host: localhost:5002
> User-Agent: curl/7.51.0
> Accept: */*
>
* HTTP 1.0, assume close after body
< HTTP/1.0 200 OK
< Content-Type: application/json
< Access-Control-Allow-Origin: *
< Content-Length: 122
< Server: Werkzeug/0.12.1 Python/3.5.2
< Date: Tue, 04 Apr 2017 07:39:48 GMT
<
[
```

```
{
    "title": "Endurance",
    "type": "training"
},
{
    "title": "10K de chalon",
    "type": "race"
}
]
* Curl_http_done: called premature == 0
* Closing connection 0
```

This is the default permissive behavior of the `crossdomain()` decorator, but you can set up fine-grained permissions for each endpoint, and restrict them to specific domains. You can even whitelist allowed HTTP verbs. Flakon also has CORS features at the blueprint level.

For our use case, allowing a domain is good enough. If your JS app is served by a Flask app the runs on `localhost:5000` for instance, you can restrict calls to that domain with the following:

```
@app.route('/api/runs.json')
@crossdomain(origins=['http://localhost:5000'])
def _runs():
    ...
```

In case a call is made from a browser with origin other than `http://localhost:5000`, the data is not returned.

Notice that in the case of rejection on a disallowed domain, the decorator returns a 403 response. The CORS protocol does not define what should be the status code when a rejection happens, so, that is an implementation choice.

 For an in-depth understanding of CORS, the MDN page is a great resource and can be found at the following link: `https://developer.mozilla.org/en-US/docs/Web/HTTP/Access_control_CORS`

In this section, we have looked at how to set up CORS headers in our services to allow cross-domain calls, which are useful in JS apps.

What's still missing to make our JS app fully functional is authentication and authorization.

# Authentication and authorization

The React dashboard needs to be able to authenticate its users, and perform authorized calls on some microservices. It also needs to let the user grant access to Strava.

We make the assumption that the dashboard only works when you are authenticated, and that there are two kinds of users: **first-time user** and **returning user**.

Following is the user story for first-time users:

> *As a first-time user, when I visit the dashboard, there's a "login" link. When I click on it, the dashboard redirects me to Strava to grant access to my resources. Strava then redirects me back to the dashboard, and I am connected. The dashboard then starts to fill with my data.*

As described, our Flask app performs an OAuth2 dance with Strava to authenticate users. Connecting to Strava also means we need to store the access token into the Runnerly user profile so we can use it to fetch runs later on.

Before going further, we need to make a design decision: do we want the dashboard merged with the DataService, or do we want to have two separate apps?

# Interacting with Data Service

We have said in `Chapter 4`, *Designing Runnerly*, that a safe approach to designing microservices is to avoid creating new ones without a good reason.

The database that holds user data is served by the DataService microservice, which is used by the Celery workers. The first option that comes to mind is to have a single Flask application, which manages that database, and serves both our end users with its HTML and JS content and other microservices with its JSON APIs.

The benefit of this approach is that we do not need to worry about implementing yet another network interaction between the dashboard and DataService. Moreover, besides the ReactJS app, there's not a lot we need to add on top of DataService to make it usable for both use cases.

However, by doing this, we are not benefiting from one of the advantages of microservices. Each microservice focuses on doing a single thing.

While it is always safer to start with a conservative approach, let's think for a minute how a split would impact our design. If the dashboard is on its own, it needs to drive DataService to create and change users' info in DataService. This means that DataService needs to expose some HTTP APIs to do this. The biggest risk of exposing a database via HTTP is that whenever it changes, the API might get impacted.

However, that risk can be limited if the exposed endpoints hide the database structure as much as possible, the opposite of CRUD-like APIs.

For example, the API to create a user in DataService could be a POST that just asks for the user's Strava token and e-mail, and returns some user ID. This information should rarely change, and the dashboard can simply act as a proxy between the users and DataService.

A significant benefit of having the Dashboard app isolated from the DataService is stability. When building an application like Runnerly, developers often reach a point where the core of the application is stable, and then they iterate a lot on the User Interface (UI) and User Experience (UX). In other words, the dashboard is probably going to evolve a lot while the DataService app should reach a stable point quite fast.

For all those reasons, having two separate apps for the dashboard and DataService sounds like a low risk.

Now that the design decision is made, let's look at how to perform the OAuth2 dance with Strava.

# Getting the Strava token

Strava provides a typical three-legged OAuth2 implementation, and **stravalib** (`https://git hub.com/hozn/stravalib`), all the tools to use it.

Implementing the dance is done by redirecting the user to Strava and exposing an endpoint the user is redirected to once granted access to Strava.

What we get in return is the user info from its Strava account along with the token access. We can store all this info in the Flask session, use it as our login mechanism, and pass the e-mail and token values to DataService so that the Celery strava worker can also use the token.

Like we did in `Chapter 4`, *Designing Runnerly*, let's implement the function that generates the URL to send the user to, as follows:

```
from stravalib.client import Client
def get_strava_url():
    client = Client()
    cid = app.config['STRAVA_CLIENT_ID']
    redirect = app.config['STRAVA_REDIRECT']
    url = client.authorization_url(client_id=cid,
redirect_uri=redirect)
    return url
```

That function takes `client_id` from the Runnerly application (generated in the Strava API settings panel) and the redirect URL defined for the dashboard, and returns a URL we can present to the user.

The dashboard view can be changed accordingly to pass that URL to the template.

```
from flask import session

@app.route('/')
def index():
    strava_url = get_strava_url()
    user = session.get('user')
    return render_template('index.html', strava_url=strava_url,
                                user=user)
```

We also pass a `user` variable if there's any stored into the session. The template can then use the Strava URL to display a login/logout link as follows:

```
{% if not user %}
<a href="{{strava_url}}">Login via Strava</a>
{% else %}
Hi {{user}}!
<a href="/logout">Logout</a>
{% endif %}
```

When the user clicks on the login link, she is redirected to Strava and back to our application on the endpoint defined by `STRAVA_REDIRECT`.

The implementation of that view can be like this

```
@app.route('/strava_redirect')
def strava_login():
    code = request.args.get('code')
    client = Client()
    cid = app.config['STRAVA_CLIENT_ID']
```

```
        csecret = app.config['STRAVA_CLIENT_SECRET']
        access_token = client.exchange_code_for_token(client_id=cid,
  client_secret=csecret, code=code)
        athlete = client.get_athlete()
        email = athlete.email
        session['user'] = email
        session['token'] = access_token
        send_user_to_dataservice(email, access_token)
        return redirect('/')
```

The stravalib library's `Client` class converts the code with a token we can store in the session, and lets us grab some info on the user using the `get_athlete()` method.

Lastly, the `send_user_to_dataservice(email, access_token)` can interact with the DataService microservice to make sure the e-mail and access tokens are stored there, using a JWT-based access.

We are not detailing how Dashboard interacts with the TokenDealer, since we have already shown it in `Chapter 7`, *Securing Your Services*. The process is similar--the Dashboard app gets a token from TokenDealer, and uses it to access DataService.

The last part of authentication is in the ReactJS code, as we will see in the next section.

# JavaScript authentication

When the Dashboard app performs the OAuth2 dance with Strava, it stores user information into the session, which is perfect to have the user authenticate the dashboard.

However, when the ReactJS UI calls the DataService microservice to display the user runs, we need to provide an authentication header.

There are the following two ways to handle this problem:

- Proxy all the calls to the microservices via the Dashboard web app using the existing session information
- Generate a JWT token for the end user, which they can store and use against another microservice

The proxy solution is the simplest one by all means, because it removes the need to generate one token per user for accessing DataService. It also prevents us from exposing DataService publicly. Hiding everything behind the dashboard means we have more flexibility to change the internals while keeping the UI compatible.

The problem with that approach, though, is that we are forcing all the traffic through the Dashboard service even when it is not needed. Ideally, updating the list of displayed runs should not be something that the Dashboard server should worry about.

The second solution is more elegant with the microservices design. We are dealing tokens, and the Web UI is just one of the clients for some microservices. However, that also means the client has to deal with two authentication loops. If the JWT token gets revoked, the Client app needs to authenticate back even if the Strava token is still valid.

The first solution is probably the best bet for a first version. Proxying calls to microservices on behalf of the user means that the Dashboard application uses its JWT token to call DataService to grab the user data.

DataService, as explained in `Chapter 4`, *Designing Runnerly*, uses the following API pattern to return runs: `GET /runs/<user_id>/<year>/<month>`.

If we make the assumption that the Dashboard keeps track of the (e-mail, user ID) tuples, the proxy view for that API can be `GET /api/runs/<year>/<month>`. From there, the Dashboard code can find back the user ID given the user e-mail currently logged into the session via Strava.

The proxy code can look like this:

```
@app.route('/api/runs/<int:year>/<int:month>')
def _runs(year, month):
    if 'user' not in session:
        abort(401)
    uid = email_to_uid(session['user'])
    endpoint = '/runs/%d/%d/%d' % (uid, year, month)
    resp = call_data_service(endpoint)
    return jsonify(resp.json())
```

The `call_data_service()` function calls the DataService endpoint with a JWT token, and `email_to_uid()` converts the e-mail to the corresponding user ID.

Last, to make sure this approach works, you need to use the `withCredentials` option on every `xhr` calls so that cookies and authentication headers are sent when AJAX calls are made.

```
var xhr = new XMLHttpRequest();
xhr.open('get', URL, true);
xhr.withCredentials = true;
xhr.onload = function()   {
  var data = JSON.parse(xhr.responseText);
  ...
} .bind(this);

xhr.send();
```

# Summary

In this chapter, we looked at how to build a ReactJS UI wrapped into a Flask application (Dashboard). ReactJS is an excellent way to build a modern interactive UI in the browser--it introduces a new syntax called JSX, which speeds up JS execution.

We also looked at how to use a toolchain based on npm, Bower, and Babel to manage JS dependencies, and transpile JSX files.

The Dashboard application uses Strava's three-legged OAuth API to connect users and get back a token from the Strava service. We made the design decision to separate the Dashboard application from DataService, so the token is sent to the DataService microservice for storage. That token can then be used by the Strava Celery worker to fetch runs on behalf of the user.

Lastly, the calls made to different services to build the dashboard are proxied through the Dashboard server to simplify the client side--which deals with a single server and a single authentication and authorization process.

The following is a diagram of the new architecture, which includes the Dashboard app:

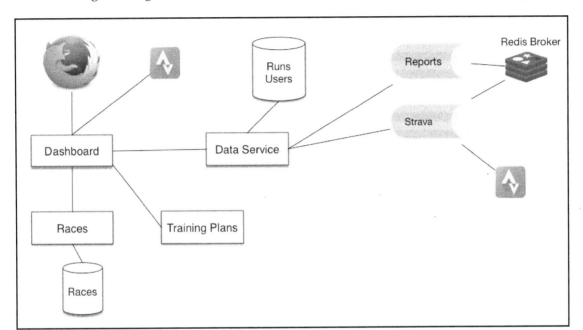

 You can find the full code of the Dashboard in the Runnerly org at `https ://github.com/runnerly/dashboard`.

With now six different Flask apps that compose it, developing an application like Runnerly can be a challenge when you are a developer.

There's an obvious need to be able to run all microservices in a single dev box without too much pain.

After a dive into how packaging works in Python, the next chapter explains how to package our Python microservices, and how to run them in development mode in a single box via a process manager.

# 9
# Packaging and Running Runnerly

When the Python programming language was first released in the early 1990s, a Python application was run by pointing the Python scripts to the interpreter. Everything related to packaging, releasing, and distributing Python projects was done manually. There was no real standard back then, and each project had a long README on how to install it with all its dependencies.

Bigger projects used the system packaging tools to release their work--whether it was Debian packages, RPM packages for Red-Hat Linux distributions, or things like MSI packages under Windows. Eventually, the Python modules from those projects all ended up in the *site-packages* directory of the Python installation, sometimes after a compilation phase, if you had a C extension.

The Python packaging ecosystem has evolved a lot since then. In 1998, **Distutils** was added in the standard library to provide essential support to create installable distributions for Python projects. Between then and now, a lot of new tools have emerged from the community to improve how a Python project can be packaged, released, and distributed.

This chapter is going to explain how to use the latest Python packaging tools for your microservices.

The other hot topic around packaging is how it fits in your day-to-day work. When building microservices-based software, you need to deal with many moving parts. When you are working in a particular microservice, you can get away with it most of the time by using the TDD and mocking approach, which we discussed in Chapter 3, *Coding, Testing, and Documenting - The Virtuous Cycle*.

However, if you want to do some realistic testing, where poking around each service is needed, you have to have the whole stack running in a single box. Moreover, developing in such a context can be tedious if you need to reinstall new versions of your microservices all the time.

It begs one question: *how can you correctly install the whole stack in your environment and develop in it?*

It also means you have to run all the microservices if you want to play with the app. In the case of Runnerly, having to open six different shells to run all the microservices is not something a developer would want to do every time they need to run the app.

In this chapter, we are going to look at how we can leverage the packaging tools to run all microservices from the same environment, and then how to run them all from a single command-line interface by using a dedicated *process manager*.

However, first, let's look at how to package your projects, and which tools should be utilized.

# The packaging toolchain

Python has come a long way in the past ten years on packaging. Numerous **Python Enhancement Proposals** (**PEPs**) were written to improve how to install, release, and distribute Python projects.

Distutils had some flaws, which made it a little tedious to release apps. The biggest pain points were its lack of dependencies management and the way it handled compilation and binary releases. For everything related to compiling, what worked well in the nineties started to get old fashioned ten years later. No one in the core team made the library evolve for lack of interest, and because Distutils was good enough to compile Python and most projects. People who needed advanced toolchains used other tools, like **SCons** (`http://scons.org/`).

In any case, improving the toolchain was not an easy task because of the existing legacy system based on Distutils. Starting a new packaging system from scratch was quite hard, since Distutils was part of the standard library, but introducing backward-compatible changes was also hard to do properly. The improvements were made in-between. Projects like **Setuptools** and **Virtualenv** were created outside the standard library, and some changes were made directly into Python.

As of today, you still find the scars from these changes, and it is still quite hard to know exactly how things should be done. For instance, the `pyvenv` command was added in Python and then removed in Python 3.6, but Python still ships with its virtual environment module, which competes with the Virtualenv project with some respect.

The best bet is to use the tools that are developed and maintained outside the standard library, because their release cycle is shorter than Python's. In other words, a change in the standard library takes months to be released, whereas a change in a third-party project can be made available much faster.

All third-party projects that are considered as being part of the de facto standard packaging toolchain are now all grouped under the **PyPA** (`https://www.pypa.io`) umbrella project.

Besides developing the tools, PyPA also works on improving the packaging standards through proposing PEPs for Python and developing its early specifications--refer to `https://www.pypa.io/en/latest/roadmap/`. In 2017, we are still in a confusing state for packaging, as we have a few competing standards, but things have improved, and the future should look better.

Before we start to look at the tools that should be used, we need to go through a few definitions to avoid any confusion.

# A few definitions

When we talk about packaging Python projects, a few terms can be confusing, because their definitions have evolved over time, and also because they can mean slightly different things outside the Python world.

We need to define, what's a Python package, a Python project, a Python library, and a Python application. They are defined as follows:

- A *Python package* is a directory tree containing Python modules. You can import it, and it is part of the module namespace.

- A *Python project* can contain several packages and other resources, and is what you release. Each microservice you build with Flask is a Python project.

- A *Python application* is a Python project that can be directly used through a user interface. The user interface can be a command-line script or a web server.

- Lastly, a *Python library* is a specific kind of Python project which provides features to be used in other Python projects, and has no direct user interface.

The distinction between an application and a library can be quite vague, since some libraries sometimes offer some command-line tools to use some of its features, even if the first use case is to provide Python packages for other projects. Moreover, sometimes, a project that was a library becomes an application.

To simplify the process, the best option is to make no distinction between applications and libraries. The only technical difference is that applications ship with more data files and console scripts.

Now that we have defined Python package, project, application, and library, let's look at how to package your projects.

# Packaging

When you package your Python project, there are three necessary files you need to have alongside your Python packages:

- `setup.py`: A special module, which drives everything
- `requirements.txt`: A file listing dependencies
- `MANIFEST.in`: A template file to list the files to be included in the releases

Let's look at each one of them in detail.

# The setup.py file

The `setup.py` file is what governs everything when you want to interact with a Python project. When the `setup()` method is executed, it generates a static metadata file, which follows the **PEP 314** format. The metadata file holds all the metadata for the project, but you need to regenerate it via a `setup()` call to get it to the Python environment you are using.

The reason why you cannot use a static version is that the author of a project might have platform-specific code in `setup.py`, which generates a different metadata file depending on the platform and Python versions.

To rely on running a Python module to extract static information about a project has always been a problem. You need to make sure that the code in the module can run in the target Python interpreter. If you are going to make your microservices available to the community, you need to keep that in mind, as the installation happens in many different Python environments.

**PEP 390** (2009) was the first attempt to get rid of the `setup.py` file for metadata. **PEP 426**, **PEP 508**, and **PEP 518** are new attempts at fixing this issue with smaller chunks, but in 2017, we still don't have tools that support static metadata, and it is probably going to take a while before everyone uses them. So `setup.py` is going to stick around for years.

A very common mistake when creating the `setup.py` file is to import your package in it when you have third-party dependencies. If a tool like PIP tries to read the metadata by running `setup.py`, it might raise an import error before it has a chance to list all the dependencies to install.

The only dependency you can afford to import directly in your `setup.py` file is Setuptools, because you can make the assumption that anyone trying to install your project is likely to have it in their environment.

Another important consideration is the metadata you want to include to describe your project. Your project can work with just a name, a version, a URL, and an author, but this is obviously not enough information to describe your project.

Metadata fields are set through `setup()` arguments. Some of them match directly with the name of the metadata, some don't.

The following is the minimal set of arguments you should use for your microservices projects:

- `name`: The name of the package, should be a short lowercase name
- `version`: The version of the project, as defined in PEP 440
- `url`: A URL for the project; can be its repository or home page
- `description`: One sentence to describe the project
- `long_description`: A reStructuredText document
- `author`, and `author_email`: The name and email of the author--can be an organization
- `license`: The license used for the project (MIT, Apache2, GPL, and so on)
- `classifiers`: A list of classifiers picked from a fixed list, as defined in PEP 301
- `keywords`: Tags to describe your project--this is useful if you publish the project to the **Python Package Index (PyPI)**
- `packages`: A list of packages that your project includes--Setuptools can populate that option automatically with the `find_packages()` method

- `install_requires`: A list of dependencies (this is a Setuptools option)
- `entry_points`: A list of Setuptools hooks, like console scripts (this is a Setuptools option)
- `include_package_data`: A flag that simplifies the inclusion of non-Python files
- `zip_safe`: This is a flag that prevents Setuptools to install the project as a ZIP file, which is a standard from the past (executable eggs)

The following is an example of a `setup.py` file that includes those options:

```python
from setuptools import setup, find_packages

with open('README.rst') as f:
    LONG_DESC = f.read()

setup(name='MyProject',
      version='1.0.0',
      url='http://example.com',
      description='This is a cool microservice based on strava.',
      long_description=LONG_DESC,
      author='Tarek', author_email='tarek@ziade.org',
      license='MIT',
      classifiers=[
          'Development Status :: 3 - Alpha',
          'License :: OSI Approved :: MIT License',
          'Programming Language :: Python :: 2',
          'Programming Language :: Python :: 3'],
      keywords=['flask', 'microservice', 'strava'],
      packages=find_packages(),
      include_package_data=True,
      zip_safe=False,
      entry_points="""
      [console_scripts]
      mycli = mypackage.mymodule:myfunc
      """,
      install_requires=['stravalib'])
)
```

The `long_description` option is usually pulled from a `README.rst` file, so you do not have to deal with including a large piece of `reStructuredText` string in your function.

 The restructured text-lint project (`https://github.com/twolfson/restru cturedtext-lint`) is a linter that you can use to verify a reST file syntax.

The other benefit of separating the description is that it's automatically recognized, parsed, and displayed by most editors. For instance, GitHub uses it as your project landing page in your repository, and also offers an inline reStructuredText editor to change it directly from the browser. PyPI does the same to display the front page of the project.

The license field is free-form, as long as people can recognize the license being used. If you use the **Apache Public Licence Version 2 (APL v2)**,it works. In any case, you should add, alongside your setup.py file, a LICENCE file with the official text of that license.

The classifiers option is probably the most painful one to write. You need to use strings from https://pypi.python.org/pypi?%3Aaction=list_classifiers, which classify your project. The three most common classifiers that developers use are the list of supported Python versions, the license (which duplicates and should match the license option), and the development status, which is a hint about the maturity of the project.

Keywords are a good way to make your project visible if you publish it to the Python Package Index. For instance, if you are creating a Flask microservice, you should use *flask* and *microservice* as keywords.

 The Trove classifier is a machine-parseable metadata that can be used, for instance, by tools interacting with PyPI. For example, the zc.buildout tool looks for packages with the Framework :: Buildout :: Recipe classifier.

The entry_points section is an INI-like string that defines Setuptools entry points, which are callables that can be used as plugins once the project is installed in Python. The most common entry point type is the console script. When you add functions in that section, a command-line script will be installed alongside the Python interpreter, and the function hooked to it via the entry point. This is a good way to create a **Command-Line Interface (CLI)** for your project. In the example, mycli should be directly reachable in the shell when the project is installed. Python's Distutils has a similar feature, but the one in Setuptools does a better job, because it allows you to point to a specific function.

Lastly, install_requires lists all the dependencies. This list of Python projects the project uses, and can be used by projects like PIP when the installation occurs. The tool will grab them if they are published in the PyPI, and install them.

Once this setup.py file is created, a good way to try it is by creating a local virtual environment.

Assuming you have `virtualenv` installed, if you run these commands in the directory containing the `setup.py` file, it will create a few directories including a `bin` directory containing a local Python interpreter, and drop you into a local shell.

```
$ virtualenv .
$ source bin/activate
(thedir) $
```

From there, running the `pip install -e` command will install the project in *editable mode*. This command installs the project by reading its setup file, but unlike install, the installation occurs in-place. Installing in-place means that you will be able to work directly on the Python modules in the project, and they will be linked to the local Python installation via its *site-packages* directory.

Using a vanilla `install` call would have created copies of the files into the local *site-packages* directory, and changing the source code would have had no impact on the installed version.

The PIP call also generates a `MyProject.egg-info` directory, which contains the metadata. PIP generates version 1.1 of the metadata spec, under the `PKG-INFO` name.

```
$ more MyProject.egg-info/PKG-INFO
Metadata-Version: 1.1
Name: MyProject
Version: 1.0.0
Summary: This is a cool project.
Home-page: http://example.com
Author: Tarek
Author-email: tarek@ziade.org
License: MIT
Description: MyProject
        ---------


        I am the **long** description.

Keywords: flask,microservice,strava
Platform: UNKNOWN
Classifier: Development Status :: 3 - Alpha
Classifier: License :: OSI Approved :: MIT License
Classifier: Programming Language :: Python :: 2
Classifier: Programming Language :: Python :: 3
```

This metadata file is what describes your project and is what is used to register it to the PyPI via other commands, as we will see later in the chapter.

The PIP call also pulls all the project dependencies by looking from them in the PyPI on `htt ps://pypi.python.org/pypi`and installs them in the local *site-packages*. Running this command is a good way to make sure everything works as expected.

One thing that we need to discuss further is the `install_requires` option. It competes with another way of listing the project dependencies, the `requirements.txt` file, which is explained in the next section.

# The requirements.txt file

One standard that emerged from the PIP community is to use a `requirements.txt` file,which lists all the project dependencies, but also proposes an extended syntax to install editable dependencies. Refer to `https://pip.readthedocs.io/en/stable/reference/pip _install/#requirements-file-format`.

The following is an example of such a file:

```
arrow
python-dateutil
pytz
requests
six
stravalib
units
```

Using this file has been widely adopted by the community, because it makes it easier to document your dependencies. You can create as many requirements files as you want in a project, and have your users call the `pip install -r thefile.txt` command to install the packages described in them.

For instance, you could have a `dev-requirements.txt` file, which contains extra tools for development, and a `prod-requirements.txt`, which has production-specific things. The format allows inheritance to help you manage requirements files' collections.

But using requirements files adds a new problem. It duplicates some of the information contained in the`setup.py` file's `install_requires` section.

To solve this new issue, some developers make a distinction between dependencies defined for their Python libraries and the one defined for their Python applications.

They use `install_requires` in their library's `setup.py` file, and the PIP requirement file in their application deployments. In other words, a Python application won't have a `setup.py` file's `install_requires` option filled with its dependencies.

But that means the application installation will require a specific installation process, where the dependencies are first installed via the requirements file. It also means that we'd lose the benefits of having requirements files for libraries .

And we've said earlier in the chapter, we do not want to make our life complicated by having two different ways to describe Python projects dependencies, since the distinction between an application and a library can be quite vague.

To avoid duplicating the information in both places, there are some tools in the community, which offer some syncing automation between `setup.py` and requirements files.

The **pip-tools** (`https://github.com/jazzband/pip-tools`) tool is one of them, and it generates a `requirements.txt` file (or any other filename) via a `pip-compile` CLI, as follows:

```
$ pip install pip-tools
...
$ pip-compile
#
# This file is autogenerated by pip-compile
# To update, run:
#
#     pip-compile --output-file requirements.txt setup.py
#
arrow==0.10.0              # via stravalib
python-dateutil==2.6.0     # via arrow
pytz==2017.2               # via stravalib
requests==2.13.0           # via stravalib
six==1.10.0                # via python-dateutil, stravalib
stravalib==0.6.6
units==0.7                 # via stravalib
```

Notice that the generated file contains versions for each package. This is called **version pinning** and is done by looking at the versions locally installed.

When declaring dependencies, it's good practice to `pin` all the dependencies before you release your project. That will ensure that you document the versions that were used and tested for the release.

If you don't use pip-tools, PIP has a built-in command called `freeze`, which you can use to generate a list of all the current versions that are installed in your Python. This is done as follows:

```
$ pip freeze

cffi==1.9.1
click==6.6
cryptography==1.7.2
dominate==2.3.1
flake8==3.2.1
Flask==0.11.1
...
```

The only problem when you pin your dependencies is when another project has the same dependencies, but is pinned with other versions. PIP will complain and fail to meet both the requirements sets and you won't be able to install everything.

The simplest way to fix this issue is to leave the dependencies unpinned in the `setup.py` file and pinned in the `requirements.txt` file. That way, PIP can install the latest version for each package, and when you deploy, specifically in stage or production, you can refresh the versions by running the `pip install -r requirements.txt` command. PIP will then upgrade/downgrade all the dependencies to match the versions, and in case you need to, you can tweak them in the requirements file.

To summarize, defining dependencies should be done in each project's `setup.py` file, and requirements files can be provided with pinned dependencies as long as you have a reproducible process to generate them from the `setup.py` file to avoid duplication.

The last mandatory file your projects should have is the `MANIFEST.in` file.

# The MANIFEST.in file

When creating a source or binary release, Setuptools will include all the packages modules and data files, the `setup.py` file, and a few other files automatically in the tarball. But files like the PIP requirements will not be included for you.

In order to add them to your distribution, you need to add a `MANIFEST.in` file, which contains the list of files to include.

The file follows a simple glob-like syntax, described at `https://docs.python.org/3/distu tils/commandref.html#creating-a-source-distribution-the-sdist-command`, where you point a file or a directory (including glob patterns) and say if you want to include or prune the matches.

Here's an example from Runnerly:

```
include requirements.txt
include README.rst
include LICENSE
recursive-include myservice *.ini
recursive-include docs *.rst *.png *.svg *.css *.html conf.py
prune docs/build/*
```

The docs/directory containing the Sphinx doc will be integrated in the source distribution, but any artifact generated locally in `docs/build/` when the doc is built will be pruned.

Once you have the `MANIFEST.in` file in place, all the files should be added in your distribution when you'll release your project. Notice that you can use the *check-manifest* distutils command to check the syntax of the file and its effect.

A typical microservice project, as described in this book, will have the following list of files:

- `setup.py`: The setup file
- `README.rst`: The content of the `long_description` option
- `MANIFEST.in`: The MANIFEST template
- `requirements.txt`: PIP requirement files generated from `install_requires`
- `docs/`: The Sphinx documentation
- `package/`: The package containing the microservice code

From there, releasing your project consists of creating a source distribution, which is basically an archive of this structure. If you have some C extensions, you can also create a binary distribution.

Before we learn how to create those releases, let's look at how to pick version numbers for your microservices.

# Versioning

Python packaging tools do not enforce a specific versioning pattern. The version field can be any string. This freedom became a problem, because projects followed their own versioning schemes and, sometimes, they were not compatible with installers and tools.

To understand a versioning scheme, an installer needs to know how to sort and compare versions. The installer needs to be able to parse the string, and know if a version is older than another one.

Early software used schemes based on the date of release, like `20170101` if your software is released on 1st January 2017. But that scheme won't work anymore if you do branch releases. For instance, if your software has a version 2, which is backward incompatible, you might start to release updates for version 1 in parallel of releases for version 2. In that case, using dates will make some of your version 1 releases appear as if they were more recent than some version 2 release.

Some software combine incremental versions and dates for that reason, but it became obvious that using dates was not the best way to handle branches.

And then, there's the problem of beta, alpha, release candidates, and dev versions. Developers want to have the ability to mark releases as being pre-releases.

For instance, when Python is about to ship a new version, it will ship *release candidates* using a **rcX** marker so that the community can try it before the final release is shipped. For example 3.6.0rc1, 3.6.0rc2, and so on.

For a microservice that you are not releasing to the community, using such markers is often an overkill--but when you start to have people from outside your organization using your software, it may become useful.

Release candidates can be useful, for example, if you are about to ship a backward incompatible version of a project. It's always a good idea to have your users try it out before it's published. For the usual release though, using candidate releases is probably an overkill, as publishing a new release when a problem is found is cheap.

 PIP does a fairly good job at figuring out most patterns, ultimately falling back to some alphanumeric sorting, but the world would be a better place if all projects were using the same versioning scheme.

PEP 386, and then 440, were written to try to come up with a versioning scheme for the Python community. It's derived from the standard **MAJOR.MINOR[.PATCH]** scheme, which's widely adopted among developers, with some specific rules for pre- and post-versions.

The **Semantic Versioning** (**SemVer**) (`http://semver.org/`) scheme is another standard that emerged in the community, which is used in many places outside Python. If you use SemVer, you will be compatible with PEP 440 and the PIP installer as long as you don't use pre-release markers. For instance, *3.6.0rc2* translates to *3.6.0-rc2* in SemVer.

Unlike PEP 440, SemVer asks that you always provide the three version numbers. For instance, **1.0** should be **1.0.0**.

Adopting SemVer is a good idea as long as you remove the dash it uses to separate the version from a marker.

Here's an example of a sorted list of versions for a project that will work in Python, and which will be close to SemVer:

- 9.0
- 0.0a1
- 0.0a2
- 0.0b1
- 0.0rc1
- 0.0
- 1.0

For your microservice project, or any Python project for that matter, you should start with the **0.1.0** version, make it clear that it's still an unstable project, and that backward compatibility is not guaranteed. From there, you can increment the MINOR number at will until you feel the software is mature enough.

Once maturity has been reached, a common pattern is to release **1.0.0**, and then start to following these rules:

- **MAJOR** is incremented when you introduce a backward incompatible change for the existing API
- **MINOR** is incremented when you add new features that don't break the existing API
- **PATCH** is incremented just for bug fixes

Being strict about this scheme with the 0.x.x series when the software is in its early phase does not make much sense, because you will do a lot of backward incompatible changes, and your MAJOR version would reach a high number in no time.

The 1.0.0 release is often emotionally charged for developers. They want it to be the first stable release they'll give to the world--that's why it's frequent to use the 0.x.x versions and bump to 1.0.0 when the software is deemed stable.

For a library, what we call the API are all the public and documented functions and classes one may import and use.

For a microservice, there's a distinction between the code API and the HTTP API. You may completely change the whole implementation in a microservice project and still implement the exact same HTTP API. You need to treat those two versions distinctly.

Both versions can follow the pattern described here, but one version will be on your `setup.py` (the code) and one may be published in your **Swagger** specification file, or wherever you document your HTTP API. The two versions will have a different release cycle.

Now that we know how to deal with version number, let's do some releasing.

# Releasing

To release your project, a simple command called `sdist` is provided in Python's Distutils.

Distutils has a series of commands that can be invoked with the `python setup.py` `<COMMAND>` command. Running the `python setup.py sdist` command in the root of your project will generate an archive containing the source code of your project.

In the following example, `sdist` is called in Runnerly's tokendealer project:

```
$ python setup.py sdist
running sdist
[...]
creating runnerly-tokendealer-0.1.0
creating runnerly-tokendealer-0.1.0/runnerly_tokendealer.egg-info
creating runnerly-tokendealer-0.1.0/tokendealer
creating runnerly-tokendealer-0.1.0/tokendealer/tests
creating runnerly-tokendealer-0.1.0/tokendealer/views
copying files to runnerly-tokendealer-0.1.0...
copying README.rst -> runnerly-tokendealer-0.1.0
[...]
copying tokendealer/tests/__init__.py -> runnerly-
tokendealer-0.1.0/tokendealer/tests
copying tokendealer/tests/test_home.py -> runnerly-
tokendealer-0.1.0/tokendealer/tests
copying tokendealer/views/__init__.py -> runnerly-
tokendealer-0.1.0/tokendealer/views
copying tokendealer/views/home.py -> runnerly-
tokendealer-0.1.0/tokendealer/views
Writing runnerly-tokendealer-0.1.0/setup.cfg
creating dist
Creating tar archive
removing 'runnerly-tokendealer-0.1.0' (and everything under it)
```

The `sdist` command reads the info from `setup.py` and `MANIFEST.in`, and grabs all the files to put them in an archive. The result is created in the `dist` directory.

```
$ ls dist/
runnerly-tokendealer-0.1.0.tar.gz
```

Notice that the name of the archive is composed of the name of the project and its version. This archive can be used directly with PIP to install the project as follows:

```
$ pip install dist/runnerly-tokendealer-0.1.0.tar.gz
Processing ./dist/runnerly-tokendealer-0.1.0.tar.gz
   Requirement already satisfied (use --upgrade to upgrade): runnerly-
tokendealer==0.1.0   [...]
Successfully built runnerly-tokendealer
```

Source releases are good enough when you don't have any extension that needs to be compiled. If you do, the target system will need to compile them again when the installation happens. That means the target system needs to have a compiler, which is not always the case.

Another option is to precompile and create binary distributions for each target system. Distutils has several `bdist_xxx` commands to do it, but they are not really maintained anymore. The new format to use is the Wheel format as defined in PEP 427. The Wheel format is a ZIP file containing all the files that will be deployed on the target system, without having to rerun commands at install time.

If your project has no C extension, it's still interesting to ship Wheel distributions, because the installation process will be faster than with `sdist`; PIP is just going to move files around without running any command.

To build a Wheel archive, you need to install the `wheel` project, then to call the `bdist_wheel` command--that will create a new archive in `dist`.

```
$ pip install wheel
$ python setup.py bdist_wheel --universal
$ ls dist/
runnerly-tokendealer-0.1.0.tar.gz
runnerly_tokendealer-0.1.0-py2.py3-none-any.whl
```

Notice that we've used the –universal flag when `bdist_wheel` was called in this example.

This flag tells the command to generate a source release that can be installed on both Python 2 and 3 if your code is compatible with both, with no extra steps (like a 2 to 3 conversion). Without the flag, a `runnerly_tokendealer-0.1.0-py3-none-any.whl` file would have been created, indicating that the release works only for Python 3.

In case you have some C extensions, `bdist_wheel` will detect it and create a platform-specific distribution with the compiled extension. In that case, `none` in the filename is replaced by the platform.

Creating platform-specific releases is fine if your C extensions are not linking to specific system libraries. If they do, there are good chances your binary release will not work everywhere, in particular, if the target system has a different version of that library. Shipping a proper binary release that will work in all circumstances is really hard. Some projects ship statically linked extensions together will all the libraries the extension is using. In general, you rarely need to ship a C extension when you write a microservice, so a source distribution is good enough.

Shipping a `sdist` and a Wheel distribution is the best practice. Installers like PIP will pick the wheel, and the project will get installed faster than with `sdist`. The `sdist` release on the other hand can be used by older installers or for manual installations.

Once you have your archive ready, you can distribute them, let's see how.

# Distributing

If you are developing in an open source project, it's good practice to publish your project to the PyPI at `https://pypi.python.org/pypi`.

Like most modern language ecosystem, this index can be browsed by installers that are looking for releases to download.

When you call the `pip install <project>` command, PIP will browse the PyPI index to see if that project exists, and if there are some suitable releases for your platform.

The public name is the name you use in your `setup.py` file and you need to register it at PyPI in order to be able to publish some releases. The index uses the first-come, first-serve principle, so if the name you've picked is taken, you will have to choose another one.

When creating microservices for an application or an organization, you can use a common prefix for all your projects' names. For Runnerly, `runnerly-` is used.

At the package level, a prefix can also sometimes be useful to avoid conflicts.

Python has a namespace package feature, which allows you to create a top-level package name (like `runnerly`), and then have packages in separate Python projects, which will end up being installed under the top-level `runnerly` package.

The effect is that every package gets a common `runnerly` namespace when you import them, which is quite an elegant way to group your code under the same banner. The feature is available through the `pkgutil` module from the standard library.

To do this, you just need to create the same top-level directory in every project, with the `__init__.py` file containing and prefixing all absolute imports with the top-level name.

```
from pkgutil import extend_path
__path__ = extend_path(__path__, __name__)
```

For example, in Runnerly, if we decide to release everything under the same namespace, each project can have the same top-level package name. For example, in the **token dealer**, it could be as follows:

- runnerly
    - __init__.py: Contains the `extend_path` call
    - tokendealer/
        - .. the actual code...

And then in the `dataservice` one, like this:

- runnerly
    - __init__.py: Contains the `extend_path` call
    - dataservice/
        - .. the actual code...

Both will ship a `runnerly` top-level package, and when PIP installs them, the `tokendealer` and `dataservice` packages will both end up in the same directory, `site-packages/runnerly`.

This feature is not that useful in production, where each microservice is deployed in a separate installation, but it does not hurt and is good to have, as it can be useful if you start to create a lot of libraries that are used across projects.

For now, we'll make the assumption that each project is independent, and each name is available at PyPI.

To publish the releases at PyPI, you first need to register a new user using the form at `https://pypi.python.org/pypi?%3Aaction=register_form`, shown as follows:

```
Manual user registration

This form allows "traditional" registration (using a password). Users who want to register with their OpenID (e.g. Google
or Launchpad account) should follow one of the links to the right.

You can use your PyPI account to log into other services supporting OpenID. You need to first log into PyPI before
logging into other services (doing it the other way is prone to phishing attacks). To log in, simply type pypi.python.org
into the field asking for an OpenID. Your OpenID is https://pypi.python.org/id/; you can also use this ID directly to log in.

              Username:
              Password:
               Confirm:
         Email Address:
   PGP Key ID (optional):              (This identifies a PGP or GPG key)
                        Register
```

Once you have a username and a password, you should create, in your home directory, a `.pypirc` file containing your credentials, like this:

```
[pypi]
username = <username>
password = <password>
```

This file will be used every time you interact with the PyPI index to create a Basic Authentication header.

Python Distutils has a register and upload command to register a new project at PyPI, but it is better to use **Twine** (`https://github.com/pypa/twine`), which comes with a slightly better user interface.

Once you've installed Twine (using the `pip install twine` command), the next step is to register your package with this command:

```
$ twine register dist/runnerly-tokendealer-0.1.0.tar.gz
```

The preceding command will create a new entry in the index using your package metadata.

Once it's done, you can go ahead and upload the releases as follows:

```
$ twine upload dist/*
```

From there, your package should appear in the index, with an HTML home page at `https://pypi.python.org/pypi/<project>`. And the `pip install <project>` command should work!

Now that we know how to package each microservice, let's see how to run them all in the same box for development purposes.

# Running all microservices

Running a microservice can be done by using the built-in Flask web server. Running the Flask apps via this script requires to set up an environment variable, which points to the module that contains the flask application.

In the following example, the application for Runnerly, the `dataservice` microservice is located in the app module in `runnerly.dataservice` and can be launched from the root directory with this command:

```
$ FLASK_APP=runnerly/dataservice/app.py bin/flask run
 * Serving Flask app "runnerly.dataservice.app"
 * Running on http://127.0.0.1:5000/ (Press CTRL+C to quit)
127.0.0.1 - - [01/May/2017 10:18:37] "GET / HTTP/1.1" 200 -
```

Running apps using Flask's command line is fine, but it restricts us to use its interface options. If we want to pass a few arguments to run our microservice, we would need to start to add environment variables.

Another option is to create our own launcher using the **argparse** module (`https://docs.py thon.org/3/library/argparse.html`), so that we can add for each microservice any option we want.

The following example is a full working launcher, which will run a Flask application via an argparse-based command-line script. It takes a single option, `–config-file`, which is the configuration file that contains everything needed by the microservice to run.

```
import argparse
import sys
import signal
from .app import create_app

def _quit(signal, frame):
    print("Bye!")
    # add any cleanup code here
    sys.exit(0)

def main(args=sys.argv[1:]):
    parser = argparse.ArgumentParser(description='Runnerly
                                     Dataservice')
    parser.add_argument('--config-file', help='Config file',
```

```
                        type=str, default=None)
        args = parser.parse_args(args=args)

        app = create_app(args.config_file)
        host = app.config.get('host', '0.0.0.0')
        port = app.config.get('port', 5000)
        debug = app.config.get('DEBUG', False)
        signal.signal(signal.SIGINT, _quit)
        signal.signal(signal.SIGTERM, _quit)
        app.run(debug=debug, host=host, port=port)

    if __name__ == "__main__":
        main()
```

This approach offers a lot of flexibility. In order to make that script a console script, you need to pass it to your setup class's function via the entry_points option as follows:

```
    from setuptools import setup, find_packages
    from runnerly.dataservice import __version__

    setup(name='runnerly-data',
          version=__version__,
          packages=find_packages(),
          include_package_data=True,
          zip_safe=False,
          entry_points="""
          [console_scripts]
          runnerly-dataservice = runnerly.dataservice.run:main
          """)
```

With this option, a runnerly-dataservice console script will be created and linked to the main() function we've seen earlier.

```
$ runnerly-dataservice --help
usage: runnerly-dataservice [-h] [--config-file CONFIG_FILE]

Runnerly Dataservice

optional arguments:
  -h, --help            show this help message and exit
  --config-file CONFIG_FILE
                        Config file

$ runnerly-dataservice
 * Running on http://127.0.0.1:5001/ (Press CTRL+C to quit)
 * Restarting with stat
 * Debugger is active!
 * Debugger pin code: 216-834-670
```

We have used the -e option earlier in PIP to run a project in develop mode. If we use the same option for all our microservices from within the same Python, we will be able to run all of them in the same box using their respective launchers.

You can create a new `virtualenv`, and simply link each development directory using -e in a `requirements.txt` file that lists all your microservices.

PIP can also recognize Git URLs, and clone the repositories in your environment for you, which makes it convenient to create a root directory with all the code inside it.

For example, the following `requirements.txt` file points to two GitHub repositories:

```
-e git+https://github.com/Runnerly/tokendealer.git#egg=runnerly-tokendealer
-e git+https://github.com/Runnerly/data-service.git#egg=runnerly-data
```

From there, running the `pip install -r requirements.txt` command will clone the two projects in a `src` directory and install them in *develop* mode, meaning that you can change and commit the code directly from `src/<project>`.

Lastly, assuming you have created console scripts everywhere you needed to run your microservices, they will be added in the virtualenv `bin` directory.

The last piece of the puzzle is to avoid having to run each console script in a separate bash window. We want to manage those processes with a single script. Let's see in the next section how we can do this with a process manager.

# Process management

We've seen in `Chapter 2`, *Discovering Flask*, that Flask-based applications, in general, run in a single-threaded environment.

To add concurrency, the most common pattern is to use a *prefork model*. Serving several clients concurrently is done by forking several processes (called workers), which accept incoming connections from the same inherited socket. The socket can be a *TCP Socket* or a *Unix Socket*. Unix sockets can be used when both the clients and the server are running on the same machine. They are based on exchanging data via a file and are slightly faster than TCP sockets, since they don't have to deal with the network protocol overhead. Using Unix Sockets to run Flask apps is common when the application is proxied via a front server like NGinx.

In any case, Unix or TCP, every time a request reaches the socket, the first available process accepts the request and handles it. Which process gets which request is done at the system level by the system socket API with a lock mechanism. This round-robin mechanism load balances requests among all processes and is pretty efficient.

To use this model for your Flask app, you can use **uWSGI** (`http://uwsgi-docs.readthedo cs.io`), for instance, which will prefork several processes with its `processes` option, and serve the Flask app from there.

The uWSGI tool is pretty amazing with a lot of options, and even has its own binary protocol to communicate through TCP. Running uWSGI with its binary protocol behind an nginx HTTP server is a great solution for serving Flask apps. uWSGI takes care of managing its processes, and interacts with nginx, with whatever HTTP proxy you use. Or directly with the end user.

The uWSGI tool, however, specializes in running web apps. If you want to deploy for a development environment, a few other processes, like a Redis instance, which need to run alongside your microservices on the same box, you will need to use another process manager.

A good alternative is a tool like **Circus** (`http://circus.readthedocs.io`), which can run any kind of process even if they are not a WSGI application, it also has the ability to bind sockets, and make them available for the managed processes. In other words, Circus can run a Flask app with several processes, and can also manage some other processes if needed.

Circus is a Python application, so, to use it, you can simply run the `pip install circus` command. Once Circus is installed, you will get a few new commands. The two principal commands are: `circusd`, which is the process manager, and `circusctl`, which lets you drive the process manager from the command line.

Circus uses an INI-like configuration file, where you can list the commands to run in dedicated sections, and for each one of them, the number of processes you want to use.

Circus can also bind sockets, and let the forked process use them via their file descriptors. When a socket is created on your system, it uses a **file descriptor** (**FD**), which is a system handle a program can use to reach a file or an I/O resource like sockets. A process that is forked from another one inherits all its file descriptors. That is, through this mechanism, all the processes launched by Circus can share the same sockets.

In the following example, two commands are being run. One will run five processes for the Flask application located in the `server.py` module, and one will run one Redis server process.

```
[watcher:web]
cmd = chaussette --fd $(circus.sockets.web) server.application
use_sockets = True
numprocesses = 5

[watcher:redis]
cmd = /usr/local/bin/redis-server
use_sockets = False
numprocesses = 1

[socket:web]
host = 0.0.0.0
port = 8000
```

The `socket:web` section describes what host and port to use to bind the TCP socket, and the `watcher:web` section uses it via the `$(circus.sockets.web)` variable. When Circus runs, it replaces that variable with the FD value for the socket.

To run this script, you can use the `circusd` command line.

```
$ circusd myconfig.ini
```

There are a few WSGI web servers out there that provide an option to run against a file descriptor, but most of them don't expose that option, and bind a new socket themselves given a host and a port.

The **Chaussette** (`http://chaussette.readthedocs.io/`) project was created to let you run most existing WSGI web servers out there via an FD. Once you've run the `pip install chaussette` command, you can run the Flask app with a variety of backend listed at `http://chaussette.readthedocs.io/en/latest/#backends`.

For our microservices, using Circus means we can simply create a watcher and a socket section per service and start them all using the `circusd` command.

The only difference is that, if we use our own launcher instead of the Chaussette console, it needs to be adapted in order to be able to run with file descriptors.

The `main()` function from the microservice can use the `make_server()` function from Chaussette and use it in case an `-fd` option is passed when launched.

```
from chaussette.server import make_server

def main(args=sys.argv[1:]):
    parser = argparse.ArgumentParser(description='Runnerly
                                    Dataservice')
    parser.add_argument('--fd', type=int, default=None)
    parser.add_argument('--config-file', help='Config file',
                        type=str, default=None)
    args = parser.parse_args(args=args)
    app = create_app(args.config_file)
    host = app.config.get('host', '0.0.0.0')
    port = app.config.get('port', 5000)
    debug = app.config.get('DEBUG', False)
    signal.signal(signal.SIGINT, _quit)
    signal.signal(signal.SIGTERM, _quit)

    def runner():
        if args.fd is not None:
            # use chaussette
            httpd = make_server(app, host='fd://%d' % args.fd)
            httpd.serve_forever()
        else:
            app.run(debug=debug, host=host, port=port)

    if not debug:
        runner()
    else:
        from werkzeug.serving import run_with_reloader
        run_with_reloader(runner)
```

And then, in the `circus.ini` file:

```
[watcher:web]
cmd = runnerly-dataservice --fd $(circus.sockets.web)
use_sockets = True
numproccoses - 5

[socket:web]
host = 0.0.0.0
port = 8000
```

From there, if you need to debug a specific microservice, a common pattern is to add a `pdb.set_trace()` call inside the Flask view you are going to call.

Once the call is added in the code, you can stop the microservice via `circusctl` in order to run it manually in another shell, so you can get access to the debug prompt.

 Circus also offers options to redirect the `stdout` and `stderr` streams to log files to facilitate the debugging and numerous other features you can find at `https://circus.readthedocs.io/en/latest/for-ops/configuration/`.

# Summary

In this chapter, we've looked at how to package, release, and distribute each microservice. The current state of the art in Python packaging still requires some knowledge about the legacy tools, and this will be the case for some years until all the ongoing work in Python and PyPA become mainstream.

But as long as you have a standard, reproducible, and documented way to package and install your microservices, you should be fine.

Having numerous projects to run a single application adds a lot of complexity when you are developing it, and it's important to be able to run all pieces from within the same box.

Tools like PIP's development mode and Circus are useful for this, as it allows you to simplify how you run the whole stack--but they still require that you install things on your system even if it's inside a Virtualenv.

The other issue with running everything from your box is that you might not use an operating system that will be used to run your services in production, or have some libraries installed for other purposes, which might interfere.

The best way to prevent this problem is to run your stack in full isolation inside a virtual box. This is what the next chapter will cover, for example, how to run your services inside Docker.

# 10
# Containerized Services

In the previous chapter, we ran our different microservices directly in the host operating system--so, all the dependencies and data that your application uses were installed directly on the system.

Most of the time, it is fine to do so, because running a Python application in a virtual environment downloads and installs dependencies inside a single directory. However, if the application requires a database system, you need that database to run on your system, unless it is just an SQLite file. For some Python libraries, you might also need some system headers to compile extensions.

In no time, your system is going to have various software running, which were installed along the way when developing your microservices. It is not a problem for your development environment as long as you don't need to work with different versions of a service you are working on. However, if some potential contributors try to install your applications locally, and are forced to install much of the software at the system level, it could be a dealbreaker.

That is where VMs are a great solution to run your applications. In the past ten years, many software projects that required an elaborate setup to run started to provide ready-to-run VMs, using tools such as VMWare or VirtualBox. Those VMs included the whole stack, like prefilled databases. Demos became easily runnable on most platforms with a single command. That was progress.

However, some of those tools were not fully open source, and they were very slow to run, and greedy in memory and CPU and terrible with disk I/O. It was unthinkable to run them in production, and they were mostly used for demos.

The big revolution came with Docker, an open source virtualization tool, which was first released in 2013, and became hugely popular. Moreover, unlike VMWare or VirtualBox, Docker can run your applications in production at native speed.

In other words, creating *images* for your application is not only for demonstration and development purposes anymore. It can be used for real deployments.

In this chapter, we present Docker, and explain how to run Flask-based microservices with it. Then, we look at some of the tools in the Docker ecosystem. We conclude the chapter by an introduction to **clusters**.

# What is Docker?

The **Docker** (https://www.docker.com/) project is a *container* platform, which lets you run your applications in isolated environments. Docker leverages existing Linux technologies like **cgroups** (https://en.wikipedia.org/wiki/Cgroups) to provide a set of high-level tools to drive a collection of running processes. On Windows and macOS, Docker interacts with a Linux Virtual Machine, since a Linux kernel is required.

As a Docker user, you just need to point which *image* you want to run, and Docker does all the heavy lifting by interacting with the Linux kernel. An *image* in that context is the sum of all the instructions required to create a set of running processes on the top of a Linux kernel to run one container. An image includes all the resources necessary to run a Linux distribution. For instance, you can run whatever version of Ubuntu you want in a Docker container even if the host OS is a different distribution.

While it is possible to use Windows, Flask microservices should always be deployed under a Linux or BSD-based system--the rest of this chapter makes the assumption that everything is installed under a Linux distribution such as Debian.

If you have already installed Docker in Chapter 6, *Monitoring Your Services*, to set up a Graylog instance, you can jump directly to the next section of this chapter, Docker 101.

If not, you can visit the *Get Docker* section of the page at https://www.docker.com/get-doc ker to install it. The *community edition* is good enough for building, running, and installing containers. Installing Docker on Linux is a no-brainer-- you can probably find a package for your Linux distribution.

For macOS, Docker uses a VM to run a Linux Kernel. The latest versions are based on **HyperKit** (https://github.com/moby/hyperkit), which leverages **bhyve**, a BSD Hypervisor. Running Docker via a VM adds a bit of overhead, but it is quite lightweight, and works well with modern hardware. Hypervisors are becoming a commodity in all major operating systems.

Under Windows, Docker uses the Windows built-in Hyper-V, which might need to be enabled. The feature can usually be enabled via a command-line shell with a DSIM call, as follows:

```
$ DISM /Online /Enable-Feature /All /FeatureName:Microsoft-Hyper-V
```

If the installation was successful, you should be able to run the `docker` command in your shell. Try the `version` command to verify your installation like this:

```
$ docker version
Client:
 Version:      17.03.1-ce
 API version:  1.27
 Go version:   go1.7.5
 Git commit:   c6d412e
 Built:        Tue Mar 28 00:40:02 2017
 OS/Arch:      darwin/amd64

Server:
 Version:      17.03.1-ce
 API version:  1.27 (minimum version 1.12)
 Go version:   go1.7.5
 Git commit:   c6d412e
 Built:        Fri Mar 24 00:00:50 2017
 OS/Arch:      linux/amd64
 Experimental: true
```

A Docker installation is composed of a Docker server (the engine that's being executed by a daemon) and a Docker client (the shell commands like `docker`).

The server provides an HTTP API, which can be reached locally through a UNIX socket (usually, `/var/run/docker.sock`) or through the network.

In other words, the Docker client can interact with Docker daemons running on other boxes.

 For managing Docker manually, the Docker command line is great. However, in case you need to script some of your Docker manipulation, a Python library like **docker-py** (https://github.com/docker/docker-py) lets you do everything from Python. It uses `requests` to perform HTTP calls against the Docker daemon.

Now that Docker is installed on your system, let's discover how it works.

# Docker 101

Running a container in Docker is done by executing a series of commands which starts a group of processes, which the tool isolates from the rest of the system.

Docker can be used to run a single process, but in practice we want to run a full Linux distribution. Not to worry, everything needed to run a full Linux inside Docker is already available.

Every existing Linux distribution out there provides a *base image*, which lets you run the distribution in Docker. The typical way you use images is by creating a `Dockerfile` (`https://docs.docker.com/engine/reference/builder/`), where you point the base image you want to use, and add some extra commands to be run to create the container.

The following is a basic example of a Docker file:

```
FROM ubuntu
RUN apt-get update && apt-get install -y python
CMD ["bash"]
```

A `Dockerfile` is a text file with a set of instructions. Each line starts with the instruction in uppercase, followed by its arguments.

In our example, there are these three instructions:

- `FROM`: Points the base image to use
- `RUN`: Runs the commands in the container once the base image is installed
- `CMD`: The command to run when the container is executed by Docker

To create that image and then run it, you can use the docker `build` and `run` commands from within the directory where the `Dockerfile` file is located. Notice the full stop (`.`) at the end.

```
$ docker build -t runnerly/python .
Sending build context to Docker daemon 6.656 kB
Step 1/3 : FROM ubuntu
 ---> 0ef2e08ed3fa
Step 2/3 : RUN apt-get update && apt-get install -y python
 ---> Using cache
 ---> 48a5a722c81c
Step 3/3 : CMD bash
 ---> Using cache
 ---> 78e9a6fd9295
Successfully built 78e9a6fd9295
$ docker run -it --rm runnerly/python
```

```
root@ebdbb644edb1:/# python
Python 2.7.12 (default, Nov 19 2016, 06:48:10)
[GCC 5.4.0 20160609] on linux2
Type "help", "copyright", "credits" or "license" for more information.
>>>
```

The -t option in the preceding code snippet adds a label to the image. In our example, the image is tagged runnerly/python. One convention is to prefix the label with the project or organization name so that you can group your images under the same namespace.

When Docker creates images, it creates a cache which has every instruction from the Dockerfile. If you run the build command a second time, without changing the file, it should be done within seconds. Permuting or changing instructions rebuilds the image starting at the first change. For this reason, a good strategy when writing these files is to sort instructions so that the most stable ones (the ones you rarely change) are at the top.

One great feature that Docker offers is the ability to share, publish, and reuse images with other developers. The **Docker Hub** (https://hub.docker.com) is to Docker containers what PyPI is to Python packages.

In the previous example, the ubuntu base image was pulled from the Hub by Docker, and there are numerous pre-existing images you can use.

For instance, if you want to launch a Linux distribution that is tweaked for Python, you can look at the Python page on the official Docker Hub and pick one (https://hub.docker.com/_/python/).

The python:version images are Debian-based, and are an excellent starting point for any Python project.

The Python images based on **Alpine Linux** (refer to http://gliderlabs.viewdocs.io/docker-alpine/) are also quite popular, because they produce the smallest images to run Python. They are more than ten times smaller than other ones, which means they are way faster to download and set up for people wanting to run your project in Docker.

To use Python 3.6 in Alpine, you can create a Dockerfile like this:

```
FROM python:3.6-alpine
CMD ["python3.6"]
```

Building and running this `Dockerfile` drops you in a Python 3.6 shell. The Alpine set is great if you run a Python application that does not require a lot of system-level dependencies or any compilation. Alpine has a very specific set of compilation tools, which are sometimes incompatible with some projects.

For a Flask-based microservice project, the Debian-based one is probably a simpler choice because of its standard compilation environment and stability. Moreover, once the base image is downloaded, it is cached and reused, so you do not need to download everything again.

 Notice that it's important to use images from trusted people and organizations on Docker Hub since anyone can upload an image. Beyond the risk of running malicious code, there's also the problem of using a Linux image that is not up-to-date with the latest security patches.

# Running Flask in Docker

To run a Flask application in Docker, we can use the base Python image.

From there, installing the app and its dependencies can be done via PIP, which is already installed in the Python image.

Assuming your project has a `requirements.txt` file for its pinned dependencies, and a `setup.py` file that installs the project, creating an image for your project can be done by instructing Docker how to use the `pip` command.

In the following example, we add two new instructions--the `COPY` command recursively copies a directory structure inside the Docker image, and the `RUN` command runs PIP via shell commands:

```
FROM python:3.6
COPY . /app
RUN pip install -r /app/requirements.txt
RUN pip install /app/

EXPOSE 5000
CMD runnerly-tokendealer
```

The `3.6` tag here will get the latest Python 3.6 image that was uploaded to the Hub.

The COPY command automatically creates the top-level app directory in the container, and copies everything from "." in it. One important detail to remember with the COPY command is that any change to the local directory (".") invalidates the Docker cache, and builds from that step.

To tweak this mechanism, you can create a .dockerignore file where you can list files and directories that should be ignored by Docker.

Let's try to build that Dockerfile as follows:

```
$ docker build -t runnerly/tokendealer .
Sending build context to Docker daemon 148.5 MB
Step 1/6 : FROM python:3.6
 ---> 21289e3715bd
Step 2/6 : COPY . /app
 ---> 01cebcda7d1c
Removing intermediate container 36f0d93f5d78
Step 3/6 : RUN pip install -r /app/requirements.txt
 ---> Running in 90200690f834
Collecting pyjwt (from -r /app/requirements.txt (line 1))
[...]
Successfully built d2444a66978d
```

Once PIP has installed the dependencies, it installs the project with the second call by pointing to the app directory. When the pip command is pointed to a directory, it looks for a setup.py file, and runs it.

In the Token Dealer project, a runnerly-tokendealer console script is added to the system when installed. We are not using Virtualenv here--it would be an overkill, since we are already in a container. So, the runnerly-tokendealer script is installed directly alongside the Python executable so that they are both reachable directly in the shell.

That is why the CMD instruction that points which command should be run when the container is executed points directly to runnerly-tokendealer.

Lastly, an EXPOSE instruction was added to let the container listen for connections to the inbound TCP port 5000--the one where the Flask app runs.

Notice that, once the port is exposed, you still need to bridge it to the host system by mapping a local port with the exposed port at runtime.

Bridging the port is done with the -p option. In the following example, the container bridges its 5000 port with the local 5555 port:

```
$ docker run -p 5555:5000 -t runnerly/tokendealer
```

The last thing we need to do for a fully functional image is to run a web server in front of the Flask application.

Let's see in the next section how we can do that.

# The full stack - OpenResty, Circus and Flask

When you release microservices as Docker images, there are two strategies for including a web server.

The first one consists of ignoring it and exposing the Flask application directly. A web server like **OpenResty** could then run in its docker container, proxying calls to your Flask container.

However, if you are using some power features in nginx, like a Lua-based application firewall as we have seen in Chapter 7, *Securing Your Services*, it can be better to include everything within the same container, together with a dedicated process manager.

In the diagram that follows, the docker container implements the second strategy, and runs both the web server and the Flask service. Circus is used to launch and watch one nginx process and a few Flask processes:

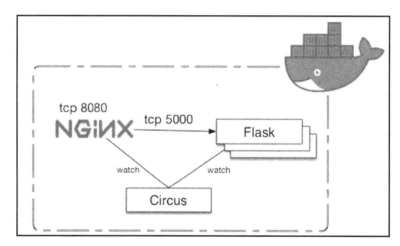

In this section, we will implement this container by adding in our `Dockerfile` the following steps:

1. Download, compile, and install OpenResty.
2. Add an nginx configuration file.
3. Download and install Circus and Chaussette.
4. Add a Circus configuration file to run nginx and the Flask app.

# OpenResty

The base Python image uses Debian's `apt` package manager, and OpenResty (the nginx distribution that includes Lua and other good extensions) is not available directly in the stable Debian repository. However, it is quite simple to compile and install OpenResty from its source release.

In the `Dockerfile`, we first want to make sure the Debian environment has all the required packages to compile OpenResty.

The following instructions first update the packages list, then install everything needed:

```
RUN apt-get -y update && \
    apt-get -y install libreadline-dev libncurses5-dev && \
    apt-get -y install libpcre3-dev libssl-dev perl make
```

Notice that the three commands in the preceding code are merged as a single `RUN` instruction to limit the number of instructions the `Dockerfile` has. By doing so, you can limit the final image size.

The next step is to download the OpenResty source code, and perform the compilation step. **cURL** is already available in the Python base image and you can pipe it with the `tar` module to decompress the OpenResty release tarball directly from its URL.

The following `configure` and `make` calls are straight from OpenResty's documentation, and compile and install everything:

```
RUN curl -sSL https://openresty.org/download/openresty-1.11.2.3.tar.gz \
    | tar -xz && \
    cd openresty-1.11.2.3 && \
    ./configure -j2 && \
    make -j2 && \
    make install
```

Once the compilation is over, OpenResty is installed in `/usr/local/openresty` and you can add an `ENV` instruction to make sure that the nginx executable is available directly in the container's `PATH` variable:

```
ENV PATH "/usr/local/openresty/bin:/usr/local/openresty/nginx/sbin:$PATH"
```

The last thing we need to do for OpenResty is to include an nginx configuration file to start the web server.

In the following minimal example, nginx proxies all calls made to the 8080 port, to the container `5000` port--as shown in the previous diagram:

```
worker_processes  4;
error_log /logs/nginx-error.log;
daemon off;

events {
    worker_connections 1024;
}

http {
    server {
        listen 8080;

        location / {
            proxy_pass http://localhost:5000;
            proxy_set_header Host $host;
            proxy_set_header X-Real-IP $remote_addr;
        }
    }
}
```

Notice that the `error_log` path uses the `/logs/` directory. It's the root directory within the container for our logs.

That directory needs to be created via a RUN instruction, and a mount point can be added thanks to the VOLUME instruction:

```
RUN mkdir /logs
VOLUME /logs
```

By doing this, you will be able to mount the /logs directory on a local directory on the host at runtime, and keep the log files even if the container is killed.

A Docker container filesystem should always be considered as a volatile volume, which can be lost at any moment.
If the processes in a container produce anything precious, the resulting data should be copied to a directory that is mounted as a volume outside the container's filesystem.

This configuration file is a *full* nginx configuration and can be used directly with nginx's -c option with this call:

```
$ nginx -c nginx.conf
```

Once nginx runs, it makes the assumption that Circus listens to incoming TCP connections on port 5000 and nginx listens itself on port 8080.

Let's now configure Circus so that it binds a socket on that port and spawns a few Flask processes.

# Circus

If we reuse the Circus and Chaussette setup from Chapter 9, *Packaging Runnerly*, Circus can bind a socket on port 5000, and fork a few Flask processes, which will accept connection on that socket. Circus can also watch the single nginx process we want to run in our container.

The first step to using Circus as a process manager in our container is to install it, together with Chaussette, as follows:

```
RUN pip install circus chaussette
```

From there, the following Circus configuration is similar to what we had in the previous chapter, except that we have one extra section for nginx:

```
[watcher:web]
cmd = runnerly-tokendealer --fd $(circus.sockets.web)
use_sockets = True
numprocesses = 5
```

```
copy_env = True

[socket:web]
host = 0.0.0.0
port = 5000

[watcher:nginx]cmd =  nginx -c /app/nginx.confnumprocesses = 1copy_env =
True
```

The `copy_env` flag is used, so both Circus and the spawned processes have access to the container environment variables. That is why the configuration calls nginx directly without indicating its path since the `PATH` variable was set in our `Dockerfile`.

Once this INI file is created, it can be launched with the `circusd` command.

With all the previous changes, the finalized `Dockerfile` for our container looks like the following:

```
FROM python:3.6

# OpenResty installation
RUN apt-get -y update && \
    apt-get -y install libreadline-dev libncurses5-dev && \
    apt-get -y install libpcre3-dev libssl-dev perl make
RUN curl -sSL https://openresty.org/download/openresty-1.11.2.3.tar.gz \
    | tar -xz && \
    cd openresty-1.11.2.3 && \
    ./configure -j2 && \
    make -j2 && \
    make install
ENV PATH "/usr/local/openresty/bin:/usr/local/openresty/nginx/sbin:$PATH"

# config files
COPY docker/circus.ini /app/circus.ini
COPY docker/nginx.conf /app/nginx.conf
COPY docker/settings.ini /app/settings.ini
COPY docker/pubkey.pem /app/pubkey.pem
COPY docker/privkey.pem /app/privkey.pem

# copying the whole app directory
COPY . /app

# pip installs
RUN pip install circus chaussette
RUN pip install -r /app/requirements.txt
RUN pip install /app/
```

```
# logs directory
RUN mkdir /logs
VOLUME /logs

# exposing Nginx's socket
EXPOSE 8080

# command that runs when the container is executed

CMD circusd /app/circus.ini
```

 In the Dockerfile example above, the SSH key are directly available in the repository to simplify the example for the book. In a real project, the production keys should be made available from outside the image through a mount point.

Assuming this Docker file is located in a /docker subdirectory in the microservice project, it can be built and then run with the following calls:

```
$ docker build -t runnerly/tokendealer -f docker/Dockerfile .
$ docker run --rm --v /tmp/logs:/logs -p 8080:8080 --name tokendealer -it
runnerly/tokendealer
```

The /logs mount point is mounted to a local /tmp/logs in this example, and the logs files are written in it.

The -i option makes sure that stopping the run with a *Ctrl + C* forwards the termination signal to Circus so that it shuts down everything properly. This option is useful when you run a Docker container in a console. If you do not use -i, and kill the run with *Ctrl + C*, the Docker image will still run, and you will need to terminate it manually via a docker terminate call.

The --rm option deletes the container when stopped, and the --name option gives a unique name to the container in the Docker environment.

Numerous tweaks can be added in this Dockerfile example. For instance, the sockets used by the Circus UIs (both web and command line) to control the Circus daemon could be exposed if you want to interact with it from outside the container.

You can also expose some of the running options, like the number of Flask processes you want to start--like environment variables--and pass them at run time via Docker with -e.

The fully working `Dockerfile` can be found at `https://github.com/Run` `nerly/tokendealer/tree/master/docker`.

In the next section, we will look at how containers can interact with each other.

# Docker-based deployments

Once you have microservices running inside containers, you need them to interact with each other. Since we are bridging the container sockets with some local sockets on the host, it is pretty transparent from an external client. Each host can have a public DNS or IP, and programs can simply use it to connect to the various services. In other words, a service deployed inside a container on *host A* can talk to a service deployed inside a container on *host B* as long as *host A* and *B* have a public address and expose the local sockets that are bridged with the containers sockets.

However, when two containers need to run on the same host, using the public DNS to make them interact with each other is less than optimal, particularly, if one of the containers is private to the host. For example, if you run a container in Docker for internal needs, like a caching service, its access should be restricted to the localhost.

To make this use case easier to implement, Docker provides a *user-defined network feature*, which lets you create local *virtual* networks. Containers can be added to them, and if they run with a `--name` option, Docker acts as a DNS resolver, and makes them available in those networks via their names.

Let's create a new `runnerly` network with the `network` command as follows:

```
$ docker network create –driver=bridge runnerly
4a08e29d305b17f875a7d98053b77ea95503f620df580df03d83c6cd1011fb67
```

Once this network is created, we can run containers in it, using the `--net` option. Let's run one container with the `tokendealer` name, like this:

```
$ docker run --rm --net=runnerly --name=tokendealer -v /tmp/logs:/logs -p
5555:8080 –it runnerly/tokendealer
2017-05-18 19:42:46 circus[5] [INFO] Starting master on pid 5
2017-05-18 19:42:46 circus[5] [INFO] sockets started
2017-05-18 19:42:46 circus[5] [INFO] Arbiter now waiting for commands
2017-05-18 19:42:46 circus[5] [INFO] nginx started
2017-05-18 19:42:46 circus[5] [INFO] web started
```

If we run a second container with the same image and a different name on the same network, it can ping the first container directly with its `tokendealer` name:

```
$ docker run --rm --net=runnerly --name=tokendealer2 -v /tmp/logs:/logs -p
8082:8080 -it runnerly/tokendealer ping tokendealer
PING tokendealer (172.20.0.2): 56 data bytes
64 bytes from 172.20.0.2: icmp_seq=0 ttl=64 time=0.474 ms
64 bytes from 172.20.0.2: icmp_seq=1 ttl=64 time=0.177 ms
64 bytes from 172.20.0.2: icmp_seq=2 ttl=64 time=0.218 ms
^C
```

Using dedicated Docker networks for your microservices container when you deploy them is good practice even if you have a single container running. You can always attach new containers within the same network, or tweak the network permissions from the shell.

 Docker has other network strategies you can look at in `https://docs.doc ker.com/engine/userguide/networking/`.

Having to deploy several containers to run one microservice requires you to make sure that both containers are properly configured when launched.

To make that configuration easier, Docker has a high-level tool called **Docker Compose**, presented in the next section.

# Docker Compose

The command-lines required to run several containers on the same host can be quite long once you need to add names and networks and bind several sockets.

Docker Compose (`https://docs.docker.com/compose/`) simplifies the task by letting you define multiple containers' configuration in a single configuration file.

This utility is pre-installed on macOS and Windows when you install Docker. For Linux distributions, you need to get the script and add it to your system. It is a single script, which you can download or even install with PIP (refer to `https://docs.docker.com/compose/i nstall/`).

Once the script is installed on your system, you need to create a YAML file named `docker-compose.yml`, which contains a `services` section to enumerate your Docker containers.

The Compose's configuration file has many options that let you define every aspect of the deployment of several containers.
It replaces all the commands one usually puts in a Makefile to set and run containers. This URL lists all options: `https://docs.docker.com/compose/compose-file/`.

In the following example, the file is placed in one of the Runnerly microservice and defines two services--`microservice`, which picks the local `Dockerfile`, and `redis`, which uses the Redis's image from the Docker Hub:

```
version: '2'
networks:
  runnerly:
services:
  microservice:
    networks:
     - runnerly
    build:
        context: .
        dockerfile: docker/Dockerfile
    ports:
     - "8080:8080"
    volumes:
     - /tmp/logs:/logs
  redis:
    image: "redis:alpine"
    networks:.
     - runnerly
```

The Compose file also creates networks with its `networks` sections, so you do not have to create it manually on your host before you deploy your containers.

To build and run those two containers, you can use the `up` command as follows:

```
$ docker-compose up
Starting tokendealer_microservice_1
Starting tokendealer_redis_1
Attaching to tokendealer_microservice_1, tokendealer_redis_1
[...]
redis_1         | 1:M 19 May 20:04:07.842 * DB loaded from disk: 0.000
seconds
redis_1         | 1:M 19 May 20:04:07.842 * The server is now ready to
accept connections on port 6379
microservice_1 | 2017-05-19 20:04:08 circus[5] [INFO] Starting master on
pid 5
microservice_1 | 2017-05-19 20:04:08 circus[5] [INFO] sockets started
microservice_1 | 2017-05-19 20:04:08 circus[5] [INFO] Arbiter now waiting
```

```
for commands
microservice_1  | 2017-05-19 20:04:08 circus[5] [INFO] nginx started
microservice_1  | 2017-05-19 20:04:08 circus[5] [INFO] web started
```

The first time that command is executed, the `microservice` image is created.

Using Docker Compose is great when you want to provide a full working stack for your microservices, which includes every piece of software needed to run it.

For instance, if you are using a Postgres database, you can use the Postgres image (`https://hub.docker.com/_/postgres/`), and link it to your service in a Docker Compose file.

Containerizing everything, even the databases, is great to showcase your software or for development purposes. However, as we stated earlier, a Docker container should be seen as a volatile filesystem. So if you use a container for your database, make sure that the directory where the data is written is mounted on the host file system.

However, in most cases, the database service is usually its dedicated server on a production deployment. Using a container does not make much sense and adds a little bit of overhead and risks.

So far in this chapter, we have looked at how to run apps in Docker containers, and how to deploy several containers per host and have them interact with each other.

When you deploy a microservice that needs scaling, it is often required to run several instances of the same service to be able to support the load.

The next section discusses various options to run several instances of the same container in parallel.

# Introduction to Clustering and Provisioning

Deploying a microservice at scale can be done by running several containers spread across one or several hosts.

Once your Docker image is created, every host that runs a Docker daemon can be used to run as many containers as you want within the limits of the physical resources. Of course, if you run several instances of the same container on the same host, you need to use a different name and socket ports for each instance to differentiate them.

The collection of containers running the same image is called a `cluster`, and there are a few tools available to manage clusters.

Docker has a built-in cluster functionality called **swarm mode** (https://docs.docker.com/engine/swarm/). This mode has an impressive list of features, which lets you manage all your clusters from a single utility.

Once you have deployed a cluster, you need to set up a load balancer so that all the instances of your cluster are sharing the workload. The load balancer can be nginx or HAProxy, for instance, and is the entry point to distribute the incoming requests on clusters.

While Docker tries to provide all the tools to deal with clusters of containers, managing them can become quite complex. When done properly, it requires to share some configuration across hosts, and to make sure that bringing containers up and down is partially automated. A service discovery feature is needed to ensure that the addition and removal of new containers is detected by the load balancer, for instance.

Service discovery and sharing configuration can be done by tools like **Consul** (https://www.consul.io/) or **Etcd** (https://coreos.com/etcd/) and Docker's swarm mode can be configured to interact with those tools.

The other aspect of setting up clusters is *provisioning*. This term describes the process of creating new hosts, and therefore, clusters, given the description of the stack you are deploying in some declarative form.

For instance, a poor mans provisioning tool can be a custom Python script that follows these steps:

1. Read a configuration file that describes the instances needed via a few Docker Compose files.
2. Start a few VMs on the cloud provider.
3. Wait for all VMs to be up and running.
4. Make sure everything needed to run services on the VM is set.
5. Interact with the Docker daemon on each VM to start some containers.
6. Ping whatever service needs to be pinged to make sure the new instances are all interlinked.

Once the task of deploying containers is automated, it can be used to spin off new VMs if some of them crash, for example.

However, doing all this work in a Python script has its limits and there are dedicated tools to handle this, like **Ansible** (https://www.ansible.com/) or **Salt** (https://docs.saltstac k.com). Those tools provide a DevOps-friendly environment to deploy and manage hosts.

**Kubernetes** (https://kubernetes.io/) is yet another tool, that can be used to deploy clusters containers on hosts. Unlike Ansible or Salt, Kubernetes specializes in deploying containers and tries to provide a generic solution that works anywhere.

For example, Kubernetes can interact with major cloud providers through their API, meaning that once an application deployment is defined, it can be deployed on AWS, Digital Ocean, OpenStack, and the like. However, that begs the question of whether this ability is useful for your project.

Usually, if you pick a cloud provider for an application, and decide, for some reason, to move to another cloud provider, it is rarely as simple as pushing a new stack. There are many subtle details that make the transition more complex, and the deployment is rarely similar. For instance, some cloud providers offer data storage solutions that are cheaper to use than running your own PostgreSQL or MySQL deployment, while others make their caching solution much more expensive than running your Redis instances.

Some teams deploy their services across several cloud providers, but in general, they do not deploy the same microservice on several providers. That would make the cluster management too complex.

Moreover, each major cloud provider offers a full range of built-in tools to manage the applications they host, including features like load balancing, discoverability, and auto-scaling. They are often the simplest option to deploy clusters of microservices.

In the next chapter, we will look at how to deploy applications using AWS.

Overall, the toolset to use to deploy microservices is dependent on *where* you are deploying. If you manage your servers, Kubernetes can be an excellent solution to automate many steps, and can be installed directly on a Linux distribution like Ubuntu. That tool can use your Docker images as its basis for deploying your application.

If you opt for a hosted solution, looking at what tools are already offered by the provider is the first step before you invest in your toolset.

# Summary

In this chapter, we looked at how microservices can be containerized with Docker, and how you can create a deployment entirely based on Docker images.

Docker is still a young technology, but it is mature enough to be used in production. The most important thing to keep in mind is that a containerized application can be trashed at any time, and any data that's not externalized via a mount point is lost.

For provisioning and clustering your services, there's no generic solution, and tons of tools, which can be combined to create a good solution. There is much innovation right now in that field, and the best choice depends on where you deploy your services, and how your teams work.

The best way to tackle this problem is to take baby steps by first deploying everything manually, then automating much where it makes sense. Automation is great, but can rapidly become a nightmare if you use a toolset you do not fully grasp.

In that vein, to make their services easier to use and more appealing, cloud providers have built-in features to handle deployments. One of the biggest players is **Amazon Web Services** (**AWS**) and the next chapter demonstrates how microservices can be deployed on their platform. Of course, the goal here is not to tell you to use AWS; there are many good solutions out there. However, it gives you a sense of what it is like to deploy your services on a hosted solution.

# 11
## Deploying on AWS

Unless you are Google or Amazon, and need to run thousands of servers, managing your hardware in some data center does not provide many benefits in 2017.

Cloud providers offer to host a solution that is often cheaper than deploying and maintaining your infrastructure. **Amazon Web Services** (**AWS**) and others have numerous services that let you manage virtual machines from a web console, and they add new features every year.

One of the latest AWS additions, for example, is **Amazon Lambda**. Lambda lets you trigger a Python script when something happens in your deployments. With Lambda, you do not have to worry about setting up a server and a cron job, or some form of messaging. AWS takes care of executing your script in a VM automatically, and you only pay for execution time.

Combined with what Docker has to offer, this kind of feature really changes how applications can be deployed in the cloud, and provide a fair amount of flexibility. For instance, you do not have to spend too much money to set up a service that might see a peak in activity and then slow down. You can deploy a world-class infrastructure that can hold an enormous amount of requests, and it stays, in most cases, cheaper than running your hardware.

Moving to your own datacenter might save you money in some cases, but it adds a maintenance burden, and it is a challenge to make your deployments as reliable as if they were running at a cloud provider.

While they make much noise in the press, Amazon or Google outages are rare events (a few hours a year at most), and their reliability is very high. The **Service Level Agreement** (**SLA**) for EC2, for example, guarantees an uptime of 99.95% per region or you get some money back. In reality, it is often closer to five nines (99.999%).
You can track cloud providers' uptime values with online tools like `https://cloudharmony.com/status-1year-for-aws`, but their results should be taken with a pinch of salt because some *partial* outages are not counted sometimes.

In this chapter, we are going to do two things:

- Discover some of the features AWS offers
- Deploy a Flask application on it

The goal of this chapter is not to deploy a complete stack, as it is too long, but to give you a good overview of how microservices can be implemented there.

Let's start with an overview of what AWS has to offer.

# AWS overview

Amazon Web Service began in 2006 with **Amazon Elastic Compute Cloud** (**Amazon EC2**), and has extended its services since then. At present (2017), there are countless services. We will not go through all of them in this chapter, but just focus on the ones you usually deal with when you start to deploy microservices:

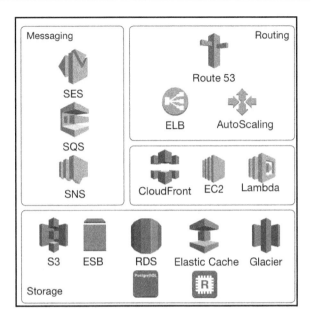

The AWS services we are interested in can be organized into four five main groups as seen in the diagram:

- **Routing**: Services that redirect requests to the right place, such as DNS services and load balancers
- **Execution**: Services that execute your code, such as EC2 or Lambda
- **Storage**: Services that store data-storage volumes, caching, regular databases, long-term storage, or CDN
- **Messaging**: Services that send notifications, emails, and so on

One extra group of service that is not displayed in the diagram is everything related to **provisioning and deployment**.

Let's have a look at each group.

 If you want to read the official documentation for an Amazon Service, the usual link to reach the root page of each service is `https://aws.amazon.com/<service name>`.

# Routing - Route53, ELB, and AutoScaling

**Route53** (https://aws.amazon.com/route53/) refers to the TCP port 53 that's used for DNS servers, and is Amazon's DNS service. Similar to what you would do with **BIND** (http://www.isc.org/downloads/bind/), you can define DNS entries in Route53, and set up the service to automatically route the requests to specific AWS services that host applications or files.

DNS is a critical part of a deployment. It needs to be highly available, and to route each incoming request as fast as possible. If you are deploying your services on AWS, it is highly recommended to use Route53 or to use the DNS provider of the company where you bought the domain, and not deal with DNS yourself.

Route53 can work in close cooperation with **Elastic Load Balancing** (**ELB**) (https://aws.amazon.com/elasticloadbalancing/), which is a load balancer that can be configured to distribute incoming requests to several backends. Typically, if you are deploying several VMs for the same microservice to create a cluster, ELB can be used to distribute the load among them. ELB monitors all instances through *health checks* and unhealthy nodes can automatically get taken out of rotation.

The last interesting service for routing is **AutoScaling** (https://aws.amazon.com/autoscaling/). This service can add instances automatically depending on some events. For instance, if one node is unresponsive or has crashed, it is detected by an ELB Health Check event that can be picked up by AutoScaling. From there, the incriminated VM can be automatically terminated and a new one started.

With these three services, you can set up a robust routing system for your microservices. In the next section, let's see what services are used to run the actual code.

# Execution - EC2 and Lambda

The core of AWS is **EC2** (https://aws.amazon.com/ec2/), which lets you create Virtual Machines. Amazon uses the **Xen hypervisor** (https://www.xenproject.org/) to run Virtual Machines, and **Amazon Machine Images** (**AMIs**) to install them.

AWS has a huge list of AMIs you can choose from; you can also create your own AMIs by tweaking an existing AMI. Working with AMIs is quite similar to working with Docker images. Once you have picked an AMI from the Amazon console, you can launch an instance, and, after it has booted, you can use SSH into it and start working.

At any moment, you can snapshot the VM and create an AMI that saves the instance state. This feature is quite useful if you want to manually set up a server, then use it as a basis for deploying clusters.

An EC2 instance comes in different series (`https://aws.amazon.com/ec2/instance-types/`). The **T2**, **M3**, and **M4** series are for a general purpose. The **T** series uses a bursting technology, which boosts the baseline performance of the instance when there's a workload peak.

The **C3** and **C4** series are for CPU-intensive applications (up to 32 Xeon CPUs), and the **X1** and **R4** ones have a lot of RAM (up to 1,952 GiB).

Of course, the more RAM or CPU, the more expensive the instance is. For Python microservices, assuming you are not hosting any database on the application instance, a `t2.xxx` or an `m3.xx` can be a good choice. You need to avoid the `t2.nano` or `t2.micro` though, which are fine for running some testing, but too limited for running anything in production. The size you need to choose depends on the resources taken by the operating system and your application.

However, since we are deploying our microservices as Docker images, we do not need to run a fancy Linux distribution. The only feature that matters is to choose an AMI that's tweaked to run Docker containers.

In AWS, the built-in way to perform Docker deployments is to use the **EC2 Container Service (ECS)** (`https://aws.amazon.com/ecs`). ECS offers features that are similar to **Kubernetes**, and integrates well with other services. ECS uses its own Linux AMI to run Docker containers, but you can configure the service to run another AMI. For instance, **CoreOS** (`https://coreos.com/`) is a Linux distribution whose sole purpose is to run Docker containers. If you use CoreOS, that is one part which won't be a locked-in AWS.

Lastly, **Lambda** (`https://aws.amazon.com/lambda/`) is a service you can use to trigger the execution of a *Lambda Function*. A Lambda Function is a piece of code that you can write in Node.js, Java, C#, or Python 2.7 or 3.6, and that is deployed as a *deployment package*, which is a ZIP file containing your script and all its dependencies. If you use Python, the ZIP file is usually a Virtualenv with all the dependencies needed to run the function.

Lambda functions can replace Celery workers, since they can be triggered asynchronously via some AWS events. The benefit of running a Lambda function is that you do not have to deploy a Celery microservice that needs to run 24/7 to pick messages from a queue. Depending on the message frequency, using Lambda can reduce costs. However, again, using Lambda means you are locked in AWS services.

Let's now look at the storage solutions.

# Storage - EBS, S3, RDS, ElasticCache, and CloudFront

When you create an EC2 instance, it works with one or several **Elastic Block Stores** (**EBS**) (https://aws.amazon.com/ebs/). An EBS is a replicated storage volume EC2 instances can mount to use as their filesystem. When you create a new EC2 instance, you can create a new EBS, and decide if it runs on an SSD or an HDD disk, the initial size, and some other options. Depending on your choices, the volume is more or less expensive.

**Simple Storage Service (S3)** (https://aws.amazon.com/s3/) is a storage service that organizes data into *buckets*. Buckets are, roughly, namespaces that you can use to organize your data. A bucket can be seen as a *key-value* storage, where a *value* is data you want to store. There is no upper limit for the size of the data, and S3 provides everything needed to stream big files in and out of its buckets. S3 is often used to distribute files, since each entry in a bucket can be exposed as a unique, public URL. **CloudFront** can be configured to use S3 as a backend.

One interesting feature is that S3 provides different storage backend depending on how often the files are written or accessed. For instance, **Glacier** (https://aws.amazon.com/glacier/) can be used as a backend when you want to store big files that are rarely accessed. One use case can be backups. It is quite easy to interact with S3 from your Python applications, and pretty common to see S3 as a data backend in microservices.

**ElasticCache** (https://aws.amazon.com/elasticache/) is a cache service that has two backends--Redis and Memcached. ElasticCache leverages Redis' shard and replication features, and lets you deploy a cluster of Redis nodes. If you host a lot of data in Redis and might go over the RAM capacity, Redis shards can spread the data across several nodes and raise Redis' capacity.

**Relational Database Service** (**RDS**) (https://aws.amazon.com/rds/) is a database service that has many database backends available; in particular, MySQL and PostgreSQL.

 AWS has an online calculator you can use to estimate the cost of your deployments; see http://calculator.s3.amazonaws.com/index.html.

The big advantage of using RDS over your database deployment is that AWS takes care of managing clusters of nodes, and offers high availability and reliability for your database without having to worry about doing any maintenance work yourself. The recent addition of PostgreSQL in RDS backends made this service very popular, and is often one of the reasons people host their application on AWS.

Another recently added backend is the proprietary, locked-in **Amazon Aurora** (`https://aws.amazon.com/rds/aurora/details/`), which implements MySQL 5.x, but is supposed to run much faster (5x faster, according to Amazon).

Lastly, **CloudFront** (`https://aws.amazon.com/cloudfront/`) is Amazon's **Content Delivery Network** (**CDN**). If you have static files you want to serve, this is the best way to do it when your users are spread all over the world. Amazon caches the files, and makes them available with the minimum latency possible by routing the client's requests to the closest server. A CDN is what you need to use to serve video, CSS, and JS files--one thing to look at, though, is the cost. If you have a few assets to serve for your microservice, it might be simpler to serve them directly from your EC2 instance.

# Messaging - SES, SQS, and SNS

For all messaging needs, AWS provides these three major services:

- **Simple Email Service** (**SES**): An email service
- **Simple Queue Service** (**SQS**): A queue system like RabbitMQ
- **Simple Notification Service** (**SNS**): A pub/sub and push notification system that works with SNS

## Simple Email Service (SES)

If you build services that send out emails to users, it is hard to make sure they all end up in their inbox. If you use the local SMTP service from the application's server that sends the email out, it takes much work to configure the system properly so that the emails are not flagged as spam by the target mail servers.

Moreover, even if you do a good job, if the server's IP is part of an IP block that was blacklisted because a spammer used an IP close to yours to send out spam, there's not much you can do besides trying to remove your IP from the blacklisting services. The worst case scenario is when you get an IP that was used by spammers before you got it.

Making sure your emails end up where they are supposed to is hard, and that is why it is often a good idea to use a third-party service that's specializes in sending emails--even if you do not host your microservices in the cloud.

There are many of them on the market, and AWS has Simple Email Service (SES) (`https://aws.amazon.com/ses/` ). Sending emails with SES simply requires you to uses SES's SMTP endpoint. They also provide an API, but sticking with SMTP is a good idea so that your services can use a local SMTP when you are doing some development or testing.

# Simple Queue Service (SQS)

SQS (`https://aws.amazon.com/sqs/`) is a subset of what you get with RabbitMQ, but it is often good enough for most use cases.

You can create two types of queue. A **First-In-First-Out** (**FIFO**) stores messages in the order they are received, and ensures that a message that's retrieved from the queue is read just once. They are useful when you want to store a stream of messages that need to be picked up by workers, like what you would do with Celery and Redis. They have a limit of 20,000 in-flight messages.

The second type (standard) is similar, except that the ordering is not entirely guaranteed. That makes it much faster than the FIFOs, and has a higher limit (120,000).

The messages stored in SQS are replicated in several AZs in the AWS cloud, making them reliable.

AWS is organized into Regions and in each Region, Availability Zones.

Regions are isolated one from each other to ensure fault tolerance and stability. AZ are also isolated but they are attached with low-latency links. Instances spread across different AZ in the same region can be used behind the same load balancer in AWS.

Since the maximum size of a message is 256 KB, the volume you can store in a FIFO queue is 5 GB, and it is 30 GB for the standard one. In other words, there are no real limitations besides the price.

# Simple Notification Service (SNS)

The last service in the messaging tools is SNS (`https://aws.amazon.com/sns/`), which offers two messaging APIs.

The first one is a pub/sub API, which can be used to trigger actions in your stack. The publisher can be one of the Amazon service or your application, and the subscriber can be an SQS queue, a Lambda Function, or any HTTP endpoint such as one of your microservices.

The second one is a push API, which can be used to send messages to mobile devices. SNS interacts, in that case, with third-party APIs such as **Google Cloud Messaging** (**GCM**) to reach phones or simple text messages via SMS.

The SQS and SNS services can be an interesting combo to replace a custom deployment of your messaging system like RabbitMQ. However, you need to check that their features are good enough for your needs.

In the next section, we are going to look at the AWS services you can use to provision and deploy services.

# Provisioning and deployment - CloudFormation and ECS

As described in Chapter 10, *Containerized Services*, there are many different ways to provision and deploy your Docker containers in the cloud, and tools like Kubernetes can be used on AWS to manage all your running instances.

AWS also offers its service to deploy clusters of containerized applications; it is called **EC2 Container Service-ECS** (https://aws.amazon.com/ecs) and leverages another service called **CloudFormation** (https://aws.amazon.com/cloudformation/).

CloudFormation lets you describe the different instances you want to run on Amazon via JSON files, and drives everything automatically on AWS, from deploying instances to autoscaling.

ECS is, basically, a set of dashboards to visualize and operate clusters deployed via CloudFormation using predefined templates. The AMI used for running the Docker daemon is tweaked for that purpose, such as CoreOS.

What's convenient with ECS is that you can create and run a cluster for a given Docker image in a matter of minutes by simply filling a couple of forms. The ECS console provides some basic metrics for the cluster, and offers features like scheduling new deployments depending on the CPU or memory usage.

Beyond the initial form-based setup, clusters deployed via ECS are driven by **Task Definitions** that define the whole lifecycle for your instances. Those definitions describe the Docker containers to run, and the behavior for some events.

# Deploying on AWS - the basics

Now that we have looked at the major AWS services, let's see how to deploy a microservice on them in practice.

To understand how AWS works, it is good to know how to manually deploy an EC2 instance, and run a microservice on it. This section describes how to deploy a **CoreOS** instance, and run a Docker container in it. Then, we will look at automated clusters' deployments using ECS. Lastly, we will see how Route53 can be used to publish your clusters of services under a domain name.

First of all, let's create an AWS account.

# Setting up your AWS account

The first step in deploying on Amazon is to create an account at `https://aws.amazon.com`. You have to enter your credit card information to register, but you can use some of the services with a *basic plan* for free for a while under some conditions.

The services that are offered for free are good enough to evaluate AWS.

Once you have registered, you are redirected to the AWS console. The first thing you need do is pick the US East (N. Virginia) region from the top-right corner menu that's under your login name. North Virginia is the region to use to set up specific billing alerts.

The second thing you should do is to configure the alarm in the **Billing Console** by visiting `https://console.aws.amazon.com/billing/home#/` (or navigating to it from the menu), and in the preferences, check the **Receive Billing Alerts** checkbox:

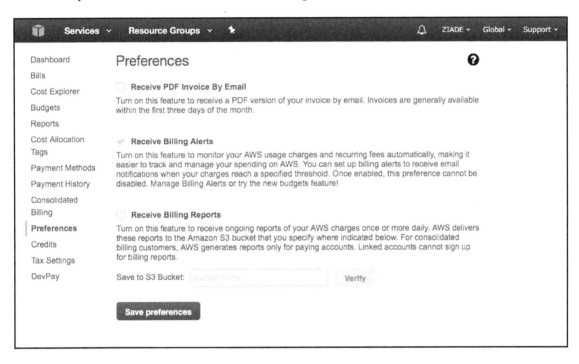

Once the option is set, you need to go to the **CloudWatch** panel at `https://console.aws.a mazon.com/cloudwatch/home`, and select **Alarms | Billing** in the left panel to create a new alert. A new popup window opens, and we can set a notification in case one of the services we use starts to cost money. Setting up $0.01 as the maximum charge does the trick. This notification prevents you from spending money if you are just doing some testing:

At any time, you can reach any service by clicking on the **Services** menu in the top-left corner. It opens a panel with all the services.

If you click on EC2, you are redirected to the EC2 console at
`https://console.aws.amazon.com/ec2/v2/home`, where you can create new instances:

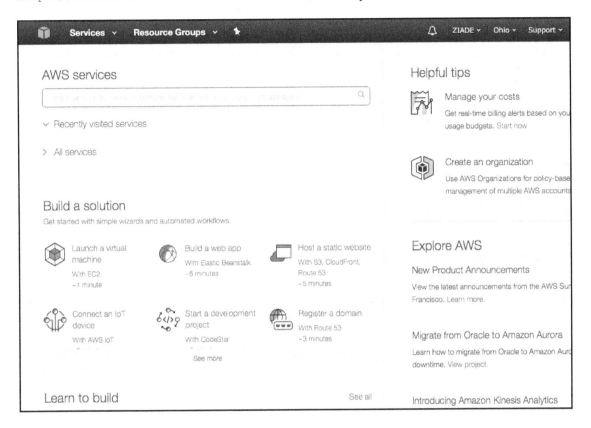

# Deploying on EC2 with CoreOS

Let's click on the **Launch Instance** blue button, and pick an AMI to run a new VM:

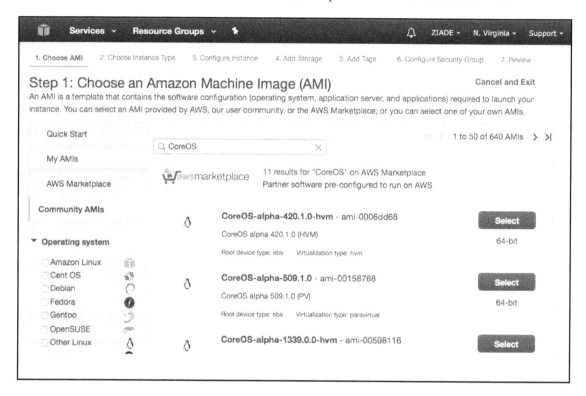

Under **Community AMIs**, you can search for an instance of `CoreOS` to list all the available CoreOS AMIs.

There are two types of AMI: **Paravirtual** (**PV**) or **Hardware Virtual Machine** (**HVM**). These are the two different levels of virtualization in the Xen hypervisor. PV is full virtualization, whereas HVM is partial virtualization. Depending on the Linux distribution, you might not be able to run all types of VMs under PV.

If you just want to play around, select the first PV AMI in the list. Then, in the next screen, pick a **t1.micro**, and go on directly with the **Review And Launch** option. Lastly, hit the **Launch** button.

Just before it creates the VM, the console asks you to create a new SSH key pair, which is a crucial step if you want to be able to access the VM. You should generate a new key pair per VM, give the key pair a unique name, and download the file. You get a .pem file, which you can add to your ~/.ssh.

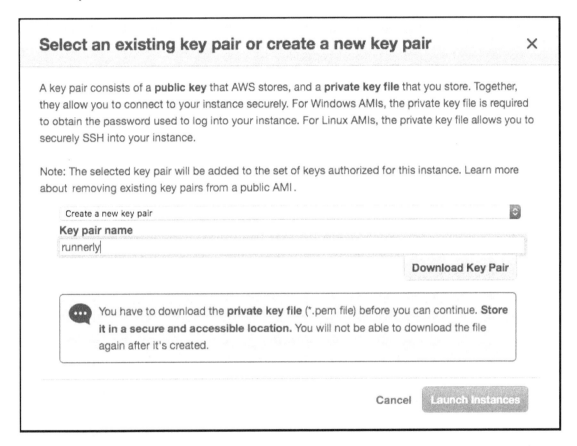

Do not lose this file, AWS does not store it for you for security reasons.

Once you have launched your instance, it is listed in the EC2 console-you can see it if you click on the **Instances** menu on the left-hand side.

You can see the status of the VM in the status checks column. It takes a few minutes for AWS to deploy the VM. Once everything is ready, you should be able to SSH into the box by using the `.pem` file as a key and the public DNS of the VM.

The default user for CoreOS is `core`, and, once you're connected, everything needed to run Docker containers is available, but will need an update. While CoreOS self-updates continuously, you can force an update of the system with `update_engine_client`, and reboot the VM with the `sudo reboot` command, as follows:

```
$ ssh -i ~/.ssh/runnerly.pem
core@ec2-34-224-101-250.compute-1.amazonaws.com
CoreOS (alpha)
core@ip-172-31-24-180 ~ $
core@ip-172-31-24-180 ~ $ update_engine_client -update
[0530/083245:INFO:update_engine_client.cc(245)] Initiating update check and
install.
[0530/083245:INFO:update_engine_client.cc(250)] Waiting for update to
complete.
LAST_CHECKED_TIME=1496132682
PROGRESS=0.000000
CURRENT_OP=UPDATE_STATUS_UPDATED_NEED_REBOOT
NEW_VERSION=0.0.0.0
NEW_SIZE=282041956
core@ip-172-31-24-180 ~ $ sudo reboot
Connection to ec2-34-224-101-250.compute-1.amazonaws.com closed by remote
host.
Connection to ec2-34-224-101-250.compute-1.amazonaws.com closed.
```

Once the VM is back, you should have a recent version of Docker, and you can try it by echoing `hello` from a **busybox** Docker container, shown as follows:

```
$ ssh -i ~/.ssh/runnerly.pem
core@ec2-34-224-101-250.compute-1.amazonaws.com
Last login: Tue May 30 08:24:26 UTC 2017 from 91.161.42.131 on pts/0
Container Linux by CoreOS alpha (1423.0.0)
core@ip-172-31-24-180 ~ $
docker -v Docker version 17.05.0-ce, build 89658be
core@ip-172-31-24-180 ~ $ docker run busybox /bin/echo hello
Unable to find image 'busybox:latest' locally
latest: Pulling from library/busybox
1cae461a1479: Pull complete
Digest:
sha256:c79345819a6882c31b41bc771d9a94fc52872fa651b36771fbe0c8461d7ee558
Status: Downloaded newer image for busybox:latest hello
core@ip-172-31-24-180 ~ $
```

If the previous call was successful, you now have a fully working Docker environment. Let's try to run a web app in it now using the `docker-flask` image from the Docker Hub:

```
core@ip-172-31-24-180 ~ $
docker run -d -p 80:80 p0bailey/docker-flask
Unable to find image 'p0bailey/docker-flask:latest' locally
latest:
Pulling from p0bailey/docker-flask
bf5d46315322: Pull complete
9f13e0ac480c: Pull complete
e8988b5b3097: Pull complete
40af181810e7: Pull complete
e6f7c7e5c03e: Pull complete
ef4a9c1b628c: Pull complete
d4792c0323df: Pull complete
6ed446a13dca: Pull complete
886152aa6422: Pull complete
b0613c27c0ab: Pull complete
Digest:
sha256:1daed864d5814b602092b44958d7ee6aa9f915c6ce5f4d662d7305e46846353b
Status: Downloaded newer image for p0bailey/docker-flask:latest
345632b94f02527c972672ad42147443f8d905d5f9cd735c48c35effd978e971
```

By default, AWS opens only port 22 for SSH access. To reach port 80, you need to go to the **Instances** list in the EC2 console and click on the Security Group that was created for the instance (usually named `launch-wizard-xx`).

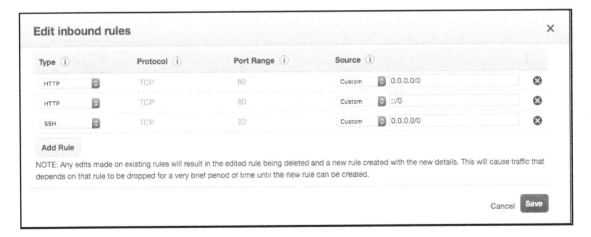

Clicking on it brings up the Security Group page, where you can edit the Inbound Rules to add `HTTP`. This immediately opens port 80, and you should be able to visit your Flask app using the public DNS in your browser.

This is what it takes to run a Docker image on AWS, and it is the basis for any deployment. From there, you can deploy clusters by creating groups of instances managed by the AutoScaling and ELB services.

The higher-level tool, CloudFormation, can take care of all these steps automatically using template definitions. However, ECS is the ultimate level of deployment automation on AWS when you are using Docker-let's see how to use it in the next section.

# Deploying with ECS

As described earlier in this chapter, ECS takes care of deploying Docker images automatically, and sets up all the services needed around the instances.

You do not need, in this case, to create EC2 instances yourself. ECS uses its own AMI, which is tweaked to run Docker containers on EC2. It is pretty similar to CoreOS, as it comes with a Docker daemon, but it is integrated with the AWS infrastructure for sharing configuration and triggering events.

An ECS cluster deployment is composed of many elements:

- An **Elastic Load Balancer** (in EC2) to distribute the requests among the instance
- A **Task Definition**, which is used to determine which Docker image needs to be deployed, and what ports should be bound between the host and the container
- A **Service**, which uses the Task Definition to drive the creation of EC2 instances, and run the Docker container in them
- A **Cluster**, which groups Services, Task Definitions, and an ELB

Deploying a cluster on ECS when you are not used to it is complex, because it requires creating elements in a specific order. For instance, the ELB needs to be set up before everything else.

Fortunately, everything can be created for you in the right ordering via the first run wizard. This wizard is displayed when you go to the ECS service on the console for the first time, and will bootstrap everything for you. Once you are on the landing page, Click on the **Get Started** button to launch the wizard.

You can check the **Deploy a sample application onto Amazon ECS Cluster** option, and get going:

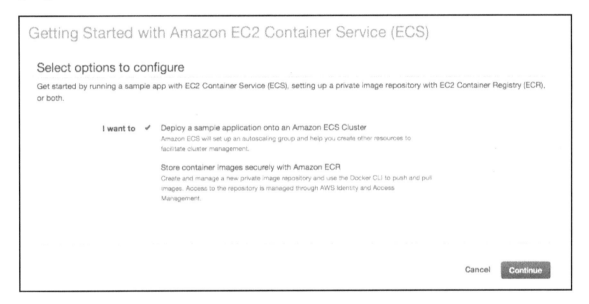

This action brings up a task definition creation dialog, where you can define a name for the task and the container to be used for that task:

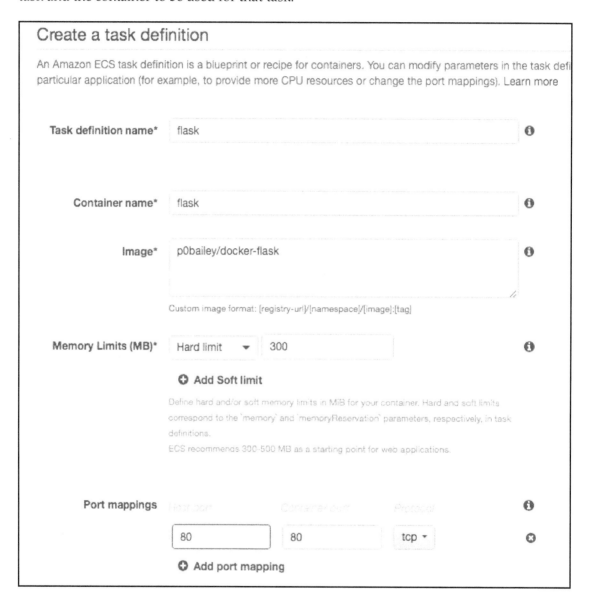

In the preceding example, we deployed the same Flask application that we deployed earlier on EC2, so we provide that image name on the container form for the task definition. The Docker image needs to be present on Docker Hub or AWS's own Docker images repository.

In that form, you can also set up all the port mapping between the Docker container and the host system. That option is used by ECS when the image is run. Here, we bind port 80, which is where the Flask docker image that we are using exposes the app.

The next step in the wizard is the **Service** configuration:

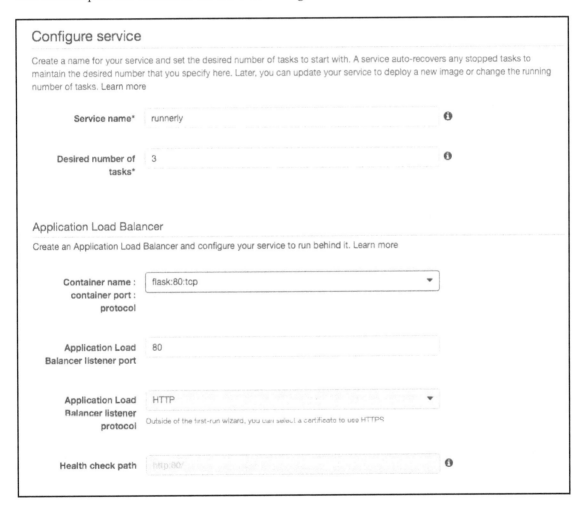

We add three tasks into that service, as we want to run three instances in our cluster with one Docker container running on each one of them. In the **Application Load Balancer** section, we use the container name and the port defined earlier. Lastly, we need to configure a cluster, where we set up an instance type, some instances, and the SSH key pair to use:

## Configure cluster

Your Amazon ECS tasks run on container instances (Amazon EC2 instances that are running the ECS container agent). Configure the instance type, instance quantity, and other details of the container instances to launch into your cluster

| | |
|---|---|
| Cluster name* | default |
| EC2 instance type* | t2.micro |
| Number of instances* | 3 |
| Key pair | runnerly |

You will not be able to SSH into your EC2 instances without a key pair. You can create a new key pair in the EC2 console.

## Security group

By default, your instances are accessible from any IP address. We recommend that you update the below security group ingress rule to allow access from known IP addresses only. ECS automatically opens up port 80 to facilitate access to the application or service you're running.

| | |
|---|---|
| Allowed ingress source(s)* | Anywhere |
| | 0.0.0.0/0 |

## Container instance IAM role

The Amazon ECS container agent makes calls to the Amazon ECS API actions on your behalf, so container instances that run the agent require the ecsInstanceRole IAM policy and role for the service to know that the agent belongs to you. If you do not have the ecsInstanceRole already, we can create one for you.

Once you validate that last step, the ECS wizard works for a little while to create all parts, and once it is ready, you end up with a **view service** button, which is enabled once all the parts are created. The **Service** page summarizes all the parts of the deployment, and has several tabs to check every service in detail. The deployment done by the ECS wizard can be summarized as follows:

- A task definition was created to run the Docker container
- A cluster of three EC2 instances was added, and in that cluster
- A Service was added to the cluster, and Task Definition was used to deploy Docker containers in the EC2 instance
- The deployment was load-balanced by the ELB created earlier

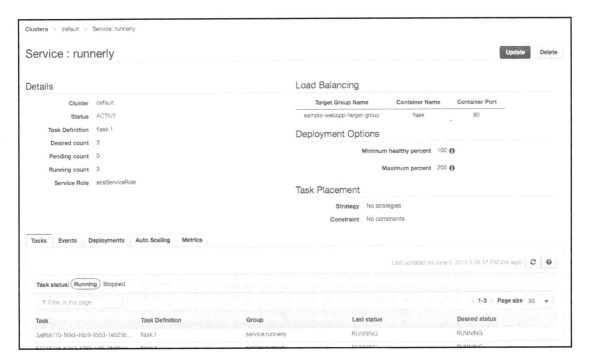

If you go back to the EC2 console, and visit the **Load Balancing** | **Load Balancers** menu on the left, you will find the newly created `ECS-first-run-alb` ELB that is used to serve your ECS cluster.

This ELB has a public DNS name, which you can use in your browser to visit your Flask app. The URL is in the form of `http://<ELB name>.<region>.elb.amazonaws.com`.

The next section explains how to link this ELB URL to a clean domain name.

# Route53

Route53 can be used to create an alias with your domain name. If you visit the service console at `https://console.aws.amazon.com/route53`, and click on the **hosted zones** menu, you can add a new hosted zone for your domain name, which is an alias to the ELB previously set.

Assuming that you already own the domain name from a registrar, you can simply redirect the domain to AWS's DNS. Click on **Create Hosted Zone**, and add your domain.

Once it is created, you can go to **Create a Record Set**, and select a type A record. The record has to be an Alias, and in the target input, a dropdown appears with the list of available targets:

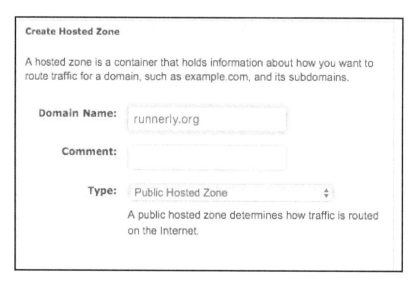

The ELB load balancer that was previously created by the wizard should appear in that list, and selecting it links your domain name to that ELB:

This step is all it takes to link a domain name to your deployed ECS cluster; and you can add more entries with a subdomain, for instance, for each one of your deployed microservice.

Route53 has DNS servers all over the world, and other interesting features like a health check that you can use to ping your ELB and underlying services regularly. In case there's a failure, Route53 can send an alarm to CloudWatch, and automatically, even fail over all the traffic to another healthy ELB if you have several ones set.

# Summary

Containerized applications are becoming the norm for deploying microservices, and cloud vendors are all following that trend.

Google, Amazon, and all the other big players are now able to deploy and manage clusters of Docker containers. So, if your application is *dockerized*, you should be able to deploy it easily. In this chapter, we have looked at how to do it in AWS, which has its service (ECS) to manage Docker images that is tightly integrated with all the other main AWS services.

Once you are familiar with all the AWS services, it is a pretty powerful platform that can be tweaked to publish not only large-scale microservices-based applications, but also smaller applications for a fraction of the price you would pay if you were running your own data center.

In the next chapter, we conclude this book by giving a few leads for going further into the art of building microservices.

# 12
## What Next?

Five years ago, choosing a Python version was driven by these two factors:

- The operating system used to deploy your applications
- The availability of the libraries your application used

One extreme example of how the operating system influences this decision is when CentOS is used. CentOS is really close to **Red Hat Enterprise Linux** (**RHEL**) minus the commercial support, and many companies that started off with RHEL and grew internal teams, ended up moving to CentOS. There are a lot of good reasons to use CentOS. This Linux distribution is popular and based on a robust set of management tools.

However, using CentOS means you cannot use the latest Python version for your projects unless you install a custom Python instance on the system. Moreover, that is often considered to be bad practice from an Ops point of view because you go out of the supported versions. For that reason, some developers were forced to use 2.6 for a very long time, and that prevented them from using the newest Python syntax and features.

The other reason people stayed on Python 2 was that a few essential libraries were still not ported to Python 3. However, this is not the case anymore--if you start a new microservice project in 2017, everything is available for Python 3.

Those two reasons to stick with older Python versions are gone nowadays; you can pick the latest Python 3, and ship your app on whatever Linux distribution is inside a Docker container.

As we've seen in `Chapter 10`, *Containerized services*, Docker seems to be the new standard for containerizing applications. But, maybe, other players will become serious alternatives, like CoreOs's **rkt** (`https://coreos.com/rkt/`). In any case, the maturity of the containers technology will be reached the day all containers engines are based on a universal standard to describe images--and that is the goal of organizations such as **Open Container Initiative (OCI)** (`https://www.opencontainers.org/`), which is driven by all the big containers and cloud players.

For all these reasons, using the latest Python 3 and Docker for your microservices is a safe bet. Your Dockerfile syntax is probably going to be very close to whatever syntax an initiative like OCI will build.

So, if Python 3.6 or the next versions have great features, nothing will prevent you from moving forward and using them for your next microservice--and as we've said throughout the book, it's fine to use different stacks or Python versions for each microservice.

In this book, Flask was picked, because that framework is excellent to build microservices, and has a vast and mature ecosystem. But since Python 3.5, web frameworks based on the **asyncio** library (`https://docs.python.org/3/library/asyncio.html`) along with the `async` and `await` new language keywords are starting to become serious alternatives.

There are good chances that in a couple of years, one of them will replace Flask as the most popular framework, because the benefits regarding the performances of I/O bound microservices are huge, and developers are starting to adopt asynchronous programming.

In this last chapter, we are going to look at how asynchronous programming works in Python 3.5+, and discover two web frameworks that can be used to build microservices asynchronously.

# Iterators and generators

To understand how asynchronous programming works in Python, it is important to first understand how iterators and generators work because they are the basis of asynchronous features in Python.

An iterator in Python is a class that implements the *Iterator protocol*. The class must implement the following two methods:

- `__iter__()`: Returns the actual iterator. It often returns `self`
- `next()`: Returns the next value until `StopIteration()` is raised

In the following example, we'll implement the Fibonacci sequence as an iterator:

```
class Fibo:
    def __init__(self, max=10):
        self.a, self.b = 0, 1
        self.max = max
        self.count = 0

    def __iter__(self):
        return self

    def next(self):
        try:
            return self.a
        finally:
            if self.count == self.max:
                raise StopIteration()
            self.a, self.b = self.b, self.a + self.b
            self.count += 1
```

Iterators can be used directly in loops, as follows:

```
>>> for number in Fibo(10):
...         print(number)
...
0
1
1
2
3
5
8
13
21
34
```

To make iterators more *Pythonic, generators* were added to Python. They have introduced the `yield` keyword. When `yield` is used by a function instead of `return`, this function is converted into a generator. Each time the `yield` keyword is encountered, the function returns the yielded value and pauses its execution.

```
def fibo(max=10):
    a, b = 0, 1
    cpt = 0
    while cpt < max:
        yield a
        a, b = b, a + b
        cpt += 1
```

This behavior makes generators a bit similar to *coroutines* found in other languages, except that coroutines are *bidirectional*. They return a value as `yield` does, but they can also receive a value for its next iteration.

Being able to pause the execution of a function and communicate with it both ways is the basis for asynchronous programming--once you have this ability, you can use an event loop, and pause and resume functions.

The `yield` call was extended to support receiving values from the caller via the `sender()` method. In the next example, a `terminal()` function simulates a console, which implements three instructions, `echo`, `exit`, and `eval`:

```
def terminal():
    while True:
        msg = yield     # msg gets the value sent via a send() call
        if msg == 'exit':
            print("Bye!")
            break
        elif msg.startswith('echo'):
            print(msg.split('echo ', 1)[1])
        elif msg.startswith('eval'):
            print(eval(msg.split('eval', 1)[1]))
```

When instantiated, this generator can receive data via its `send()` method:

```
>>> t = terminal()
>>> t.next()     # call to initialise the generator - similar to send(None)

>>> t.send("echo hey")
hey

>>> t.send("eval 1+1")
2

>>> t.send("exit")
Bye!
Traceback (most recent call last):
  File "<stdin>", line 1, in <module>
StopIteration
```

Thanks to this addition, Python generators became similar to coroutines.

Another extension that was added to `yield` is *yield from*, which lets you chain-call another generator.

Consider the following example, where a generator is uses two other generators to yield values:

```
def gen1():
    for i in [1, 2, 3]:
        yield i

def gen2():
    for i in 'abc':
        yield i

def gen():
    for val in gen1():
        yield val
    for val in gen2():
        yield val
```

The two `for` loops in the `gen()` function can be replaced by a single *yield from* call as follows:

```
def gen():
    yield from gen1()
    yield from gen2()
```

Here's an example of calling the `gen()` method until each sub generator gets exhausted:

```
>>> list(gen())
[1, 2, 3, 'a', 'b', 'c']
```

Calling several other coroutines and waiting for their completion is a prevalent pattern in asynchronous programming. It allows developers to split their logic into small functions and assemble them in sequence. Each `yield` call is an opportunity for the function to pause its execution and let another function take over.

With these features, Python got one step closer to supporting asynchronous programming natively. Iterators and generators were used as building blocks to create native coroutines.

# Coroutines

To make asynchronous programming more straightforward, the `await` and `async` keywords were introduced in Python 3.5, along with the `coroutine` type. The `await` call is *almost* equivalent to *yield from*, as its goal is to let you call a coroutine from another coroutine.

The difference is that you can't use the await call to call a generator (yet).

The async keyword marks a *function*, a for or a with loop, as being a native coroutine, and if you try to use that function, you will not retrieve a generator but a coroutine object.

The native coroutine type that was added in Python is like a fully symmetric generator, but all the back and forth is delegated to an event loop, which is in charge of coordinating the execution.

In the example that follows, the asyncio library is used to run main(), which, in turn, calls several coroutines in *parallel*:

```python
import asyncio

async def compute():
    for i in range(5):
        print('compute %d' % i)
        await asyncio.sleep(.1)

async def compute2():
    for i in range(5):
        print('compute2 %d' % i)
        await asyncio.sleep(.2)

async def main():
    await asyncio.gather(compute(), compute2())

loop = asyncio.get_event_loop()
loop.run_until_complete(main())
loop.close()
```

What's compelling about such an application is that, besides the async and await keywords, it looks like plain sequential Python--making it very readable. And since coroutines work by ceding control and not by interrupting, it's deterministic and the events occur in the same way every time it runs unlike programming with threads.

Notice that the asyncio.sleep() function is a coroutine, so it is called with the await keyword.

If you run this program, you will get the following output:

```
$ python async.py
compute 0
compute2 0
compute 1
compute2 1
compute 2
```

```
compute 3
compute2 2
compute 4
compute2 3
compute2 4
```

In the next section, we will take a closer look at the `asyncio` library.

# The asyncio library

The **asyncio** (`https://docs.python.org/3/library/asyncio.html`) library, which was originally an experiment called **Tulip** run by Guido, provides all the infrastructure to build asynchronous programs based on an event loop.

The library predates the introduction of `async`, `await`, and native coroutines in the language.

The `asyncio` library is inspired by Twisted, and offers classes that mimic Twisted *transports* and *protocols*. Building a network application based on these consists of combining a transport class (like TCP) and a protocol class (such as HTTP), and using *callbacks* to orchestrate the execution of the various parts.

But, with the introduction of native coroutines, callback-style programming is less appealing, since it's much more readable to orchestrate the execution order via `await` calls. You can use coroutine with `asyncio` protocol and transport classes, but the original design was not meant for that and requires a bit of extra work.

However, the central feature is the event loop API and all the functions used to schedule how the coroutines will get executed. An event loop uses the operating system I/O *poller* (*devpoll, epoll, and kqueue*) to register the execution of a function given an I/O event.

For instance, the loop can wait for some data to be available in a socket to trigger a function that will treat the data. But that pattern can be generalized to any event. For instance, when *coroutine A* awaits for *coroutine B* to be finished, the call to `asyncio` sets an I/O event, which is triggered when *coroutine B* is over and makes *coroutine A* wait for that event to resume.

The result is that if your program is split into a lot of interdependent coroutines, their executions are interleaved. The beauty of this pattern is that a single-threaded application can run thousands of coroutines concurrently without having to be thread-safe and without all the complexity that it entails.

To build an asynchronous microservice, the typical pattern is like this:

```
async def my_view(request):
    query = await process_request(request)
    data = await some_database.query(query)
    response = await build_response(data)
    return response
```

An event loop running this coroutine for each incoming request will be able to accept hundreds of new requests while waiting for each step to finish.

If the same service were built with Flask, and typically run with a single thread, each new request would have to wait for the completion of the previous one to get the attention of the Flask app. Hammering the service with several hundred concurrent requests will issue timeouts in no time.

The execution time for a single request is the same in both cases, but the ability to run many requests concurrently and interleave their execution is what makes asynchronous applications better for I/O-bound microservices. Our application can do a lot of things with the CPU while waiting for a call to a database to return.

And if some of your services have CPU-bound tasks, `asyncio` provides a function to run the code in a separate thread or process from within the loop.

In the next two sections, we will present two frameworks based on `asyncio`, which can be used to build microservices.

# The aiohttp framework

The **aiohttp** (http://aiohttp.readthedocs.io/) framework is a popular asynchronous framework based on the `asyncio` library, which has been around since the first days of the library.

Like Flask, it provides a request object and a router to redirect queries to functions that handle them.

The `asyncio` library's event loop is wrapped into an `Application` object, which handles most of the orchestration work. As a microservice developer, you can just focus on building your views as you would do with Flask.

In the following example, the `api()` coroutine returns some JSON response when the application is called on `/api`:

```
from aiohttp import web

async def api(request):
    return web.json_response({'some': 'data'})
app = web.Application()
app.router.add_get('/api', api)
web.run_app(app)
```

The aiohttp framework has a built-in web server, which is used to run this script via the `run_app()` method, and, overall, if you are used to Flask, the biggest difference is that you do not use decorators to route requests to your views.

This framework provides helpers like those you find in Flask, plus some original features such as its *Middleware*, which will let you register coroutines to perform specific tasks such as custom error handling.

# Sanic

**Sanic** (`http://sanic.readthedocs.io/`) is another interesting project, which specifically tries to provide a Flask-like experience with coroutines.

Sanic uses **uvloop** (`https://github.com/MagicStack/uvloop`) for its event loop, which is a Cython implementation of the `asyncio` loop protocol using **libuv**, allegedly making it faster. The difference might be negligible in most of your microservices, but is good to take any speed gain when it is just a transparent switch to a specific event loop implementation.

If we write the previous example in Sanic, it's very close to Flask:

```
from sanic import Sanic, response

app = Sanic(__name__)

@app.route("/api")
async def api(request):
    return response.json({'some': 'data'})

app.run()
```

Needless to say, the whole framework is inspired by Flask, and you will find most of the features that made it a success, such as Blueprints.

Sanic also has its original features, like the ability to write your views in a class (HTTPMethodView) that represents one endpoint, with one method per verb (GET, POST, PATCH, and so on).

The framework also provides middleware to change the request or response.

In the next example, if a view returns a dictionary, it will be automatically converted to JSON:

```python
from sanic import Sanic
from sanic.response import json

app = Sanic(__name__)

@app.middleware('response')
async def convert(request, response):
    if isinstance(response, dict):
        return json(response)
    return response

@app.route("/api")
async def api(request):
    return {'some': 'data'}

app.run()
```

This little middleware function simplifies your views if your microservice produces only JSON mappings.

# Asynchronous versus synchronous

Switching to an asynchronous model means you will need to use asynchronous code all the way down.

For example, if your microservice uses a Requests library that is not asynchronous, every call made to query an HTTP endpoint will block the event loop, and you will not benefit from asynchronicity.

And making an existing project asynchronous is not an easy task because it changes the design completely. Most projects that want to support asynchronous calls are redesigning everything from scratch.

The good news is that there are more and more asynchronous libraries available, which can be used to build a microservice. On PyPI, you can search for `aio` or `asyncio`.
This wiki page (`https://github.com/python/asyncio/wiki/ThirdParty`) is also a good place to look at.

Here's a short list of those that are relevant to building microservices:

- `aiohttp.Client`: Can replace the `requests` package
- `aiopg`: PostgreSQL driver on top of **Psycopg**
- `aiobotocore`: AWS client--might be merged with the official boto3 project at some point
- `aioredis`: Redis client
- `aiomysql`: MySQL client, built with PyMySQL

In case you cannot find a replacement for one of your libraries, `asyncio` provides a way to run blocking code in a separate thread or process via an executor. This function is a coroutine, and uses a `ThreadPoolExecutor` or a `ProcessPoolExecutor` class from the `concurrent` module under the hood.

In the example that follows, the `requests` library is used via a pool of threads:

```python
import asyncio
from concurrent.futures import ThreadPoolExecutor
import requests

# blocking code
def fetch(url):
    return requests.get(url).text


URLS = ['http://ziade.org', 'http://python.org', 'http://mozilla.org']

# coroutine
async def example(loop):
    executor = ThreadPoolExecutor(max_workers=3)
    tasks = []
    for url in URLS:
        tasks.append(loop.run_in_executor(executor, fetch, url))
```

```
        completed, pending = await asyncio.wait(tasks)
        for task in completed:
            print(task.result())

    loop = asyncio.get_event_loop()
    loop.run_until_complete(example(loop))
    loop.close()
```

Each call to `run_in_executor()` returns a `Future` object, which can be used to set some synchronization points in your asynchronous program. The `Future` objects keep an eye on the state of the execution, and provide a method for retrieving the result once it is available.

 Python 3 has two `Future` classes that are slightly different, and that can be confusing. The `asyncio.Future` is a class you can use directly with the event loop, while `concurrent.futures.Future` is a class that is used in the `ThreadPoolExecutor` or `ProcessPoolExecutor` class.
To avoid any confusion, you should isolate the code that is working with `run_in_executor()`, and get back the results as soon as they are available.
Keeping Future objects around is a recipe for disaster.

The `asyncio.wait()` function can wait for all the Futures to complete, so the `example()` function here will block until all the Futures return. The `wait()` function can take a timeout value, so the function returns a tuple composed of the list of completed Futures and the ones that are still running. When not using a timeout, it waits indefinitely (unless you have a general timeout on the socket library).

You can use processes instead of threads, but, in that case, all the data that goes in and out of your blocking function needs to be pickable. To avoid blocking code altogether is the best option, particularly, if the code is I/O bound.

That said, if you have a function that is CPU bound, it can be worthwhile to run it in a separate process to use all the CPU cores available, and speed up your microservice.

# Summary

In this final chapter, we have looked at how we can write microservices using asynchronous programming in Python. While Flask is a great framework, asynchronous programming might be the next big revolution in Python for writing microservices that are usually I/O bound.

There are more and more asynchronous frameworks and libraries based on Python 3.5 and beyond, which makes this approach appealing.

Switching from Flask to one of these frameworks for one of your microservices can be a good way to experiment with limited risks.

# Index

implementing 113
model 100
splitting 114, 120
Strava token, obtaining 108
template 101, 103, 105
view 101, 103, 105

# N

Nameko
  URL 146
network strategies, Docker
  reference 269
nginx content pack
  URL 168
nginx
  about 23
  function, adding 191
Node.js
  about 24
  URL 213, 215
Nose
  URL 82
npm
  URL 215
  using 215, 217
ntpdate service 133

# O

OAuth2
  about 98, 171, 172, 173, 174
  URL 98, 171
Object-Relational Mapper (ORM) 35
Open API 2.0
  using 117
Open Container Initiative (OCI)
  URL 302
Open Source Software (OSS) 14
Open Web Application Security Project (OWASP)
  about 188
  URL 188
OpenResty
  about 190
  concurrency limiting 193
  configuring 263, 264, 265
  features 195

Lua 190
nginx 190
rate limiting 193
URL 190, 195
OpenStack community
  URL 201
Operation person (Ops) 22
out-of-memory killer (oomkiller) 163

# P

packaging toolchain
  about 230, 231
  definitions 231, 232
  project, distributing 245, 246, 247
  project, releasing 243, 244, 245
  Python project, packaging 232
  versioning 240, 241, 242, 243
Paravirtual (PV) 288
Paste project 81
PBKDF2
  reference 110
PEP (Python Environment Proposal)
  URL 46
performance metrics
  about 163
  code metrics 166
  system metrics 163
  web server metrics 168
Periodic Task feature
  reference 108
pika-pool
  URL 144
Pika
  URL 143
Pip 63
pip-tools
  about 238
  URL 238
Postgres image
  URL 271
preflight mechanism 218
process management 250, 251, 252, 253, 254
Protocol Buffers (protobuf)
  about 136
  URL 136

CPSIA information can be obtained
at www.ICGtesting.com
Printed in the USA
FSHW04n0207300318
46215FS